Andrew Ryan Scoggins

STRIVING TOGETHER PUBLICATIONS

A GLORIOUS CHURCH

A STUDY OF THE ORIGIN,
IDENTITY, HERITAGE,
AND INTEGRITY OF THE
NEW TESTAMENT
CHURCH

MIKE GASS

Copyright © 2009, 2013 by Striving Together Publications. All Scripture quotations are taken from the King James Version.

First published in 2009 by Striving Together Publications, a ministry of Lancaster Baptist Church, Lancaster, CA 93535. Striving Together Publications is committed to providing tried, trusted, and proven books that will further equip local churches to carry out the Great Commission. Your comments and suggestions are valued.

All rights reserved. No part of this book may be reproduced, stored in a retrieval system, or transmitted in any form or by any means—electronic, mechanical, photocopy, recording, or otherwise—without written permission of the publisher, except for brief quotations in printed reviews.

Striving Together Publications
4020 E. Lancaster Blvd.
Lancaster, CA 93535
800.201.7748

Cover design by Andrew Jones
Layout by Craig Parker
Edited by Joan Parish, Paul Chappell, and Cary Schmidt
Editing assistance by Sarah Michael

ISBN 978-1-59894-074-9

Printed in the United States of America

DEDICATION

This book is dedicated to the Lord first of all for by Him all things consist! May He use it as He sees fit. In addition, this book is dedicated to the friends and members of the Harvest Baptist Temple of Medford, Oregon. At the writing of this book, my brother Bob and I have had a wonderful and profitable ministry since 1977, due in large part to the commitment and love for the Lord and His work that these dear saints have demonstrated for more than thirty years. Thank you for your heart, your faithfulness, and your example. We love you all.

SPECIAL THANKS

I want also to make mention of those closest to me in ministry and life. First to my wife, Marilyn. What a wonderful and precious gift God gave me when he brought you into my life. I love you! Out of our life together we have been blessed with three wonderful children, all grown up and serving the Lord. To my daughter, Amber, you have been the delight of my life. To Ryan, you never cease to amaze me, and to Matthew, you are the gem in the rough. May God bless you in your ministries. Finally, I would be amiss if I didn't acknowledge and thank my kinsman brother after the flesh, Pastor Bob Gass, with whom I have had the privilege of serving the Lord these many years. Thank you for your encouragement and your example as a pastor and friend.

Table of Contents

Acknowledgments VII
Foreword. IX
Preface XIII

Part One—The Origin of the New Testament Church
1. The Framework: John the Baptist 11
2. The Founder: Jesus Christ 21
3. The Facilitators: The Apostles 29
4. The Formula: The Great Commission 35
5. The Fulfillment: The World! 43

Part Two—The Identity of the New Testament Church
6. The Church: An Assembly 57
7. The Concept: Correct Terminology 65
8. The Compliance: Scriptural Baptism 71
9. The Character: Scriptural Identification 79

Part Three—The Heritage of the New Testament Church
10. The Primitive Church: Early Christianity 105
11. The Medieval Church: Anabaptism 139
12. The Protestant Reformation: The Reformers. 169
13. Reformation Consequences: Evangelicalism 185
14. Migration to Freedom: The Baptists. 203

Part Four—The Integrity of the New Testament Church
15. The Testimonies of Historians and Persons of Note 239
16. The Testimony of the Scriptures 247
    Conclusion 265

Notes 271
Bibliography 287
Glossary 291
Appendix I—Societies of Human Origin 297
Appendix II—Traditions of Human Origin in the
   Roman Catholic Church. 301
Appendix III—Six Reasons to Reject the Universal
   Church Theory 305
Appendix IV—The Historic Baptist Distinctives 309
Index 311
Scripture Index 321

ACKNOWLEDGMENTS

I would like to thank the several people who have helped in the editing of this project from its early days. My good friend Dusty Brian was a great help in the beginning although he probably questioned my sanity. Thank you Dusty for redeeming the time.

There were several members of the Harvest Baptist Temple who over a period of time have also added their judgment and insight. Deserving of special thanks are Mark and Trinia Thompson, Diane Allen, Vickie Garrison, and Mr. Marti Cotè who became not only my loyal critic but also my much needed professor. Thank you Marti for your honest and diligent service on our behalf!

Long-time friends, Pastor Bill Rench of Temecula, California, and Pastor Jeff Hodges of Alamogordo, New Mexico, are both well acquainted with our subject and were great resources for help and advice.

A good secretary is such a great help in a project such as this. Jaci Smalley will hate that I have mentioned her name, but she is truly one of the best.

I also want to thank Pastor Paul Chappell whose ministry has made this book a possibility rather than just a dream. Thank you Brother Chappell for your heart and vision.

Brother Cary Schmidt, you have truly exemplified the ideal of Lancaster Baptist Church. As a servant leader you have been a great blessing in more ways than you may know. As the man who directs the day-to-day operations of Striving Together Publications, you have continued to be a source of encouragement and wisdom to me. Thank you for your direction and counsel.

In addition to these individuals with whom I have had personal contact, I know that there have been many whose names I do not know who are the faithful and loyal employees of Lancaster Baptist Church and Striving Together Publications and who have spent much time and effort in the details of bringing this book to publication. Thank you for your assistance and dedication to the cause of Christ.

FOREWORD

The work you hold in your hands is the culmination of many years of study, research, and teaching. Mike Gass has done a marvelous job of documenting the history of authentic, New Testament churches since the time of Jesus Christ. There are many things I greatly appreciate about this book.

First, I appreciate the subject matter! I truly love the New Testament church. The local, New Testament church is God's idea, and Jesus gave His life for it. It is His institution for accomplishing His work on planet Earth. From the time of Christ to the present day, God's promises and plan for the church hold true. The gates of Hell shall not prevail against it. Authentic local churches are still alive and well all around the world. And it is my great privilege to serve as the pastor of a healthy local church where God is changing lives on a regular basis.

Second, I appreciate the doctrinal integrity of these pages. Mike Gass goes to great lengths to accurately define and describe the local church in biblical terms. The biblical model of local church ministry has been lost among so many groups today, and yet it is this biblical model that God still blesses. The more we can understand and duplicate the work of local churches as defined in the book of Acts and in other New Testament epistles, the more we will see God's hand of blessing return to our efforts.

Third, I appreciate the spirit of these pages. Regardless of your spiritual background, this book addresses an important matter with respect and forthrightness. The tone of these pages is authoritative yet positive and encouraging. As you read, you will learn much about the history of various movements—including the independent Baptist movement—and you will have a deeper and more biblical appreciation for God's plan in local church ministry. You will gain a greater level of discernment in appreciating what Christians have stood for through the centuries and also in identifying error as it has unfolded over the last two thousand years.

For many readers, this book will challenge your thinking—in a wonderful, biblical way. I urge you to read it with an open heart and seriously consider the biblical and historical evidence that Mike Gass presents. Let the truth that you read build your faith and strengthen your commitment to the right kind of church in our day.

Our Baptist heritage is precious. Thousands upon thousands of those who have gone before us have died for the faith that they held dear. These courageous believers through the centuries refused to unite or endorse modern movements of their day because of doctrinal impurity. They remained passionate and true to the faith once delivered to the saints. May their fire become ours, and may the cause of Christ continue to be handed down to future generations.

These pages will give you a fresh and biblical understanding of God's original intent for His church. As you read, you will be challenged with Bible doctrine, historical documentation, and practical application. This book will strengthen your heart for that which is so near to God's heart—the local church.

It is our privilege at Striving Together Publications to partner with Mike Gass in the creation and publication of this vital book, *A Glorious Church*. May God use it to strengthen your commitment to Christ and to His local church. Thank you for reading!

Dr. Paul Chappell
Lancaster, California
April 2009

"Thou hast given a banner to them that fear thee, that it may be displayed because of the truth. Selah."
—Psalm 60:4

PREFACE

I once heard a man say that when an author has written multiple books on a particular subject other than his first, all that follows are simply a re-hash of what he has previously written. It is his first book that is the most important to read. He went on to say that men write their first books partly out of frustration, that a story has not been told or that an old story has been forgotten. They feel compelled to set the record straight or at least enter into the debate. So it is with this book.

After finishing three years of seminary I was excited to fulfill my calling in the ministry. Like most of my peers, I felt that the time spent in seminary was well served and that it had properly prepared me to launch out into the ministry. My brother Bob and I—after much prayer and preparation—moved three thousand miles in the summer of 1977 to plant an independent Baptist church in the Northwest. A few short years later in Medford, Oregon, our church was well established, growing, and about to build its first buildings. We were both amazed and grateful for what God was doing. As people were saved, baptized, and added to the church, it was not long before we were faced with some issues that we could not remember ever being addressed in school. In reality, it was probably more the application of certain principles than the absence of training. But at the same time, I couldn't remember even the principles being addressed in a practical way. I concluded that Bible college doesn't prepare you for everything and simply placed these questions on the back burner.

As time went on we faced these same issues over and over, and I often wondered if any of my friends in the ministry were facing similar questions. To my surprise, the questions I was struggling with didn't seem to matter to many of my peers. But they did matter, at least it seemed like they should. I knew things were to be done decently and in order in the church, and I knew the issues I was struggling with had to have answers. But I just was not seeing them in the Scriptures. I have learned since those early days that rather than expanding our understanding, sometimes education actually limits or hinders our understanding. I mean a man only knows what he knows. That is not to say a man shouldn't grow. He should and he must, especially in the ministry. But sometimes a man comes to understand something in a way that actually becomes the reason why he is unable to grow beyond the point he finds himself. Let me give you a personal illustration.

Before entering seminary, I had already completed my undergraduate schooling in the field of science. Throughout my education I was taught to accept the theory of evolution and all of its supporting theories. But they were not just theories, they were the "facts!" These so-called "facts" conflicted with my faith as a Christian. I found myself resolving the conflict by simply compartmentalizing my Christianity, separating it from my chosen profession. However, my general acceptance of the theories of evolution kept coming into conflict with my belief that the Bible should be taken literally. Did God create the universe in a literal six-day week or did He not? I found myself questioning God rather than science. This I could not do! I resolved to believe God even if I did not have all the answers. You see, one false premise will always lead a man to other false premises, and once error is accepted as a fact it becomes very difficult to break free of its influence on one's thinking. Not long after this struggle I was introduced to the scientific arguments of creationism by one of my professors, and for me, the debate was ended. By the way, this personal struggle took place in a liberal arts Bible college where most of my professors believed in the evolutionary theory in one form or another.

Many Christians today are unable to move forward in their understanding of Scripture because they have come to accept a false premise of one sort or another. In turn, the false premise affects their thinking in relation to a Bible subject, for example the New Testament church. It's like having a puzzle where some pieces fit as they are designed while others do not. You may eventually get an image with which you are happy, and if any image is the goal then I guess you have accomplished your purpose. But if the purpose of putting a puzzle together in the first place is to duplicate the image on the front of the box, then shouldn't that be the goal?

Not surprisingly, many Christians have been told what the image ought to look like and have even forced the pieces together to get that image, but it is not the one the Bible gives. The result of this kind of thinking is that a man can't move beyond a certain point because what he believes actually acts as a block in his progress. This was the kind of block I had experienced as a young preacher. My understanding of the New Testament church had been handicapped by my education, not to mention years of indoctrination from a variety of sources. My understanding of the New Testament church was at odds with Scripture, and the pieces just did not fit the image found in the Bible.

Now here are some of the issues I struggled with as a young preacher. First, what was the nature of the New Testament church? How do we properly define the church? Has the New Testament church always existed since its founding in its original form? Has it changed, and if it has, can it still be the church that Jesus started? Was the church described in the New Testament invisible or was it visible or was it both at the same time? If it was invisible, how do we reconcile the language of the Bible that seems to contradict this conclusion? How are believers to be added to the church? Is membership even required? Is membership a biblical expectation or just a human tradition? Are there any limitations on those we receive? What part does baptism play? Is baptism merely an outward sign of an inward change? Are we expected to receive all those who desire admission regardless of the timing and mode of their baptism? Does every church have the proper authority to baptize its converts?

Furthermore, what about doctrinal diversity; does it matter? Are all believers part of the body of Christ regardless of their doctrinal persuasion? If so, to what extent do we allow for doctrinal diversity and still consider a church legitimate? Can a man believe anything as long as he holds to the fundamentals? What do we consider the "fundamentals"? Is fellowship among the brethren the standard by which we measure our commitment to the ministry or is our loyalty to truth the measure?

Also, in regard to the Lord's Table, who do we admit to the Table? Is the Table open to all or is it limited in some way? Is it the Lord's Table or is it ours? Is the Table a Christian ordinance or a local church ordinance? Can we observe the Table in any way we choose?

These are but some of the questions that I and every minister of the Gospel must answer in order to correctly carry out his calling as God intended. Over a period of years, I became determined to answer these questions from a biblical perspective. I did not believe

Preface

that these were unimportant questions. These matters deserved better than to be treated with indifference.

So, with Bible in hand as the measure of all things, I began to search for materials to read, and to my surprise I found that most of the books I found on these subjects were books written in much earlier times. Many of them were from the eighteenth and nineteenth centuries and were only available as reprints that were not widely circulated. I began to build a library of these books and materials as they became available to me. After more than twenty years of study, I have come to the conclusion that this material must be addressed afresh, published, and disseminated as God allows. Other good men have published excellent works dealing with these subjects in part. However, more needs to be done. So, we have embarked in our own meager effort to expose God's people afresh to principles that are rooted in Scripture and evidenced by the hallowed history of Christ's church through the centuries.

I am greatly appreciative of the encouragement I have received from the Striving Together Publishers of Lancaster Baptist Church in Lancaster, California, and for their support in this project. I hope the reader will read this work with an open heart and a hungry soul. I realize that some of the book's positions will be new to some, but they represent the historical position of the New Testament church as defined herein. Thank you for your interest.

Evangelist Mike Gass
Medford, Oregon
April 2009

PART 1 ONE

The Origin of the New Testament Church

PERSONAL OBSERVATIONS

The Origin of the New Testament Church

It is not unusual for most men to arrive at an opinion based upon their own personal observation. This is true especially when certain facts crucial to their understanding may be missing. It is possible for someone to arrive at a proper conclusion through personal observation, but it is more likely that he will come to a wrong conclusion when information is missing. His experience may be limited, his knowledge incomplete, or the framework of his personal observation may not be a full representation of reality. Regardless of the reason, the result is the same. Personal observation often leaves men with something short of the full truth. When it comes to the subject of church history, specifically the *origin* of the New Testament church, the tendency of most Christians is to define and identify the church as it appears to them in real time. Their understanding is the result of their own personal observation. However, their personal observation alone does not guarantee that the conclusions they reach are biblically correct.

Across our great land in almost every city—and sometimes on almost every street corner—there is a church. All of them claim to have the truth, or at least a large enough portion of it to be legitimate in their claim to be a *church*. The reality is that for the most part, these churches do not agree with each other in doctrine or practice. Based upon this personal observation alone we might conclude that God, therefore, must be the author of this confusion. Yet we all realize that this cannot be true according to 1 Corinthians 14:33. It makes no sense logically or biblically. How can God be the source of such confusion? Nevertheless, we find ourselves in a dilemma. Our Christian culture demands that we accept the claims of everyone, yet we are not convinced intellectually that everyone deserves that credibility. Just how do we determine such credibility?

In the current Christian culture it seems that everyone has been given the right to claim legitimacy by virtue of the claim itself. Doctrinal integrity is rarely the issue. It is more a matter of *live and let live* or *don't ask and don't tell*. Any debate is seen as unloving or unkind, and to challenge someone's claim of legitimacy is considered divisive. There has rarely been a time when there has been more confusion on this subject than today. We need to return to an honest and unbiased study of God's Word concerning the New Testament church. It is our desire to do just that. We begin by examining the New Testament church in light of its true beginnings. And although the origin of the New Testament church is a historical fact, it is the Bible that renders both the historical and doctrinal accounts that are necessary for a proper context of the matter. That is not to say that history in a secular sense does not play an important and necessary role in our understanding, but it is the Word of God—the Holy Bible—that is our primary source of information. History can easily be interpreted according to prejudice, but the Bible stands upon its own claims without the admixture of prejudice. Whom do we trust to give us the truth without an admixture of error?

In my lifetime the world has become a very cynical place. Few people genuinely trust their fellow human beings. Even in the Christian community there seems to be little trust. I understand that we are all sinners and that our hearts are desperately wicked, but I also know that if a man is in Christ, he is a new creature! Certainly, when we get saved some things ought to change about us. Still we do not find many people we feel we can fully trust. Could it be that we have tolerated lying for so long in our culture, both publicly and personally, that there is little trust placed in the words that anyone speaks today? We are not sure that the man even exists who will speak the truth without an agenda or hidden motive. Consequently, if a man should speak the truth, his words are simply placed on the table of opinion with no more merit than any other opinion.

This distrust has generally brought about a very important change in how many Christians seek out a place to worship God. Rather than examine the beliefs of a church, many look for an emotional connection first or exclusively. They look for a church that can make their worship experience more meaningful. Doctrinal substance is rarely a priority in that assessment. This lack of doctrinal emphasis has not always been the case in America. There was a time when sound doctrine was very important to the average Christian. The pervasive attitude today seems to be, "You can't believe anyone anyway," or "Things are always changing, and because no one is really sure of anything, it is just best to be non-denominational in your thinking." In other words, we are not sure who is right, and it does not really matter to us anymore anyway.

This "neutral" position that frames some good non-denominational thinking is rooted in a distorted view of the Bible. It is often a view that the Bible may be interpreted as one pleases and all sincere conclusions are equally valid (even if contradictory!). Scripture states that, *"no prophecy of the scripture is of any private interpretation"* (2 Peter 1:20). That simply means that God in His wisdom and authority said exactly what He meant to say. Our responsibility is not to put a "spin" on what God has said, but to obey it! We are not to approach the Scriptures as if God's real intentions were to hide the truth or make it difficult to understand. Somewhere along the line we have ignored the fact that any variance from God's intended thought is error. It is for this reason that Peter (2 Peter 1:16) reassures the reader that *"we have not followed cunningly devised fables."* He was acknowledging that the potential exists to fabricate error. When a man arrives at a conclusion that is at odds with God's intention and then refuses to adjust his error, he has prejudiced his understanding. Such an approach to the Bible lends itself to fabrication.

Historically it is apparent that when men's conclusions are at odds with the clear teaching of the Word of God, men simply devise systems of religion that reflect what they desire to be true. Rather than adjust their conclusions in light of Scripture, they often create religious systems that are so intricate that it becomes very difficult to unravel the doctrinal mess that results. The truth is perverted, the simple are led astray, the mature become more cynical, and the "simplicity" of the Gospel is lost. Peter called these beliefs "fables" (fabrications). Today, it seems that the more intricate the fable, the more believable it becomes. It is as though we believe the more complex something is, the more likely it came from God. To some, the less something can be understood or proven by Scripture, the more spiritual it becomes. The recent interest in the spurious *Da Vinci Code* illustrates this principle quite well.

I recently came across a quote by one of the leaders of the new Emergent church movement. If you are not yet familiar with this movement, I believe you will be in the near future. It is as dangerous a movement as Christianity has ever seen. The quote comes from Leonard Sweet, theologian, mentor, and leader in the Emergent church movement, and demonstrates the kind of rambling doublespeak that far too often has come to typify Christian dialogue. Speaking of being culturally relevant, Mr.

Sweet says, "New Lights offer up themselves as the cosmions of a mind-of-Christ conscience. As a cosmion incarnating the cells of a new body, New Lights will function as transitional vessels through which transforming energy can renew the divine image in the world, moving postmoderns from one state of embodiment to another." Here, much is said; little, I suspect, is meant; and clarity is certainly not the aim of the statement. It is intellectual elitism. But the quote does illustrate how men allure and entangle others with the use of nonsensical, obscurantist language while almost saying something.

As for the New Testament church, there is nothing more misunderstood in the Christian world. It is impossible to separate the New Testament church from the person and work of Jesus Christ. Yet many Christians treat the church with indifference, rarely examining the Scriptures to validate their own understanding or to challenge the gainsayer. The New Testament church and our proper understanding of it will determine our attitudes toward such things as soulwinning, discipleship, service, giving, and a host of other things involved in responsible Christian living. The psalmist said, *"If the foundations be destroyed, what can the righteous do?"* (Psalm 11:3). The church is foundational to the kingdom work of Christ on this earth and will be until Christ returns. However, if the biblical concept of the church continues to erode as it has for the last four hundred years, the end result cannot be good. I fear the religious trappings of that Great Whore of the Revelation are almost finished and that her attire is about to be completed! Soon she shall ride.

> *...and I saw a woman sit upon a scarlet coloured beast, full of names of blasphemy, having seven heads and ten horns. And the woman was arrayed in purple and scarlet colour, and decked with gold and precious stones and pearls, having a golden cup in her hand full of abominations and filthiness of her fornication: And upon her forehead was a name written, MYSTERY,*

> BABYLON THE GREAT, THE MOTHER OF HARLOTS AND ABOMINATIONS OF THE EARTH.
> —REVELATION 17:3–5

Since the Protestant Reformation, Christianity has been deluged with movements that claim to have re-discovered one truth or another. Every time someone claims to have unearthed some neglected or new truth, there are always people who flock to him (or her), eager it seems to create a new celebrity. Gathering enough people, he starts a new movement. The movement, seeking legitimacy, ultimately identifies itself as a *church*. Convincing enough people, they build *churches*. After building enough churches they are called a **denomination**. Let the denomination exist long enough and it gains the respect of its peers (other denominations). Once the movement is respected by its peers, it is legitimized regardless of the correctness of its views. Its views are simply a matter of interpretation.

The story of the Tower of Babel makes for a great illustration at this point. It is here that men once decided to devise their own plan in contradiction to the clearly revealed will of God to *"replenish the earth"* (Genesis 9:1). The Tower of Babel stands as a monument to the confusion that results when men refuse to simply and humbly obey God. There are two statements important to note in the biblical account in Genesis 11. First, the justification for the disobedience was to build a tower whose top may reach to Heaven. Now these

---

DEFINING THE TERMS

Denomination: *The word denomination literally means "to name." In a religious sense, it is an effort to distinguish a religious group by name whose doctrinal uniqueness warrants an identity separate from those that already exist. Mathematically it represents a number that has been divided or multiplied by another.*

were not foolish or unlearned men. They did not believe they could actually build a tower that would reach Heaven. But, they believed that adding religious trappings to their rebellion would gain them the support of the people. Furthermore, connecting Heaven to the project would raise their efforts to a lofty and noble gesture. This gesture, in turn, would most certainly obligate God to lend His support to their ambitions.

There was a second statement made in connection to the tower that is very revealing. The statement reveals the true motive. They said, *"and let us make us a name"*! You see, they desired to make for themselves a name—a legacy. They desired greatness among their peers and needed to build a kingdom on earth. The kingdom required a movement! That in turn required them to deceive others into believing it was the will of God. The project could not be completed without the sweat equity of the masses. The deception was complete; the project commenced; but God was not happy. Rather than obey the clear revelation of God to replenish the earth, they set off on their own path to build a kingdom of human origin. Ultimately, confusion was the result!

Confusion results every time men devise their own systems of religion. Some men create what they believe best represents the divine. It is always of human origin, rooted in philosophy rather than theology. On the other hand, in the Christian faith some men devise their systems by some peculiar interpretation of the Scriptures. Again, towers are built, and names are made, but confusion is always the result.

From where does all the doctrinal diversity come? The Bible says several things concerning this, but here are three reasons. First, we are told that God gives all believers a spirit *"of a sound mind"* (2 Timothy 1:7). That is, there is not a single Christian who is incapable of understanding biblical truth. It is not the depth of the Word of God, but its breadth which most Christians fail to master. Without a broad understanding of the Bible, confusion is more likely, and the believer becomes more susceptible to doctrinal error. However, the Christian who understands the importance of the whole counsel of God will do his due diligence in comparing Scripture with Scripture in their proper context.

Second, Paul told young Timothy that if one is to be *"approved unto God,"* rather than to be *"ashamed,"* he must be *"rightly dividing the word of truth"* (2 Timothy 2:15). The obvious fact is that many have perverted the truth either knowingly or unknowingly because they did not rightly divide the truth. This failure to properly divide the Word of truth results in error.

Third, the Bible says that in the *"latter times some shall depart from the faith, giving heed to seducing spirits, and doctrines of devils"* (1 Timothy 4:1). Thus, we are warned that not all doctrine that men come to believe is doctrine from God or His Word! Satan is a master at deception. That little word *some* is a reference to God's people, not the lost. Indeed, many of God's people have departed from the simple faith of the New Testament and placed their hope in the vain traditions of human origin.

As we consider the origin of the New Testament church, I hope you will take it as a fresh re-introduction to the subject. I say this because I know that for many Christians this will seem like such an insignificant subject to cover—you have already settled that matter long ago. Be patient with me, and together let's make sure all the pieces of the puzzle are where they should be. We will deal with some issues later in this book that will require a sound understanding of the church that Jesus built. We will begin with a rather unusual character in his day named John the Baptist.

CHAPTER ONE

The Framework: John the Baptist

It is important to emphasize again that *"God is not the author of confusion"* (1 Corinthians 14:33). Everything God does reveals itself in the context of structure and order, not chaos. When we consider the origin of the New Testament church, we see it exemplify this order. The church did not appear by accident or happenstance, as many would believe. Upon careful examination of the Scriptures, we find that the initial framework for the New Testament church actually appeared long before the day of **Pentecost**. That framework originated with John the Baptist.

John the Baptist was an unusual character in the Bible. According to Jesus, he was without peer in his own day in that there was none *"born of women"* any greater than John (Matthew 11:11). John probably did not fully understand the great significance of his work of preparation on behalf of the Saviour in relation to the creation of the church, but his ministry and its importance should not be overlooked. We can summarize John's ministry in four ways: (1) His Mission; (2) His Authority; (3) His Method; and (4) His Credibility.

His Mission

The Bible says that John was God's *"messenger"* sent to *"prepare… the way of the Lord, make his paths straight"* (Mark 1:1–3). This was a fulfillment of a passage in the book of Malachi (Malachi 3:1–3). Christ's earthly ministry began with the cleansing of the temple. However, the passage also states that God would send a messenger who would *"prepare the way"* before Him (see also Isaiah 40:3 and John 1:23). The *"messenger"* was John of course. The *"messenger"* is further described in Malachi as *Elijah* (Malachi 4:5). These prophecies were written some four hundred years before the time of John the Baptist. Jesus confirmed that John was indeed the fulfillment of this prophecy in Matthew 17:11–12. Years before, the angel who announced John's birth to his father Zechariah also confirmed the fulfillment of the prophecy in Luke 1:11–17.

John the Baptist was a man with a mission! From a human perspective, the references in the book of Malachi alone should have alerted the religious leaders that the kingdom was at hand. Their Messiah was about to be revealed, but their hearts were hardened. Rather than see Jesus as the Christ, they saw Him as a competitor. Envy and jealousy filled their hearts. Thus, John's ministry was directed toward the common people. He was sent to *"make ready a people prepared for the Lord"* (Luke 1:17). The apostles were no doubt among those whom John's ministry had affected. This preparation was both spiritual and physical in nature. In understanding this two-fold preparation, we understand the God-given mission of John the Baptist.

Spiritually, John prepared the way of the Lord by renewing the Old Testament focus on **the kingdom of Heaven**.

His message and announcement that the kingdom of Heaven was at hand caused no small stir. This message of repentance was manifested in two very important ways. There was first the *preaching* of repentance followed by a *baptism* unto repentance.

To make the *"paths straight"* John was to bring down the high things and bring up the low things. That which was crooked he was to make straight, and the rough places were to be made smooth (Luke 3:4–5). John did this through the preaching of repentance. According to Acts 17:30, there was a time when God winked at (i.e., overlooked) the ignorance of man that was rooted in the fallen nature. That is not to say that the sin of man was ignored or that God viewed man's sin as less egregious, but simply that the plan of redemption was not fully complete. Once the Gospel of the kingdom was introduced by John (Mark 1:1), God *"commandeth all men every where to repent"* (Acts 17:30). In other words, God

DEFINING THE TERMS

Pentecost: *Pentecost was celebrated by the Jews as the fiftieth (GK pentekostos) day after the presentation of the first harvested sheaf of the barley harvest, i.e., the fiftieth day from the first Sunday after Passover (Leviticus 23:15). It was known among the Jews as the "feast of weeks" (Exodus 34:22; Deuteronomy 16:10) and also as "the day of the first fruits" (Numbers 28:26; Exodus 23:16).*

The Kingdom of Heaven: *The kingdom of Heaven speaks of a divine or heavenly order of government, a theocracy. In relation to men, it refers to the divine authority that God exercises among men. Its primary use is found in Matthew because his Gospel is directed to the Jew. Elsewhere in the Gospels, the term kingdom of God is dominant. Whereas the former often has a historical connection, both terms deal with the redemptive work of God in real time whereby the authority of God is established in the hearts of men as evidenced in Jesus' discussion with Nicodemus (John 3).*

desired a straight and unrestricted path to every man's heart and life. To repent was to be "converted" (to be turned). That is, every man was to be turning away—every one from his iniquities (Acts 3:19, 26). Those who responded to the message were then baptized as evidence that they had not only accepted the message but also the focus of the kingdom, the coming Messiah.

Physically, John prepared the way of the Lord as a direct result of his message of repentance. That is, he gathered together the physical or human material out of which the Lord formed the first church known to us as the church which was at Jerusalem. We are introduced to these men in Luke 6. All of them except Judas Iscariot, who is described as the traitor (Luke 6:16), were likely the disciples of John first. At the very least, they had repented and were baptized under the preaching ministry of John. They were thus numbered among those looking forward to the coming of the kingdom. They were a spiritually-prepared people made *ready* by the ministry of John the Baptist.

His Authority

In Luke 20, Jesus was asked a question by the chief priests and scribes. They had challenged His authority as well as the words He had spoken. Jesus responded by saying that if they could first answer His question, then He would answer theirs. He then proceeded to ask, *"The baptism of John, was it from heaven, or of men?"* They reasoned within themselves that if they said that John's authority to baptize was contrived in his own heart and mind as they believed, then the people around them would stone them because the people counted John a prophet. On the other hand, if they acknowledged that his authority came from Heaven or God, then Jesus would surely confront them with their resistance to John's God-ordained mission. In frustration they responded, *"they could not tell."* So

Chapter One—The Framework: John the Baptist

Jesus Himself raises the issue of proper authority when His own authority was questioned.

Submission to authority is exactly why Jesus, who was without sin, was baptized by John. If the baptism of John was from Heaven, then to submit to it would *"fulfill all righteousness."* It demonstrates even our Lord's attitude toward proper authority. John himself verified that his authority to baptize came from *"above."* In John 1:33 he said, *"…but he that sent me to baptize with water, the same said unto me…."* This matter of proper authority is essential to our understanding of the New Testament church. For if any church claiming to have Heaven's blessing or authority in fact does not have it at all, then that church is scattering rather than gathering the harvest.

This issue was raised one other time in connection with John when he learned of the success of Jesus' ministry as *"all men come to him"* rather than to John. John's response was typical, *"He must increase, but I must decrease"* (John 3:30). But he also said, *"A man can receive nothing, except it be given him from heaven,"* and thus taught us a lesson on proper authority (John 3:27). Authority comes from above…Heaven…GOD!

Another example of this principle is seen in the response of the Roman centurion who had asked Jesus to heal his dying servant (Matthew 8). When Jesus said that He would go and heal him, the centurion declared that he himself was a man under Roman authority and when he commanded a man to go, he went; and when he commanded a man to come, he came. These actions came because he was a man *under* authority! So he simply asked Jesus to speak the word, and he believed his servant would be healed. Jesus Himself was amazed at the man's understanding of proper authority. Other examples of this principle could be used, but the lesson should be obvious. One does not take authority upon himself. Authority is something that is given from above; it is vertical not horizontal. Men tend to take things into their own hands and then ask God to bless their plans as they attempt to build towers that will reach to Heaven. Although it is often done under the guise of piety and humility, or noble intention, it is still rebellion! We were not placed here on this earth to build a monument to our own glory. The name we should seek to exalt is not our own, but that of the Saviour. How often has the work of God been confused and estranged from mankind because someone wanted to carve out his own little niche? This type of action is not the kingdom of God coming down to man; it is man establishing his own kingdom on earth!

So, any claim to legitimacy must rise and fall on parameters established by divine authority. Without that authority, all we have is a kingdom or organization of human origin.

His Method

As we have seen, John clearly acknowledged that his practice of baptizing those whom had received his message of repentance came from the Heavenly Father. The means of this instruction, whether by revelation, angel or vision, we cannot tell. However, the means does not require our understanding. What is important is that we understand that the work of God is not carried on by self-willed men but by the direction of God. With the multitude of examples provided in the Scriptures, we are compelled to understand that the work of God is always defined by His specific directions. In other words, John was to not only *"prepare the way of the Lord,"* but he was also given the responsibility of introducing Jesus to the world! Baptism was the means or method God chose to accomplish this task. Baptism is a symbol of death, burial, and resurrection, and as such would symbolize the death and resurrection of Jesus Christ.

When John was asked to explain the practice, he declared that *"he* [Christ] *should be made manifest to Israel"* (John 1:31). The word *manifest* here means to make something or in this case *someone* "obvious." Now this meaning makes perfect sense when we come to realize that Jesus was the only man who has ever been resurrected from the grave under His *own power* (see John 2:19–22)! Others such as Lazarus came forth from the grave, but Jesus was the only one who came out of the grave under His own power. He raised Himself from the dead according to John 2. Baptism then points men to the reality of a resurrected Christ and that He alone can save from the penalty of sin and death. Because He was able to save Himself, certainly He is able to save others. Baptism means far more than an "outward sign of an inward change." My, how we attempt to bring attention and glory to ourselves, even in being saved and baptized. The emphasis of baptism is not for our personal benefit or glory but to draw attention to Christ as the Saviour of the world as proven by His resurrection. It is a witnessing tool, a clear testimony by the one being baptized to those who witness the event, that Jesus is *"the resurrection, and the life"* (John 11:25)!

Of course, in addition to this, we understand that baptism identifies us with Christ (Romans 6). Here the Bible clearly teaches us that believers are to *"walk in newness of life"* because of the life they now have in Christ. The old man is to be reckoned dead and the new man *"alive unto God through Jesus Christ our Lord."* Baptism thus pictures not only the death of the old man but also this new life in Christ by the power of His resurrection. So, the point of Romans 6 remains the resurrection of Christ.

His Credibility

I suppose most Christians consider John the Baptist as simply an interesting figure in the Gospels with no real significance or purpose. The apostles themselves held him in very high regard. Not long after Judas committed suicide, Peter was gathered together with the remaining disciples and spoke in reference to Psalm 109:8, *"let another take his* [Judas'] *office."* In his statement he gave three criteria for the selection of a replacement to Judas:

> *Wherefore of these men which have companied with us all the time that the Lord Jesus went in and out among us, Beginning from the baptism of John, unto that same day that he was taken up from us, must one be ordained to be a witness with us of his resurrection.*
> —ACTS 1:21–22

The first requirement was that the individual would be someone who had followed Jesus very closely (*"companied with us"*). Although he was not numbered among the original twelve, he would need to be a part of that larger body of people who followed Jesus day by day. They would certainly be familiar with all the teachings of Christ and thus would be able to communicate those things to others.

The second requirement would be regarded as equally important and is found in the latter part of this verse. That is, the man would have to be an eyewitness to the resurrected Lord. How could someone be counted as one of the twelve if they were not a witness to the fact that Jesus had risen from the dead?

Now in the context of the first two requirements, we have the third. The first two are logical expectations, and most would accept this to be so. But if the first two are logical conclusions, so must be the third, and I have purposely dealt with them out of order. The third requirement was that of a proper baptism (*"beginning from the baptism of John"*). The replacement of Judas must have a proper baptism. Remember, by John's own testimony as well as the example of Jesus, we know that John's baptism was from Heaven. It had divine sanction. Peter and the other disciples considered the baptism of John essential. It was a reference point for them at a time when they were still coming to a complete understanding of their role in the church. Without a proper baptism by a proper authority,

Chapter One—The Framework: John the Baptist

the replacement of Judas would fail to meet the standard that God had established in John. In addition, they were fully aware that in the Great Commission Jesus had specifically required the church to baptize its converts. How could the replacement be expected to baptize others when he had not been baptized himself?

Furthermore, since this was part of the criteria, I think it is safe to conclude that John had likewise baptized all of the disciples. We know that all the disciples met the first two requirements. It would be just a little bit hypocritical to require something of a new man that they had not willingly submitted to themselves. Again, even Jesus was baptized of John and thus *"fulfilled all righteousness."* In John 4:1 we read that the Pharisees believed that Jesus made and baptized more disciples than John. But in verse 2, a clarification is made that it was the disciples of Jesus who administered baptism to His converts rather than Jesus Himself. Once again, it would seem unreasonable to assume that the apostles had not been baptized themselves prior to their responsibilities described in this passage.

John's credibility is thus established by the action of the disciples in replacing Judas, and their actions reveal their understanding of John's divine purpose. John's credibility, in turn, hinges upon the authority under which he ministered. Without that authority from above, John is like the thousands throughout history seeking their own glory, building names for themselves while they attempt to build something that will reach Heaven.

So in connection with the New Testament church, what do we learn from an examination of the ministry of John the Baptist? First, we see that everything God does has order to it. Nothing is done in confusion. The way of the Lord was a prepared path. Second, we see that all authority must come from above. It is wrong to assume God's blessing in the absence of proper authority. That authority must come from above. Third, the work of God should always point men to the Saviour, not religious exercise. John knew his place, and as Jesus increased, he willingly decreased. Finally, by

John's example we learn that the credibility of any man should be determined by his allegiance to the truth of Scripture rather than to the traditions of men. These basic principles form a framework by which the New Testament church is to be understood by God's people. They are essential for a proper understanding of the New Testament church both historically and in the present day.

As important as John the Baptist was in relation to the principles we have just enumerated, we are not at all suggesting that he was the founder of the New Testament church. That honor belonged to Jesus alone. John played out his role and as a faithful steward simply prepared the way of the Lord spiritually. Jesus was the founder of the New Testament church. It was and is His church. As we examine Christ's relationship to His church in the next chapter, we will see how these principles play an integral part in the formation of the first church.

CHAPTER TWO

The Founder: Jesus Christ

Sometime during or near the second year of our Lord's ministry, Jesus declared to the disciples that He would build His church. Upon the occasion of Peter's testimony that he believed Jesus to be the "Christ," Jesus said, *"...thou art Peter, and upon this rock I will build my church; and the gates of hell shall not prevail against it"* (Matthew 16:18).

There is a play on words here in this statement. Simon's surname, Peter (Greek *petros*), is a word that means "stone" (a small rock) and speaks of Peter's inherent weakness and instability. But the reference to *"this rock"* (Greek *petra*) meaning a large rock, is an obvious reference to the confession that Peter had just made, that Jesus was the *"Christ, the Son of the living God"* (Matthew 16:16). As such, Jesus declared that His church would be established upon the fact that He is the Christ, the anointed of God. In other words, Jesus was the founder of the New Testament church, and His authority to do so came from above.

The debate among Christians for the last four hundred years has been how one is to define that church. That is, whether to define it as visible and **local**, or as invisible and universal. The issue is clarified when one remembers that the Greek word *ecclesia*, which is translated "church" in our English Bible, literally means "a called-out assembly." In order to meet this definition, the New Testament church must be understood as a local, autonomous (self-governing) congregation or assembly of believers gathered together in a given location with a common purpose. The fact that believers are expected to assemble together (Hebrews 10:25) implies a common purpose. If there is no reason to assemble locally, then the New Testament church loses its reason to exist at all. That reason is found in the Great Commission (Matthew 28:18–20)—the command to take the Gospel into the world and disciple those who come to a saving knowledge of Jesus Christ.

Furthermore, it makes no sense to speak of the New Testament church in terms of being invisible. We know that God is not the author of confusion and that the church is commanded to do all things decently and in order. If the church is to be understood as invisible, the structure and order of its obligation to carry out the Great Commission is obviously missing. Thus, we are of necessity

DEFINING THE TERMS

Local: *The term local is used often in this book. It refers to the existence of New Testament churches that are visible rather than invisible. In other words, they are local in the sense that they have a particular location that is identifiable either in theory or context.*

Ecclesia: *The Greek word* ecclesia *originates from two words* kaleo *meaning "to call" and* ek *meaning "out." Thus the word literally means "to call out." It refers to the fact that the church is composed of a people called out from the world to Christ.*

forced to conclude that a local and autonomous church was what Jesus had in mind when He said, *"the gates of hell shall not prevail against it."* After all, the first church at Jerusalem was both local and autonomous.

Jesus Christ: the Head

> *...and gave him to be the head over all things to the church, Which is his body, the fulness of him that filleth all in all.*—EPHESIANS 1:22–23

> *And he is the head of the body, the church...that in all things he might have the preeminence.*
> —COLOSSIANS 1:18

As the founder of His own unique New Testament church, Jesus is also described in the Scriptures as the *"head"* of that church. When the Bible speaks of a *head*, it is speaking of the individual who by all right and authority is the director or ruler of the church. Now, in conjunction with the head, there is a body. That body must be understood as individual local assemblies of believers. Furthermore, Jesus is the head over all things to the church. Thus, in the proper context of the local New Testament church, we would describe Jesus as the head of the affairs of each local assembly of believers. The analogy ought to be obvious. Although we will examine this principle in some detail later, it is important to note that the Scripture uses the human body as an illustration to describe the local New Testament church. Just as the human body has a head which directs the activities of the body, so Jesus directs the affairs of a local New Testament church.

Now, we must realize a very important principle which many fail to understand. If Jesus is supplanted or replaced as head, we no longer have the same church or body. Whether He is replaced by a man or group of men (as in an organization or hierarchy), once Jesus is removed from His sovereign authority over the local church, we no longer have the same church described in the New Testament. It is only by being the head of each assembly that Christ maintains His rightful preeminence in this God-given institution.

Jesus Christ: the Foundation

> ...I have laid the foundation, and another buildeth thereon. But let every man take heed how he buildeth thereupon. For other foundation can no man lay than that is laid, which is Jesus Christ.
> —1 CORINTHIANS 3:10–11

We now turn our attention to the foundation upon which the New Testament church was established. According to his own testimony, it was the Apostle Paul who laid the doctrinal foundation of the early church. This doctrinal foundation came to Paul by the revelation of God. It was not the personal invention of the apostle. Rather, Paul is speaking here of the proper installment of sound doctrine. Those who were to follow after him must build on the existing foundation, not add to it or reconfigure it. They were to build using gold, silver, and precious stones as opposed to wood, hay, and stubble. The reference to wood, hay, and stubble is speaking of error or unsound doctrine, which does not find its origin in the teachings of the prophets of the Old Testament or the apostles of the New Testament. This is in contrast to the gold, silver, and precious stones of sound doctrine. Jesus Christ is the foundation, whereas the doctrine of the Old and New Testaments are the building blocks of ecclesiastical integrity that testify of Christ. Thus, we see a warning to those who would not heed this call for doctrinal integrity—their works would not stand the test of fire. In turn, they would lose reward. This admonition could well be taken today in light of the fact that so many insist that doctrinal integrity is not important. Indeed, to many, any effort to arrive at the truth of Scriptures as *the standard* is dismissed as futile as well as bigoted!

Jesus Christ: the Chief Cornerstone

...Jesus Christ himself being the chief corner stone;
—EPHESIANS 2:20

As the founder of the New Testament church, Jesus is also described as the Chief Cornerstone. It was the practice in the ancient world as a new building was about to be erected to place a large cornerstone at a location from which the foundation might be properly aligned. Without that reference point, the building would have absolutely no hope of ever being correctly aligned. Now when the Bible speaks of Jesus as the Chief Cornerstone, it is drawing an analogy from this ancient practice. Christianity, in the context of the doctrinal parameters of the New Testament church, is to be properly aligned according to the Chief Cornerstone. The doctrine of the church is to be the doctrine of the New Testament and not that of some later origin.

Jesus said that those things He spoke were things He had received from the Heavenly Father (see John 7:16). Furthermore, Jesus taught the disciples that they were to teach all nations *"all things whatsoever I have commanded you"* (Matthew 28:20). The Spirit of truth would not only lead them into all truth, but would also bring to their remembrance the things Jesus had taught them in the three and a half years He ministered among them. Does this not compel us to accept that truth is not something that is simply in the eyes of the beholder? Rather, it is something clearly taught in Scripture. Without realizing this fact, the church is not properly aligned on the cornerstone. This is at the very heart of the confusion that exists today in Christianity. Rather than every man *doing* what is right in his own eyes, every man is *believing* what is right in his own eyes! The New Testament has ceased to be the primary source of truth. Instead, it becomes the ratification of that which one has already come to believe. *All too often the real source for those beliefs is from somewhere other than the Word of God.* The emphasis placed on the value and importance of truth in the epistle of 2 John underscores this very point.

Jesus spoke of this problem in Luke 11 and again in Matthew 6:

> *The light of the body is the eye: therefore when thine eye is single* [healthy], *thy whole body also is full of light; but when thine eye is evil* [unhealthy], *thy body also is full of darkness. Take heed therefore that the light which is in thee be not darkness. If thy whole body therefore be full of light, having no part dark, the whole shall be full of light, as when the bright shining of a candle doth give thee light.*—LUKE 11:34–36

> *…If therefore the light that is in thee be darkness, how great is that darkness!*—MATTHEW 6:23

Here we have a metaphor based on an ancient belief that light enters the body through the eye. If the eye is healthy and functions as it should, then the whole body is full of light. If, however, the eye is evil or unable to do its job, the body will in turn be filled with darkness. The context of these statements is the admonition of our Lord that lighting a candle and then placing it under a cover benefits no one; the benefit of the light is *"that they which come in may see the light."* Jesus is warning of the danger of false doctrine that results in darkness in a man's life. But that darkness does not stop there. Just as a lighted candle placed on a candlestick benefits all who enter into its light, so the darkness of false doctrine, propagated by its adherents, deceives all those who enter into it. Those who are seeking light (truth) find only darkness (error)!

For example, if a man places a pair of sunglasses over his eyes, everything he looks at will be colored according to the tint in those

Chapter Two—The Founder of the Church: Jesus Christ

glasses. His body (according to the analogy) will then be filled with the effect of the sunglasses. In the same way, if a man filters everything he reads in the Holy Scriptures by a pre-conceived set of beliefs derived from a source outside the Bible, he fills his life spiritually with darkness. By so doing, he not only limits his own access to the truth; but by propagating his beliefs, he offers the promise of light to others when he has none to give. If the light that is in a man be darkness indeed, how great is that darkness!

Truth must be derived from a correct source, and that source for the Christian is the Word of God, which has not been filtered through a set of pre-determined beliefs of human origin. Though men may or may not proclaim the truth, our responsibility is to examine everything we hear in light of the Scriptures. Our loyalties are not to rest with a man or a movement, no matter how well intentioned, but with Christ. It is Christ alone who is our Chief Cornerstone!

Once we come to accept the fact that the New Testament church is divine in its origin and that Jesus was its founder, then it becomes reasonable for us to make the case that no man has the right to alter the church and make it into something that Christ never intended it to be. It is His church not ours! Yet as it will be shown later, it seems that throughout the centuries men have more often than not attempted to re-create the church after their own image or liking. We are assured that before Jesus left this earth, He put in place all that was necessary for the church to be the church. Nothing has been left to imagination; nothing has been left to speculation. The Founder has not left us blind and faltering.

Having understood that Christ is the founder of His church, we will now turn our attention to the apostles. As we will see, the apostles play a crucial role in the development of the New Testament church. It is by them, humanly speaking, that we have received the canon of Scripture in the form of the New Testament. By divine inspiration, they laid the doctrinal foundation of the New Testament according to the will of the "Chief Cornerstone." Thus its authority originates from above. It is upon that foundation alone we are to build the local New Testament church.

If men could only see the damage and confusion they inevitably create by dethroning the Saviour and placing themselves as the "head," perhaps the historical scene would be different than it is. That is not to say that men who violate this principle are always guilty of rebellion in the strictest sense or that their motives should always be suspect. Indeed, the reality is more likely that men take such action in ignorance, believing they are a help rather than a hindrance to the kingdom. But the results are the same—confusion with new foundations being laid.

CHAPTER THREE

The Facilitators: The Apostles

Their Calling

We have seen that God sent a man named John to prepare the way of the Lord. John did this faithfully, although his ministry was cut short. We summarized the ministry of John the Baptist earlier in two ways. First, he spiritually prepared the way of the Lord by virtue of the message of repentance. Second, John prepared the way of the Lord physically by gathering together the individuals whom Christ would later use in the creation of the New Testament church.

In both the Gospels of Mark and Luke, we are given the details of our Lord's selection of those men who would become the "apostles," or *sent ones*. Once again, let us remember that it is likely that those who followed Jesus had followed John previously. For example, in John 1:35–51, we are given the account of John's testimony that Jesus was the Lamb of God. He made that declaration in the presence of two of his own disciples, one of whom was Andrew, Simon Peter's brother. Andrew in turn introduced Peter to Jesus. According to Luke 5:10, James and John, the sons of Zebedee, were partners with Andrew and Peter in a fishing business in the city of Capernaum (Mark 1:21, 29). It was here that upon a miraculous catch of fishes, these four men forsook all and followed Jesus. These four, along with Philip, were from the city of Bethsaida which was located on the Sea of Galilee, as was Capernaum (John 1:43–44). The Bible says that Jesus went into Galilee and found Philip, and *"saith unto him, Follow me."* Philip then brought Nathanael (identified elsewhere in the Scriptures as Bartholomew). It was this small group of men who accompanied Jesus to the wedding in the city of Cana (John 2) where the first of many miracles took place. It was after the events of that day at the wedding of Cana that His disciples first *"believed on him."*

Now John, the Bible says, came into all the country about Jordan preaching the message of repentance. According to the Scriptures (John 3:23), John baptized at Aenon near Salim where there was *"much water."* It was here that the above-mentioned disciples were probably baptized unto John's baptism, for Aenon is not far from the Sea of Galilee. Jesus would also be baptized by John, but later in the Judean wilderness near Bethabara. To get a sense of the magnitude of John's ministry and its effect, we read in Mark 1 that there went *"out unto him all the land of Judaea, and they of Jerusalem, and were all baptized of him in the river of Jordan, confessing their sins"* (Mark 1:5). It is not unreasonable to expect from this statement that wherever John preached the message of repentance that great multitudes came out of the cities to the Jordan to hear this message. They were afterwards baptized unto repentance, and that among these, the future disciples of our Lord were numbered and baptized! As we have already suggested—given the fact that Peter makes John's baptism a prerequisite for the selection of the replacement for Judas after his suicide—it is reasonable to conclude that all the disciples had been baptized by John. Remember also, even our Lord was baptized of John in order to *"fulfill all righteousness."* This statement concerning

Christ's baptism was made in reference to John's testimony that he baptized by commandment of the Heavenly Father (John 1:33). Thus we see that John was used of God to gather together certain individuals whom Jesus would later appoint as His apostles. It was these men whom Jesus used to establish the institution of His church on this earth. This institution would carry the Gospel throughout the world in fulfillment of the Great Commission given to it in Matthew 28.

For the actual selection of the twelve from among the larger number of disciples, our attention is drawn to the early ministry of Jesus. As with John, we see that our Lord's ministry was greeted with great enthusiasm by the common people. The Bible says that there followed Jesus *"great multitudes of people from Galilee, and from Decapolis, and from Jerusalem, and from Judea, and from beyond Jordan"* (Matthew 4:25). However, as of yet an inner circle had not been formed. Out of the hundreds of disciples, who would form the inner circle? In the Gospels of Mark (3:13–14) and Luke (6:12–13) we are given the details. The Scriptures tell us of a night spent in prayer to His Heavenly Father. The next day Jesus called His disciples, and out of them He chose twelve whom He *"named apostles."* We see that Jesus chose out of His many disciples twelve special men who would be trained by Himself to be sent out later to take the Gospel into the world and to form local churches as God gave the increase.

Their Place

The very first church mentioned by name in the New Testament was the *"church which was at Jerusalem"* (Acts 8:1). Although the church is first mentioned in the book of Acts, the apostles are described as being gathered together in an upper room in John 20. We see them again in Acts 1 as they select a replacement for Judas and yet again on the day of Pentecost. Among the 120 present on those occasions were the apostles. The Apostle Paul states that, *"God hath set some in the church, first apostles"* in 1 Corinthians 12:28.

Now this statement is not just a reference to the position of importance that the apostles occupied, but perhaps more importantly, it is a reference to their order. It is clear from 1 Corinthians 12:18 that *"God set the members every one of them in the body, as it hath pleased him."* The apostles were thus the first members of the church that would become known to us as the church which was at Jerusalem. We see therefore their esteemed place in the creation of the church. Others would be added to these men, and a large increase to the membership was experienced on the day of Pentecost. Some three thousand new souls were added to this church that day alone. It is for this reason in part that we believe the church existed before the day of Pentecost. If this is not the case, then Acts 2:41 makes little sense, for it declares that those saved and baptized on the day of Pentecost *"were added unto them about three thousand souls."* To what were these new converts *added* if it was not to the local church at Jerusalem? The verses that follow make it clear that they *"continued stedfastly in the apostles' doctrine and fellowship, and in breaking of bread, and in prayers."* Indeed, verse 47 in the same passage identifies the church as the beneficiary of their addition.

In John 20:19–23, Jesus appeared in the midst of the assembled believers in the upper room. In this meeting He breathed on them and commanded them, *"receive ye the Holy Ghost."* This was His church! At that moment the institution of the church received the energizing presence of the Holy Spirit. That supernatural presence came in power on the day of Pentecost and enabled the apostles to capture the attention of the Jews *"dwelling at Jerusalem"* (see Acts 2:5, 14). Where before they were filled with fear, now they were fearless!

The day of Pentecost then, rather than being the advent of the church, was really the advent of world evangelism. Israel had generally failed to fulfill this responsibility during its long history in the Old Testament. Now, the Spirit-filled institution of the church was given that task. The apostles, as the first representatives of the church at Jerusalem, spoke on that Pentecost, and three thousand were saved and baptized. As we have already noted, those who were converted and baptized were added to that local church, for no other existed at that time. The apostles initiated the global advancement of the Gospel. Their work was empowered by the Spirit of God and orchestrated in and through the local church.

Their Importance

Now just how important are the apostles to the New Testament church? In Ephesians, Paul, once again dealing with the doctrine of the local New Testament church, says the following:

> *Now therefore ye are…fellowcitizens with the saints, and of the household of God; And are built upon the foundation of the apostles and prophets, Jesus Christ himself being the chief corner stone; In whom all the building fitly framed together groweth unto an holy temple in the Lord: In whom ye also are builded together for an habitation of God through the Spirit.*
> —EPHESIANS 2:19–22

As we have already discussed, there is only one foundation, and that foundation is Christ Jesus. In this passage of Scripture however, the Apostle Paul introduces us to the importance of doctrinal integrity. In relation to the chief cornerstone, the foundation is now seen in its doctrinal character. We are thus reminded of the need to maintain doctrinal purity. As the local church fulfills its responsibilities of evangelism and the discipleship of those who come to Christ, purity of doctrine is of the utmost importance.

The apostle describes the New Testament church as a building in process that requires things be "fitly framed together." The church at Ephesus was an example of this process. The phrase "fitly framed together" not only speaks of the joining of both Gentile and Jew in the local church, but more importantly, the necessity of having purity of doctrine. Thus, our attention is drawn to the role the apostles and Old Testament prophets played in the formation of God's building plan in the kingdom. The spiritual groundwork having been established by the prophets of the Old Testament, the apostles gave to the church the doctrines revealed to them by inspiration. Furthermore, the Holy Spirit would honor a New Testament church with His presence by abiding in their midst corporately, just as the church of Corinth had been taught earlier (see 1 Corinthians 3:9, 16–17).

Now the organization of the church was not an end in itself. As a living organism it was to reproduce itself; life always begets life and that after its own kind. The church of Jesus Christ is no different. The Gospel was to be taken into a lost and dying world, and the commission to do so came directly from the Lord. The disciples soon understood this fact as the Gospel made its way into places like Samaria, Ethiopia, Syria, and to the extremities of their immediate world. If Pentecost was not the agent of this understanding, certainly Gentile conversions outside Jerusalem would serve to prove the point. Once this was understood by the apostles, the Gospel became a window through which they could view the world through God's eyes. They caught a glimpse of eternity from God's perspective.

This Great Commission—as we often refer to it—contains the divine formula by which the Gospel was to be taken into the world. Listen, there are no loose strings here! This Commission is a centuries-old tried and tested formula. We would do well to remind ourselves that God did not devise a plan that may need adjustment as time goes on as determined by its success or failure. God instituted a formula that is designed to produce the result He desires. Our responsibility is to carry out the Great Commission as it was delivered to the first century church.

CHAPTER FOUR

The Formula: The Great Commission

The primary purpose of the local New Testament church is the spread of the Gospel to every corner of the earth. The local church does have other very important roles to play in the spiritual development of those who have been brought to Christ. However, without the focus of evangelism, the church is likely to decay into nothing more than a social club or, at best, a community service organization. The sad truth is that this has already happened in many places.

The reality is that the church has been given a commission. That "Great Commission" is at the very heart of the work of the local church. Some may view this commission as a side issue or as an indirect result of other activities more important, but this is not the case according to the Scriptures. Our Lord came to the world to "*seek and to save that which was lost*" (Luke 19:10). Jesus claimed that He alone was the way, the truth, and the life and that no man could come to the Father except through Him (John 14:6).

Furthermore, Christ maintained that unless a person experienced the truth of redemption personally, he would never be free from the burden and guilt of sin before God (see John 8:32). Tragically, he would never have eternal life. The Great Commission compels us as individuals to be soul conscious. Every Christian has a solemn obligation before God to make every effort to communicate the Gospel to those who cross his path.

But remember, this message of redemption is intended for the world—the whole world! It would be nearly impossible for any one individual to accomplish such a great task alone. For this reason, God in His wisdom instituted the New Testament church. The local church creates a vehicle for individuals to unite together in a global cause. What the individual may not be able to accomplish alone, he can now accomplish corporately with other believers in his local church. In addition, there remains the collective possibility of churches of like faith and practice uniting in a similar way in the same cause.

An organized effort is not an ecumenical effort, however. **Ecumenism** goes against the grain of Scripture. New Testament churches of like faith and practice may participate in a united effort to accomplish the spread of the Gospel. The support of missionaries would be an apt example of this principle. But to unite with churches that have replaced the doctrines or practice of the New Testament with human tradition would be very difficult to

DEFINING THE TERMS

Ecumenism: *Ecumenism refers to the effort by some to further religious unity among various Christian churches and organizations regardless of their doctrinal differences or polity. It sometimes is used in an even broader sense to include religious groups outside the historic context of Christianity.*

justify scripturally. By definition, that is what ecumenism requires. Uniting ecumenically is to imply that doctrine is not important and that despite our doctrinal differences, we should make every effort to pull together and reach the lost. But may I remind the reader that it is the "TRUTH" that *"shall make you free"* (John 8:32).

When the truth is compromised, two things happen. First, the recipient hears an adulterated version of the truth. An adulterated version of the truth is not the truth at all and is therefore another Gospel. The Bible clearly condemns such competing "gospels" (see Galatians 1:6–9).

Jesus said in the Gospel of Matthew that as the seed of the Gospel is sown into the world, it will produce fruit in some men. Not all men to be sure, but some. Those in whom it produces fruit are those who have receptive hearts. Those receptive hearts are described as those who hear and understand the message (Matthew 13:23; Luke 8:15).

Now if fruit-bearing requires one to understand the Gospel in its purity, it makes sense that the Gospel proclaimed must be the true Gospel in the first place. It implies that he who proclaims the Gospel has the responsibility to be honest in what he proclaims. If the Gospel of some is nothing more than the propagation of vain traditions and cunningly devised fables, this simply promotes confusion. If these things are true, they dispel the notion of ecumenical unity in the spread of the Gospel. Because ecumenism by definition and practice condones doctrinal diversity, it is actually a vehicle of discord and confusion.

One of the marks of the end times is deception. Even our Lord warned believers that *"many shall come in my name, saying, I am Christ…go ye not therefore after them"* (Luke 21:8). The Apostle Paul cautioned young Timothy that *"evil men and seducers shall wax worse and worse, deceiving, and being deceived"* (2 Timothy 3:13). In the book of Titus, Paul honestly admits that before knowing Christ, all men are *"foolish, disobedient, deceived"* (Titus 3:3). However, the

Bible also makes the point that although the mystery (of redemption) had been hidden from the ages as well as from generations, the truth has now been made manifest (Colossians 1:25–27). Ephesians 3:8–13 teaches the same. *"But if our gospel be hid, it is hid to them that are lost"* (2 Corinthians 4:3). That is exactly why we are under a divine mandate to clearly and exactly proclaim the truth of the Gospel. In fact, the Apostle Paul pointed to this very fact when he said the following:

> *But have renounced the hidden things of dishonesty, not walking in craftiness, nor handling the word of God deceitfully; but by manifestation of the truth commending ourselves to every man's conscience in the sight of God.*—2 CORINTHIANS 4:2

When the Gospel is hidden, it is because Satan has *"blinded the minds of them which believe not, lest the light of the glorious gospel of Christ…should shine unto them"* (2 Corinthians 4:4). The point here is that any time the Gospel is not honestly communicated in terms set by God alone, Satan is behind the confusion. As for those who perpetuate error, Jesus asked this question, *"Can the blind lead the blind? shall they not both fall into the ditch?"* (Luke 6:39).

The second consequence of the compromise of truth is division. Division among the brethren is not a good thing. Discord is not of God; however, if contending *"for the faith which was once delivered unto the saints"* (Jude 3) causes division between men, division may be warranted. The truth is inclusive by agreement only. When men ignore the truth and substitute in its place vain tradition, no matter how cunningly devised it may be, it is still not the truth! Those who recognize that fact are going to separate from those who propagate the error.

Some say that the problem with modern Christianity is the willingness of some to separate over issues of truth and error, and that those divisions demonstrate the absence of a loving spirit toward the brethren. To love God first and foremost is the greatest of all the commandments (Matthew 22:37–38). Men ought always to *"obey God rather than men"* (Acts 5:29)! We are never admonished in the Scriptures to accommodate error or those who propagate it in an effort to maintain peace among the brethren. Instead, we are to reprove it and them. Jesus Himself made this very clear as He addressed the woman at the well in John 4. He said that God desires men who will worship Him in spirit and in *truth*. It is possible to stand for the truth with a Christ-like, loving spirit and a kind attitude. It is not unloving to stand for the truth, but it is terribly unloving to propagate error and thereby lead others to confusion and possibly to eternal damnation.

Why is it that the one who stands for something, the one who strives lawfully for excellence and purity, seemingly is most often criticized for being unloving? It is the ecumenicalists who breed the confusion, not those who stand upon the supreme authority of Scripture. The Bible says, *"Can two walk together, except they be agreed?"* (Amos 3:3). A faithful man cannot be expected to walk in agreement with those who have little regard for the Bible and the truth contained within. By the way, without such faithful men the truth might have seen its demise centuries ago. From the earliest days, there have been those who would pervert the truth and replace it with their own thoughts. The fact is that we have been commanded that, *"an heretick after the first and second admonition reject; Knowing that he that is such is subverted, and sinneth, being condemned of himself"* (Titus 3:10–11).

Again, we are admonished in the Scriptures that God is not the author of confusion and all things are to be *"done decently and in order"* (1 Corinthians 14:40). God has not left the spread of the Gospel to accident or fate. Rather, God is a God of order. We see this in the matter of the Great Commission. Matthew 28:18–20 reads:

> *…All power is given unto me in heaven and in earth. Go ye therefore, and teach all nations, baptizing them in*

the name of the Father, and of the Son, and of the Holy Ghost: Teaching them to observe all things whatsoever I have commanded you: and, lo, I am with you alway, even unto the end of the world. Amen.

The divine formula to evangelize the world is found in these verses spoken by Jesus to the apostles at the conclusion of His earthly ministry. However, it is important to realize that although He spoke these words to the eleven, the commission was obviously meant to apply to more than just them. Jesus gave this commission knowing that these men would die, most by martyrdom. If the commission were given to and meant just for them, then when they died, their commission would have died with them. This conclusion is not reasonable.

The fact that Jesus promised to be with them always even unto the end of the world leads us to conclude that Jesus was referencing something that would be perpetual—something whose influence and work would extend beyond the lives of the apostles. We believe that to be the institution of the New Testament church.

In the first century there were not *many* churches, each with its own peculiar brand of the Gospel. There was but *one* church and *one* faith. These New Testament churches were both independent and autonomous. That is, they were self-governing. Although the apostles manifested a great deal of spiritual oversight while they lived, it is also quite clear that it was never God's intention for a human hierarchal system to be instituted. However, considering their common faith and practice, local churches could also function in a collective sense. That is, they could unite in a common effort, and this they did as opportunity permitted. The collective support of Paul's missionary journeys and the support of the saints in Jerusalem during a period of persecution justify this conclusion. It is that collective institution—composed of local, visible churches whose doctrine is apostolic in origin—that God has sovereignly ordained to spearhead the task of world evangelism. As each

Chapter Four—The Formula: The Great Commission

local church body assembles, disciples, concentrates its finances, and sends out its ambassadors for Christ, it is fulfilling the Great Commission. That is God's formula!

The authority for such activity comes from the Lord Himself, for Jesus said, *"All power* [authority] *is given unto me...Go ye therefore."* Authority according to the Bible always comes from above as Jesus states here. The authority to evangelize comes from above to the church, and our obligation is to take the Gospel into the world regardless of what the "world" thinks of this. Furthermore, the local church is to *"teach all nations,"* not just a select few, thus mandating world evangelism. Please note that baptism is to follow the teaching (and the inferred acceptance of that which is taught) and not precede the teaching. What is *taught*, by the way, is the truth, not error or any admixture of truth and error! That teaching or doctrine was not to be selective. Jesus said, *"Teaching them to observe **all things** whatsoever I have commanded you."* If we are to be taught all things, then our discipleship should include all things without any admixture of error or the vain traditions of men. The Christian is to observe or obey because these teachings (doctrines) of Christ are in fact commandments.

Now as Jesus concluded the Great Commission, He reassured the church that He would always be intimately involved with the work of the church. He said, *"...lo, I am with you alway, even unto the end of the world."* Thus, we are given a great divine promise that our success does not depend upon human instrumentality alone but upon the direct involvement of God Himself. Each local New Testament church therefore is to concern itself with its "Jerusalem" first. Simultaneously, however, it is to continue its advance into its Judaea (region) and its Samaria, and ultimately the uttermost part of the world (Acts 1:8). This way, each local church is not only meeting its own local responsibilities of evangelism, but also its larger regional, national, and global responsibilities. So, it should be abundantly clear that God's desire is to see that the Gospel is taken into the world and thus fulfill the Commission.

In one way, the history of Christianity should really be a history of its evangelism. It should be about its effort and progress in taking the Gospel of Jesus Christ into a lost world so that men might be saved and brought into a right relationship with God. Evangelism is its prime directive, but more often than not, that has not been the case. It has more often been about power, prestige, and prosperity.

However, it is obvious that someone has been faithful to the Great Commission, for the Gospel continues in its purity to this very day even though counterfeits exist. How did this come about? Certainly the blessing of God has been ever present, but there have also been those down through the centuries who understood the mandate of the Great Commission and have engaged the world on a personal level. They have won others to Christ and discipled those whom they have won.

Where was the Great Commission initiated, and how is the local church connected to it? The answer to this question needs to be understood in the historical setting of Pentecost.

CHAPTER FIVE

The Fulfillment: The World!

The ultimate purpose of the New Testament church was to spread the Gospel throughout the world, beginning with Jerusalem. That effort was—and still is—to be a united one, insomuch as each local church is composed of individual members united together for the common task of evangelism. Local churches of like faith and practice were allowed in the Scripture to join efforts. After all, the support of the Apostle Paul in his missionary efforts was obviously a corporate effort by first century churches throughout the Roman empire. But it demonstrated the responsibility of each local church in the effort of world evangelism. As we have already noted, the involvement on both a personal and corporate level is expected and even demanded by our Lord in the work of evangelism (Matthew 28:18–20).

Someone might ask, "Why is the Great Commission not perceived as an individual responsibility but as a church responsibility?" God requires that everything be done *"decently and in order."* To speak of the fulfillment of the Great Commission as only an "individual Christian" responsibility leaves the work of evangelism to accident. The structure and order is missing. That each Christian is responsible to personally participate in an aggressive effort to win others to Christ is not debatable. But in His wisdom, God has provided that the local church be the organized vehicle for evangelism. This order has now been maintained for almost two thousand years and is promised by God to continue.

Questions as to whether the church began on the day of Pentecost were briefly discussed earlier, but allow me to now expand on the thought. In John 17:4, Jesus made a very interesting statement concerning the work He came to do. In this statement a timeline of sorts is revealed that provides us with additional insight as to when the church began. As He prayed to the Father for the work of the ministry He said, *"I have glorified thee on the earth: I have finished the work which thou gavest me to do."* What was the work that He had finished? It was not the work of redemption, for the Cross was still in the future, although not far. When our Lord hung between Heaven and earth on the Cross, He said something very similar just before He gave up the ghost. He said, *"It is finished"*! It should be obvious that Jesus was referring to the redemptive work of God on the Cross. That work of redemption sealed the purpose of God in Christ and purchased salvation for every man who would repent and ask to be saved (Romans 10:9, 13).

However, that does not answer our question. What work had Jesus "finished" before the work of redemption on the Cross? Besides the work of redemption, the only other declaration of our Lord that was made was in connection to the establishment of the church (Matthew 16:18). When one is reminded that Jesus said He came to build His church and that the gates of Hell would not prevail against it, then we realize what Jesus was saying in John 17. His church existed previous to the day of Pentecost. It was in place and operational before Jesus reached the Cross. This idea will no

Chapter Five—The Fulfillment: The World!

doubt unnerve some. But although this passage (John 17:4) is often ignored or unrealized, it is actually a very crucial passage in the understanding of the church.

Pentecost is a very important date in the history of the church. Great controversies continue to this very day concerning the events as well as the meaning of those events in relation to the church. Some would have us believe that it reveals the necessity of speaking in tongues; others would have us believe that it demonstrates the necessity of baptism in order to be saved (making salvation a matter of works rather than grace). We could give other examples, but they would simply serve to remind us that error breeds more error. If we just take the account of Acts 2 at face value without reading into it a theological prejudice, certain things become clear.

First, the Bible says that when the day of Pentecost was fully come, *"they"* were all with one accord in *"one place."* Now the question that comes to mind is, "Who are the 'they' referred to in this verse?" The answer is found in Acts 1:13, 15–16. It was a group of about 120 people gathered together in an upper room. They included the eleven apostles, Mary the mother of Jesus and His brothers, and certain other men and women. These *"all **continued** with one accord in prayer and supplication."* It is evident from the grammar, as well as the noted repetition of the activity (Acts 1:4, 6, 13; 2:1 etc.), that this gathering together in that one place was an ongoing habit of this fledgling church. This is by definition a New Testament church. They have assembled in a given location; they have met for prayer and supplication; they have conducted the business of the early church (Acts 1:15–26) according to sound doctrine; the Spirit of God is present (John 20:19–22) and Peter preaches a message.

What else is missing? This is a New Testament church in action. All that remains is that the apostles be endued with power at Jerusalem (Luke 24:49). This is confirmed by Acts 1:8. On the day of Pentecost we see these events unfold (Acts 2). The apostles as well as those in attendance in the upper room were all filled with the Holy Ghost (Acts 2:4). But please note that is not to say the gift of the Holy Spirit had not already been given (see John 20:19–23). The gift of the indwelling presence of the Holy Spirit had already been imparted. The day of Pentecost displays the power of the Spirit's presence in a person's life when he is involved in the work of evangelism. Please see Acts 4:33, 6:8, and 8:10 to confirm this thought. That power is still meant to be manifested in a Christian's life as he attempts to communicate the Gospel to the lost. Sadly, this is not always the case, and I believe there are reasons for that.

Thus, the New Testament church had its origin before the day of Pentecost. That church is identified by definition and activity as the church which was at Jerusalem. So what of Pentecost? With the issue of the origin of the New Testament church settled, we can now place in perspective the question of the events of Pentecost. To briefly state the point again, Pentecost, rather than being the origin of the church, is the origin of global evangelism. It is the first opportunity that the church had to proclaim the Gospel to a lost and dying world, the result of which was that some three thousand people were saved and then baptized. But the marching orders of the Great Commission did not begin and end with the events of the day of Pentecost—Pentecost was the beginning. The cloven tongues make it abundantly clear that the Gospel was to be taken into the world. Cloven means divided. The disciples could now speak with languages they had not previously understood. You see the only limitation the disciples faced in their effort to take the Gospel to the world was the language barrier imposed by God upon the peoples of the world because of their willfulness (Genesis 11). This limitation would initially be overcome by this gift of tongues in the early church. This gift was not an ecstatic language that only God or angels could understand, as some would have us believe. That neither fits the description nor the results of the gift. It is obvious that those present on the day of Pentecost—although they originated from a variety of nations and kingdoms—all heard and understood the Gospel in their native tongues. Taken at face value, the apostles were obviously proclaiming the Gospel in those languages. We accept this as a supernatural work of God because, previous to this event, these languages were not spoken by or known to the apostles (thus the wording in the King James Version, "*unknown tongue*").

This gift was necessary at the time but was never meant to be a permanent means to spread the Gospel. Once the writing of the Holy Bible was complete, a temporary gift would no longer be required nor would it be legitimate. This is exactly the meaning of 1 Corinthians 13:9–12. The reality is that the last book of the Bible was not completed until the writing of the "Revelation" by the Apostle John. It was penned somewhere very near the close of the first century almost forty years after 1 Corinthians was written. So Paul, under divine inspiration, wrote, "*when that which is perfect is come, then that which is in part shall be done away.*" I believe Paul was referring to the completion of the canon of Scripture. The Second Coming of Christ is not in reference because it does not fit grammatically. The words "*that which*" denote an object, not a person. Thus the special but temporary gift of tongues became unnecessary by the time we reached the end of the first century with the completion of the Bible. Proverbs 22:20–21 underscores this very fact as does 2 Peter 1:19–21 and Hebrews 2:1–4 in the New Testament. That is, the written Word of God is the final authority. When the Scriptures were completed, they replaced any and all temporary gifts having to do with the proclamation of the Word of God by the New Testament church.

So began the initial efforts of fulfilling the Great Commission. From Pentecost the Gospel was taken into the world. It began in Jerusalem but was then taken simultaneously to Judaea, Samaria, and "*unto the uttermost part of the earth*" (Acts 1:8). The latter part of this commission continues to this very day by every Bible believing church through its world-wide missions outreach.

We have taken some time now to understand the structural order and function of the New Testament church. But the question remains, how do we identify the New Testament church today? This was a simple matter in the first century when only one church existed. Of course it was legitimate, for it was the original. It was the standard by which all others would be measured. That is not to say that the church at Jerusalem was perfect in all aspects. However, its foundation was pure. Its doctrines were untainted and remained so until men began to challenge their veracity in an effort to alter them. So if first century doctrines were pure, what of the people? Well, the facts reveal that the people were not perfect, but that is really not the issue. It is truth that must be the constant, for it is truth that anchors the soul.

In a Christian world—where we are surrounded by religious societies vying for favor—how do we identify that church which Jesus started in our own day? There are some "parameters" that help us identify the New Testament church in every century. In the next section, we will take some time to investigate these parameters that the Bible reveals about the identity of a New Testament church.

PART TWO

The Identity of the New Testament Church

PERSONAL OBSERVATIONS

The Identity of the New Testament Church

In many ways, when we deal with a subject like the New Testament church, the greatest barrier to understanding what the Bible genuinely teaches is all the misinformation that has existed for centuries. When people come to believe that error is truth, they will attempt to scripturally justify and protect what they have come to believe. Now, this does not mean they have the truth; it simply means they believe they have the truth. The fact is, there is an abundance of diverse positions held by Christians today on any given subject. Common sense would dictate that the majority of these positions could not possibly be correct. Why? Again, because God is not the author of confusion.

Realistically, as error increases, error diversifies. The result? Error is ever expanding. As error expands, so does the competition for credibility. Over time, all this diversity creates a shift in attitude toward error in general because of its sheer volume. It seems useless to deal with the error because it is difficult to put a handle on it or a face to it. Who is to blame? Names like the "Mormons" or the "Jehovah Witnesses" make it easier to identify the offending party. But, what of all the doctrinal diversity within the context of evangelical Christianity? We tend to ignore this. Believers are far less able or willing to identify error and confront it in their own backyard. The Christian community—by its unwillingness to appear judgmental or bigoted—refuses to challenge questionable doctrines, choosing rather to let "the tares" continue to grow and let God worry about the problem. This is exactly what Peter described in 2 Peter 2:1–2. He warned of false teachers among God's people who *"shall bring in damnable heresies, even denying the Lord that bought them"* that, *"many shall follow their pernicious ways; by reason of whom the way of truth shall be evil spoken of."* In other words, eventually a point is reached when it is the truth that comes under attack! It is the truth that seems judgmental. It is the truth that appears bigoted. Diversity has produced an attitude shift and truth has become the tyrant.

In the first century this was not the case. While the apostles lived, and even under the leadership of the first generation descendents of the apostles, error was not tolerated within the confines of the New Testament church. There was one faith (doctrine), and all professing believers adhered to the doctrine of the apostles or were not permitted to retain membership in the church. The understanding of this fact is crucial to our ability to identify the early church. You see, in the first century every church believed the same thing. There was no diversity of doctrine, and as we have already emphasized, error was not tolerated. We do not mean to say that error did not exist at all, for at times it did. But, the apostles dealt with the error. Those guilty of error were either corrected by admonition or dismissed once it was demonstrated that they were determined to continue in their error. In such cases fellow Christians were expected to withdraw fellowship from the guilty party (i.e., 1 Corinthians 5; 1 Timothy 6:5; Titus 3:10;

2 Thessalonians 3:6; Revelation 2:14–16). The guilty were expelled because they were viewed as dissemblers and as divisive (see also Galatians 1:8,9; 1 Timothy 1:3; 2 John 10; Jude).

In the event that an entire church had become infected with error, God would deal with them Himself. This is the impact of the warnings given to the seven churches of Revelation 2–3. The admonition to the church at Ephesus contains the warning that God would remove their candlestick out of its place, unless they repented (Revelation 2:5). In other words, a New Testament church may corporately drift so far from the truth that spiritual recovery is impossible. In such cases, God is forced to remove their influence (candlestick or light) from the kingdom. Apparently, at least some of the seven churches of Revelation 2–3 were moving in that direction. The churches of Galatia seemed to be similarly infected, and they were challenged by the Apostle Paul to recover themselves from those who were perverting the Gospel (Galatians 1:6–9). A secondary warning contained in each of the letters to the seven churches applies to Christians of each successive generation until the Lord returns. We are to *"hear what the Spirit saith unto the churches."*

This doctrinal continuity is obvious in that we see no denominational distinctives in the first century. Also, we see no unique denominational identity. In other words, there wasn't a need to have a name over the door! The early church was simply identified by its location in a particular city, whether in someone's home or some secret meeting place. When we use the term *local* church it is to this fact we are referring. When the Apostle Paul addresses a particular letter to a church or churches, he identifies the church as the church that is at Corinth or Ephesus. Sometimes he refers to them as the churches which are in Galatia or Asia. These churches all held to the same doctrinal standard. As such, there was no need to identify them beyond their specific location in the Roman world.

We see another indicator of this in the book of Acts when we find that the disciples of Jesus were simply called Christians. They were not identified by any unique doctrinal deviation from the norm. Why? There was no doctrinal deviation from the norm! You might say, "I wish that were true again, that all God's people could just be called Christians and that we could do away with all this denominational stuff!"

Yes, it would be wonderful and someday that will happen. One day our Lord will rule this old earth with a rod of iron, and truth will be exalted. But remember, the reason we have denominations is because traditions of human origin are made into the doctrines of God. To eliminate the confusion, we must lay aside the human tradition and let the Bible have the sole authority over our doctrinal positions. For centuries now, the Christian community in general has been unwilling, for whatever reason, to do that very thing.

Stubbornness is a terrible thing. Rebellion is truly as the sin of witchcraft. A man involved in the occult may recognize a power greater than himself and even yield to it. But in so doing, he also submits to a lesser power than God and thereby reveals a stubborn heart of rebellion. In the same way, any Christian who chooses a particular doctrinal persuasion is acknowledging the existence of sound doctrine (which he believes his to be). But if his doctrine is found wanting in the light of Scripture and he refuses to discard his position for the sake of truth, he has revealed a stubborn heart of rebellion. Pride is the culprit rather than mere ignorance.

As suggested earlier, men tend to judge Christianity in light of their present experience rather than by the revelation of Scripture. Seeing the doctrinal diversity in Christianity, many assume it must be of God. They presume that something has gone wrong, but apparently God doesn't really mind. This fatalistic attitude fails to consider accountability before God and that such accountability is individualistic. We are each held responsible for what we believe. How can we pass on the truth to a new generation if we do not hold to the truth ourselves? Remember, the sincerity of a person's convictions does not make them correct!

Solomon once wrote, *"I know that, whatsoever God doeth, it shall be for ever: nothing can be put to it, nor any thing taken from it: and God doeth it, that men should fear before him"* (Ecclesiastes 3:14). It is clear from this verse that when God does something, it is done right; it is done perfectly the first time around. Because it is always perfect, it removes any need for correction. The reason for this exactness, this perfection of God, is that men might respect God. God is not a failure. God does not "tinker" with the universe always attempting to achieve perfection. However, every time someone changes what God has done, he is saying that God cannot be trusted to do things right, that they must be improved upon if they are to be fit for man's consumption. Every new and false doctrine that spawns a new movement, which in turn produces a new church, is saying God cannot be trusted. The first church, the New Testament church, was founded by Christ. It was perfect in all ways except the people. It had a perfect Head, a perfect Cornerstone, a perfect Foundation, and a perfect doctrine. There was one body (the local church), one Spirit, one Lord, one faith (the doctrine), one baptism (immersion), one God and Father of all (Ephesians 4:3–6)! We endeavor to maintain unity (v. 3) in the church by our commitment to these truths. Diversity does not breed unity; that is a fallacy!

Therefore, a church is known by its doctrinal parameters, and this was true of the first church. If the apostles had altered the doctrines they had received from Christ, then the church would have ceased to exist as Christ had originally intended. If the doctrine is changed, then the church is changed. It ceases to be what it was before those changes. The practice may not change. Christians may still worship, give, sing, etc. But, because the beliefs have changed, eventually the practice will change. When Christians replace the dogma of the New Testament with traditions of human origin, they have effectively removed Christ as the head as well as the cornerstone of the New Testament church.

Jesus promised that the gates of Hell would not prevail against His church (Matthew 16:18)! However, since the term *church* is often used in a much broader sense than what the Bible describes and has become so inclusive, we are compelled to focus some attention on a proper understanding of the word. Once again, our definition must come from the Bible rather than popular Christian culture. What we find after some due diligence is that the Bible seems to be at odds with the popular understanding of the word *church*. Still, our responsibility is to recognize the sole authority of the Word of God in all such matters. As we examine the meaning of the word *church*, our goal is to communicate a biblical perspective even at the risk that it may clash with the popular Christian culture.

CHAPTER SIX

The Church: An Assembly

The original English word *church* (kirk) is probably derived from the Greek word *kurios* meaning Lord. In the old English it referred to the worshippers of Christ or the Lord as well as to their places (i.e., structures) of worship. As you can see, it was a very appropriate word to use in connection with believers and their worship of Christ. The use of this word *church* in our modern English translation is not meant to imply an understanding or definition different from that found in the New Testament. Indeed, the word assumes that an *assembly* of believers has gathered together in a given location in order to worship the Lord. It actually is a very good rendition into English of the Greek word *ecclesia*. However, over the centuries the word has been redefined to mean things that by definition are not New Testament at all. Without a proper understanding of the New Testament definition, we sacrifice clarity, hindering our ability to correctly understand many passages in the Bible. Certainly in our modern vernacular the word *church* has widely come to refer to just about any religious organization or group. In its authentic, historical and biblical context the word *church* is very specific and precise. Yet, Satan has effectively broadened and diluted its significance as well as its use. Sadly, this word doesn't mean to most people today what it has meant to the Bible-believing Christians throughout the centuries.

J.A. Shackelford, author of *Compendium of Baptist History*, states: "By some writers it [the church] is made to include 'the entire body of professed Christians.' By others it means 'the spiritual congregation, or aggregate of the regenerate, including the saints in Heaven, the saints on earth and the saints yet to come.' The general use of the word at present justifies both of these definitions, but a scriptural use does not, nor was the word so used in the time of Christ and His apostles. In fact the word *church* is not found in the Greek New Testament, nor was it used for some two hundred years after the New Testament was written."[1]

So, the Greek word that is translated in our English Bible (KJV) as the word *church* is the Greek word *ecclesia*. In the first century, this word was not an uncommon word. It was often used in the secular language. It meant an assembly or congregation of people gathered together for a common purpose or to accomplish a common goal. The root words carry with them the idea of being "called out." For example, it is sometimes used in secular literature to speak of the gathering of townspeople, citizens of a village or city. They would be "called out" in order to reach a consensus on a decision or direction that would be taken to benefit the whole of the people. What makes this word important to us is that our Lord declared in Matthew 16:18 that He was going to build His church. The fact that Jesus said, *"I will **my** church; and the gates of hell shall not prevail against it"* marks a difference between what had already existed and what He was going to do. It would be *His* church. In other words, it would be different than other assemblies commonly known to the disciples by virtue of its own

Chapter Six—The Church: An Assembly

unique purpose and parameters. It would be a collection of both Jew and Gentile, individuals called out of the world to be formed and integrated into local bodies or assemblies. Jesus would be the spiritual head as well as the doctrinal cornerstone of those bodies. When spoken of in a corporate sense, they would be considered an institution.

Now it may not be necessary to say this, but sometimes the obvious is the very thing we miss. An assembly is not an assembly unless it has assembled! A congregation is not actually a congregation unless it has congregated. In other words, it must convene! A New Testament church (*ecclesia*) must convene in order to meet the requirements of its own definition. This cannot be done invisibly!

In our American culture, we often find the English language changing, sometimes without any reasonable explanation. Our culture has created a very fluid language. At any moment words we take for granted as meaning one thing suddenly mean something entirely different. A few years ago I was speaking in a local church in southern California. After the sermon, two young men approached me. Both of them looking very typical of the young people of that time, but just the same, they both demonstrated a good spirit and treated me with respect and I them. As they approached me, the first thing one of the young men said was, "That was a gnarly message!" The other young man quickly agreed, and I was prompted to ask what he meant by "gnarly."

The young man began to struggle with how to explain to me, this middle-aged man (over the hill!) what he meant by his remark. Now I knew exactly what he meant, but it was obvious that he was using the word "gnarly" incorrectly. I found it very interesting that although he knew what he meant, he found it difficult to define his own choice of words. As he struggled, his friend, realizing his companion's dilemma, attempted to help by saying that he agreed and the message was indeed "nebular." This helped clear things considerably as you might well guess. Apparently, a stellar ball of gases found somewhere in the cosmos, better reflected my effort in the pulpit that Sunday morning than I would want to admit. We all had a good laugh at no one's expense and parted company.

The incident however, does demonstrate the fluid nature of the use of the English language. The definitions of some words that fall peril to the popular culture are often obliterated for new "cool" meanings that none but the young will understand (thus the infamous generation gap).

Although any language is susceptible to such change, the popular language of the first century did not promote such fluidness. In other words, the definitions of words did not quickly change at the whim of the popular culture. So then, when Jesus said that He would build His church we must accept the dictionary definition of the Greek word *ecclesia*. This definition, as used both in secular literature and ecclesiastical literature, does not speak of invisibility. Thus, the concept of the New Testament church as conceived by Jesus and validated by the apostles was not a universal, invisible church. They were visible assemblies of God's people in given localities, each having a common purpose.

The Greek word *ecclesia* (assembly) is used 117 times in the New Testament. Of those 117 occasions, 112 times it is used in connection with God in one of three different ways. First, it is overwhelmingly used to refer to specific, visible and local churches. In fact, of the 112 references, 94 times it refers to local, visible assemblies. That is, we know where these assemblies were located, whether by reference to a region, a city, or a home in which they were meeting. Among many possible examples, let's focus on a verse in 1 Corinthians 16.

In the opening verses, Paul addresses the subject of the "collection." He says, *"Now concerning the collection for the saints, as I have given order to the churches of Galatia, even so do ye. Upon the first day of the week let every one of you lay by him in store, as God hath prospered him..."* (1 Corinthians 16:1–2). It is obvious in this example that Paul is addressing a specific local church, the church in the city of Corinth. Furthermore, other local churches are referenced in the region of Galatia and corporately are all admonished to receive collections as God had prospered each individual in the body. This was a real church with real people passing real offering plates on the particular day of the week (Sunday).

The word *ecclesia* is also sometimes used institutionally. When Jesus declared that He would build His church (Matthew 16:18), He was speaking to the apostles. Again when Jesus gave the Great Commission (Matthew 28:18–20), He spoke to the apostles. But the apostles have long since gone on to be with the Lord. Does that mean the Great Commission died with them? Of course not! We have previously pointed this out. Jesus was speaking of His church as an institution, that it would perpetually exist beyond the limitations of any one human life until the end of the age.

You see, institutions always have parameters. It is important to understand this fact in light of the common belief today that the one "true church" is an invisible, universal church. When you identify the church of our Lord as an invisible and universal entity, there is no need to have parameters. By its very nature, it lends itself to confusion. Adherents may believe anything they want, and doctrinal purity is seen as divisive when it conflicts with beliefs of human origin.

Institutions, on the other hand, do not lend themselves to such confusion because they have parameters. For example, when we speak of the institution of government we know that the parameters of government generally involve local government (city and county), state government, federal government and more recently, even a global government. Although we speak of government in an institutional sense, we know that government is always identified in tangible or physical terms.

When one speaks of the institution of learning or education, we know that we are not speaking of some mystical invisible entity without boundaries or reality. Rather, we speak of the institution in real terms with real parameters. What are these terms? They are primary, secondary, college, etc. Primary (elementary) school is generally defined as K–6; secondary (junior and senior high) school as 7th–12th; college as 13th. We never think of this institution in imaginary terms!

Again, another familiar example is the institution of marriage. How would we define marriage? Marriage is the uniting of one man and one woman in the lawful and holy state of matrimony (both of these parameters are required, by the way). We may not be able to see all those at any given time who have entered into this state, but that does not mean they are invisible. It just means we are physically unable to see them all at one time. If you then speak of all those living in the state of lawful and holy matrimony as invisible, you are implying something that just is not true! We know they physically exist, so when we speak of them corporately, we identify them as belonging to an institution. Now this is the appropriate way to speak of the New Testament church. The Apostle Paul even uses the church as an appropriate illustration of marriage in the book of Ephesians, and speaks of marriage and the church institutionally (Ephesians 5:22–33) in both cases.

Therefore, the church in a corporate or institutional sense is not invisible, nor is it universal. When speaking of New Testament churches in a corporate sense—meaning in general rather than any one particular church—the term *institution* is appropriate. Its corporate union is determined first by its physical parameters, that is, it is a general reference to local, visible New Testament churches (assemblies), and second by its apostolic doctrinal parameters. If you change or ignore first century doctrine, you no longer have a first century, New Testament church. Furthermore, just because you cannot physically see all those local New Testament churches which make up the institution does not mean they are invisible any more than we would speak of all those who are married as being invisible.

Chapter Six—The Church: An Assembly

So you see, there is a basic difference of opinion theologically on exactly what Jesus meant when He said that He would build His church. Was this church "universal" and "invisible" or was it "local" and "visible"? Once again, the great error in the former is that the "universal/invisible" concept breeds confusion by its very definition. Because it requires no physical or doctrinal parameters, the whole structure of such a concept is left up to the whim of the individual. Furthermore, for one to maintain allegiance to such a concept, one must believe that the Bible gives no clear doctrinal definition or structure to the New Testament church. This leaves Christians in every generation to their own devises and requires them to carve out their own definition and structure. This makes absolutely no sense at all. May I remind the reader that our God is immutable? He is the same yesterday, today and forever.

We are admonished in the Scriptures to *"give the more earnest heed to the things which we have heard, lest at any time we should let them slip"* (Hebrews 2:1). In the first century, God's people took this kind of admonition seriously. They *"continued stedfastly in the apostles' doctrine"* (Acts 2:42), realizing that, *"grievous wolves [shall] enter in among you, not sparing the flock, Also of your own selves shall men arise, speaking perverse things, to draw away disciples after them"* (Acts 20:29–30). So what has changed, first century Christianity or modern day Christians?

The third way the word *ecclesia* is used in the Bible is found in Hebrews 12:23. In this passage, the apostle speaks of a future date when there would be a *"general assembly and church of the first-born."* In other words, there will someday be a "churching" or gathering together of the church in eternity. The word ecclesia is used here in a two-fold way—first as a gathering or an assembly together in a visible location (Heaven) and second in an institutional (corporate) sense.

I hope that you are getting a sense of how important definitions are to our study. We should not take them lightly. Words mean something! By them we communicate to one another either successfully or unsuccessfully and so it is with God. It is often in the failure to understand the proper meaning of words and terms in the Bible that error finds root. After years of dealing with this subject I have discovered that much of the error concerning the New Testament church originates in our misappropriation of certain phrases in the Bible. Many believers associate and even define the church by these phrases and although they are certainly important concepts, they must be understood properly. We will now examine these terms.

CHAPTER SEVEN

The Concept: Correct Terminology

With the evidence pointing to a proper description of the New Testament church as being "local and visible" rather than "universal and invisible," why, might one ask, is there so much confusion on the subject? The answer lies within the fact that so many do not understand the concept of the local church in relation to other very relevant phrases found in the New Testament. If one properly understands these concepts and how they relate to this subject, then the structure and order of such things will be clarified.

The Family of God

The first phrase we will address, whose misunderstanding has brought much confusion in the proper concept of the local church, is the *family of God*. There are other expressions of this type found in various places in the Scriptures such as the *"household of faith"* and the *"saints of the living God."* But all of them have in mind the same concept. The *family of God* is a term that includes all the children of God whether in Heaven or living on earth at any point in time. We see this statement in the book of Ephesians 3:15, *"Of whom the whole family in heaven and earth is named."* This is not a reference to mankind in general. In other words, it is not referring to the so-called "brotherhood of man." Rather, it is a direct reference to the redeemed of the Lord as revealed in Ephesians 2:19:

> *Now therefore ye are no more strangers and foreigners, but fellowcitizens with the saints, and of the household of God;*

Some of the family have gone on to meet the Lord face to face and to ever live in His presence. Others of us who remain alive in Christ have yet to experience this face-to-face meeting. But, whether departed or presently remaining, we all are a part of and make up the family of God by virtue of our faith in Christ Jesus. This concept would include both the Old Testament and New Testament saints, for they all compose the *"household of faith."*

It is this concept that so many confuse with the term *church* and thus, incorrectly apply the term *universal* to identify it. Truly, the saved of all the ages are saved the very same way—repentance and faith in Christ. We might even say that all the redeemed are saved universally the same way. But the *family of God* and the *church* are not synonymous. To say or imply that anyone who claims to be saved is a part of the church, regardless of the means or validity whereby that claim is made, is ridiculous. Inclusion in the *family* does not automatically mean inclusion in the *church* as defined in the New Testament.

The Kingdom of God

The *kingdom of God* is a phrase that often occurs in the New Testament especially in the Gospels and most often in the book

Chapter Seven—The Concept: Correct Terminology

of Luke. It is presently a spiritual kingdom that will one day be manifested as a physical one (Mark 14:25; Luke 21:31). It refers to all the children of God living and breathing on this earth at any given time. Of course when we speak of the children of God, we are referring to all those who have entered that spiritual kingdom the Bible way, that is, through repentance and salvation by grace through faith in Jesus Christ alone with absolutely no admixture of works.

Jesus urged the people of His day that the kingdom was at hand and that they should repent and receive the Gospel (Mark 1:14–15). In Matthew 6:33, Jesus clearly stated that the kingdom was to be sought first. He said that it was not easy for a rich man to enter into it (Matthew 19:24) but He also said that publicans and harlots would enter into it before the religionists of His day (Matthew 21:31). Jesus said that the kingdom does not come with observation (Luke 17:20) because the kingdom of God is within you (i.e., a spiritual work) (Luke 17:21). Jesus encouraged the rich young ruler that he was not far from entering into the kingdom (Mark 12:34) but He also said that unless a man receives the kingdom as a little child, he shall in no wise enter therein (Luke 18:17).

Jesus commanded His disciples to *preach the kingdom* (Luke 9:2) but ultimately declared that the kingdom would be taken from the Jews and given to a people (Gentile) who would bring forth the fruit thereof (Matthew 21:43).

In other words, the kingdom of God is a reference to the spiritual work of God in men's lives in real time. It is a reference to the born-again experience that is brought about by the miraculous work of the Holy Spirit in response to repentance and faith toward Christ (see Nicodemus, John 3). This is a one-time experience just as physical birth is a one-time experience. Without being *born again*, no man enters into the heavenly kingdom when he leaves this temporal life here on earth. We might add at this point—so that there is no misunderstanding—that the church a man attends has nothing to do with whether or not he can be saved. Regardless of the church a man attends, if the Bible plan of salvation is presented to him with no admixture of error, he can be saved.

The Church of God

The *church of God* is a reference to local visible assemblies whose doctrinal distinctives are apostolic in origin and whose members have been scripturally baptized (Acts 2:1, 37–42). As explained previously, when we use the term in an institutional sense, we are speaking about New Testament churches, corporately or in general. By this definition it should be obvious that we are being very specific. As we have already taken the time to demonstrate, not every assembly of believers comprises or should be identified as a New Testament church. The doctrinal parameters must be correct, and in order to be legitimate, the initial entrance into that church must be scripturally sound.

The correct definition of these three terms now forces us to arrive at certain conclusions. First, not every member of the human race is a part of the family of God; one must be born again to enter the family. Second, not every member of the family of God is a part of the kingdom of God; one must be saved and currently living on the earth in real time. Third, not every believer is a part of the church of God because not every believer has complied with scriptural baptism. It is imperative that we understand the Bible concept of scriptural baptism. Much error has been propagated over the centuries by a variety of Christian societies as men refuse to accept the simplicity of the ordinance. It is at this point that many church societies either align themselves with the Bible or take up their positions in support of some human tradition.

The ordinance of baptism is a shadow! It cannot save or wash away sin. It is merely a picture of the death, burial and resurrection of the Lord Jesus Christ. It is a picture of the new life the believer

Chapter Seven—The Concept: Correct Terminology

has in Christ and because of Christ, but it does not produce that life. However, because there has been so much error in connection with this ordinance we must make sure we know what the Bible says concerning the subject. For a church to claim some degree of legitimacy, it must be right here. There can be no compromise.

Baptism as prescribed in the New Testament requires four things. First, it requires a proper candidate. Next, it requires a proper mode or means, and then to administer the ordinance, a proper authority must be involved. Finally, scriptural baptism requires a proper motive on the part of the candidate. These four principles are essential for a proper understanding of the ordinance. In the next chapter we will examine these more closely.

CHAPTER EIGHT

The Compliance: Scriptural Baptism

What is scriptural baptism and why is it so important? There are actually three reasons for its importance. First, the Lord commands it of all believers (Matthew 28:18–20). It is often referred to as the first act of obedience after one has been saved. Second, it is a testimony to the redemptive plan of God through Christ, and third, according to the Scriptures, all things are to be done decently and in order. The work of God does not exist apart from order, nor does it go forward in disarray.

A Proper Candidate

Scriptural baptism involves four distinct elements. The first element is the New Testament requirement that one be a *proper candidate*. In other words, one must be born again before he/she is baptized. One is not a proper candidate without being saved. Many take this for granted in their understanding. But much, if not most, of mainstream Christianity in the world believes that there is some saving merit attached to baptism—a belief that water baptism somehow washes away the sin nature inherited from Adam. This mistaken doctrine is identified as *baptismal regeneration*. This belief, that one does not need to personally receive Christ into the heart before he/she is baptized, has led countless millions into a self-deceived eternity without Christ. The Bible teaches nothing like this. Rather, the Bible clearly teaches that only after an individual is saved is the ordinance of baptism to be administered, and then only by a proper local church authority (Matthew 28:18–20).

A Proper Mode

The second element of compliance to the ordinance of scriptural baptism involves the *proper mode* of baptism. A few years ago, I had the privilege of going to Israel and visiting the Jordan river. While there, we watched as many people from various countries were being baptized in that river. I was a little amused that so many wanted to be baptized in that river. It was as if people thought it held some great mystical secret of divine blessing. As I observed one particularly large group from Russia, I noticed that as the people approached the pastor, he would ask them a question and they in turn would whisper something in his ear. It became obvious from what followed that he was asking them in what manner they preferred to be baptized. Some had chosen to be sprinkled, some to have water poured over their head (affusion), while still others had just their faces placed in the water (in an effort to protect their hair). Some were baptized three times forward, others three times backward; some dunked themselves by sitting down into the water. They were all so very excited as they exited the river, and their friends were shouting what sounded to be words of encouragement.

This scene I have described to you would cause little grief to most Christian people today. Yet, once again it demonstrates the

Chapter Eight—The Compliance: Scriptural Baptism

great confusion that exists today among Christians. The Greek word *baptizo* literally means "to immerse"! It does not mean sprinkle, pour, or partially immerse. It is only through *immersion* that we are able to demonstrate the death, burial, and resurrection of our Lord. This is the proper mode of baptism and this alone! We are clearly commanded in the Great Commission of Matthew 28 to baptize converts. As already noted, it is often referred to as the first commandment of a new believer, and it is difficult to imagine the blessing of God on a man's life without following this first commandment. When John baptized, he baptized in a place where there *"was much water"* (John 3:23). Why? Because Bible baptism requires enough water to immerse. When Jesus was baptized of John, the Bible depicts Jesus *"coming up out of the water"* (Mark 1:10) and thus speaks of His immersion in water. There can be no compromise on this issue. Baptism by definition, by example and by command requires that a man be immersed. Any other mode is not baptism at all.

A Proper Authority

When Jesus spoke to His disciples and outlined the formula that would take the Gospel into a lost and dying world—that is, the Great Commission—He knew that these men would not live long lives. Indeed, John was the only one of these men who would live out his life without being murdered. Still, Jesus made the statement in this commission that He would be with them *"alway, even unto the end of the world"* (Matthew 28:20).

Truly, Jesus has been and will be—as long as this present age continues—intimately involved with the work of the New Testament church on this earth. He has never left that work to flounder under its own human devices. The ordinance of baptism is an integral part of the function of a New Testament church, and its ecclesiastical integrity is maintained by its proper administration.

But the question that arises has to do with who has the proper authority to administer the ordinance of baptism.

The ordinances, of which there are only two—baptism and the Lord's Table—are not sacraments. That is, they have absolutely no *saving value*. As most evangelicals will readily agree, the ordinance of baptism is *symbolic* in that it pictures the death, burial and resurrection of our Lord. But, just as important, although often neglected, is the fact that it is also *regulatory*. The ordinance is not just a Christian ordinance in the sense that anyone, in any way may administer it. The New Testament church alone is granted the proper authority to administer the ordinance of baptism in the Great Commission. Remember, all things are to be done *"decently and in order,"* for *"God is not the author of confusion"*! Throughout the New Testament, it is the local church or a representative under the authority of a New Testament church that administered the ordinance of baptism to a proper candidate. By the way, that includes the baptisms of the Ethiopian eunuch, Cornelius and Saul (later, Paul). To make baptism merely a Christian ordinance—meaning that anyone, in any way, may administer or receive it—is an obvious violation of Scripture, for it lends itself to confusion and disorder.

Now what do I mean by *regulatory*? The New Testament church is described in the book of Ephesians as a wife that He desires to present *"to himself a glorious church, not having spot, or wrinkle, or any such thing; but that it should be holy and without blemish"* (Ephesians 5:27). For any church to maintain the kind of purity that is described in this verse, it must protect itself from those who would contaminate the church with error. We are warned more than once in Scripture that men would arise in the midst of the church and teach false doctrine (see Acts 20:29–31; Titus 1:9–11; 2 Timothy 4:1–4; 2 Peter 2:1–3). If we are warned against wolves in our midst, certainly we may conclude that we are to be watchful as people enter our midst. You see, in part, baptism was given by our

Chapter Eight—The Compliance: Scriptural Baptism

Lord to maintain purity within the body. When one is baptized in a local church, he is testifying to his confidence in the purity of its doctrine. By virtue of that purity it has the authority to administer the ordinance. He thereby submits to its authority (whether real or unreal) as it administers the ordinance. In this way, baptism becomes a gate whereby one enters into the membership of a church and thereby demonstrates his submission to their proper authority (real or unreal). But, what of this authority?

As we have previously demonstrated, authority in these matters always comes from above. One cannot just claim that authority and proceed with the work of God. This (real) authority comes from God and is bestowed upon His church—the New Testament church as defined by the Scriptures. If a church advocates a doctrine foreign to the first century church, it is disqualified as a New Testament church. If a church has as its origin a date later than the first century, it is equally suspect. Thus, if a man is baptized in a church that cannot meet the criteria of the New Testament, he has not been baptized at all, for that church did not have the authority to baptize him in the first place. So, as people come to a local New Testament church from such a church whose doctrines are of human origin, it is proper to correctly administer the ordinance of baptism. This is not re-baptism, but merely the correct administration of the ordinance. In this way we maintain the doctrinal purity and integrity of a local New Testament church.

In passing, perhaps a brief comment concerning the second ordinance would be appropriate here. The ordinance of the Lord's Table not only commemorates the vicarious suffering and death of Christ but, like baptism, also serves in a regulatory function.

The conduct and spirit of the members of a local church is extremely important to the spiritual wellbeing of the body as a whole. We know that the Spirit of God can be grieved by the actions and attitudes of believers when they fail to walk circumspectly (Ephesians 4:30). In His wisdom, God has designed the memorial of the Lord's Table in such a way that believers are compelled to resolve spiritual issues before they become public matters. As each man is asked to *"examine himself"* that he might not be as one that *"eateth and drinketh unworthily"* and thereby *"eateth and drinketh damnation* [judgment] *to himself"* (1 Corinthians 11:28–30), the purity and spiritual wellbeing of the body is maintained when the proper steps are taken to resolve these matters before God. Thus, the Table serves not only as a memorial function but a regulatory one as well.

Furthermore, the admonition given by the Apostle Paul above clearly indicates that the Table should be served within the confines of the local church only. This is made clear by the statement, *"when ye come together in the church"* (1 Corinthians 11:18, 20, 33). It is obvious that the apostle has in his mind the local church as it gathers together (*ye:* plural). It should go without saying that the Table should be served by the proper authority—a New Testament church. We might also conclude that the proper administration of the Table would best fit the biblical criteria by a "restricted" or even "closed" polity. This has the added benefit of protecting those who come from other backgrounds from assuming that there is some saving merit in the ordinance. *"Wisdom is profitable to direct"* (Ecclesiastes 10:10).

A Proper Motive

A right attitude of the individual being baptized means that he has accepted Christ as his Saviour and understands that the first step of obedience is baptism. For this to take place scripturally, he must be baptized by the authority of a New Testament church. It is the doctrine of that church, not the name over the door that determines its identity and its proper authority as a New Testament church. Now please do not misunderstand. A name is very helpful in identifying a New Testament church in some instances, but a

Chapter Eight—The Compliance: Scriptural Baptism

name can be a source of deception. Many religious organizations (i.e., churches) of human origin have patronized God by attaching to their organization names that identify them with something having to do with the kingdom. For example, "the Church of the Latter Day Saints" or "Jehovah's Witnesses" would illustrate the point quite easily for most of us. But still a person must realize that when he submits to the authority of any church in the ordinance of baptism, he is saying that he believes that church has the God-given and proper authority to baptize him. The candidate believes his doctrine to be correct. That is exactly the underlying message that is communicated in the account of Pentecost in Acts 2. Not only did they gladly receive Peter's words, but they "*continued stedfastly in the apostles' doctrine.*" It should go without saying, but it is obvious that they "*continued stedfastly*" because they believed those words to be true and that their source was not human but divine!

The sad irony in a day when so much diversity exists is how a newly saved man is to know who is telling the truth. His understanding and knowledge is certainly not complete. He must trust that those who represent themselves as possessors of the truth really do have the truth without spot or blemish. By receiving the ordinance at their hand he is becoming a member of their church; he is becoming what they are, believing what they believe! His motive may be pure but what of their motives? This underscores the problem of legitimizing doctrinal diversity as if it were intentional by God.

But what do we see demonstrated in the Bible? The template for believers in every generation is found on its pages. We are to follow that model. God does not require of His children something He does not clearly reveal. Furthermore, we have no obligation before God to follow human tradition whether it is familial or ecclesiastical in form. The Bible is our sole rule of faith and practice. Logic compels us as Christians to turn to the Bible for answers. It is from the Bible then that one ascertains the identity of the New Testament church.

Everything we have discussed up to this point is merely a point of view, if the connection cannot be made to the New Testament church in a practical sense. As we have already suggested, the New Testament communicates certain "parameters" that serve as touchstones that in turn enable us to identify a New Testament church. Although many Christians may take them for granted, they are crucial to our ability to understand and identify a New Testament church in our own day.

CHAPTER NINE

The Character: Scriptural Identification

The New Testament Model

In Acts 2, we have the model for the New Testament church to follow. It is not a difficult model to understand, yet so many today have failed to grasp the simplicity by which the church is to operate. We find ourselves in Jerusalem on the day of Pentecost in about AD 30 (biblical chronology). The church of Jerusalem already exists. This is obvious from the simple statements found in Acts 1:13 where the pronoun "they" is used to refer to the group gathered together in the upper room (see also Acts 1:14, 15, 26; 2:1, 14). By now, this young church is composed of the twelve apostles (Mathias having been added to their number in Acts 1:25–26) as well as some 120 others (Acts 1:15). Jesus has already met with them prior to this event (see John 20:19–29). Although they are fearful, Jesus has reassured them of His presence and even imparted to them the gift of the Father, the Holy Spirit (John 20:21–22). Then on the day of

Pentecost as the disciples are gathered in the upper room, suddenly the Spirit of God falls upon each of them. Jesus had promised the manifestation of this power in Acts 1:8 and clearly stated that it would enable them to be witnesses.[1*] The details of Acts 2 that follow verify the reality of His promise.

The power of God's presence (Acts 2:2–4) manifested itself in two ways—first, figuratively, by the presence of *"cloven tongues like as of fire"* sitting upon each of them. This indicated that they would be given a special and unique gift that would enable them to proclaim the Word of God with great convicting power (as of fire). Second, it soon became quite obvious that these cloven tongues of fire represented a new reality—that the apostles at least would be able to speak in languages they had not previously learned or spoken. Again, these were not ecstatic languages, nor were they some divine prayer language. But they were the dialects of people present in Jerusalem on the day of Pentecost (Acts 2:5). The result of this divine intervention was that three thousand people repented and were saved on that day.

[1*] A close reading of the events described in Acts 1 and 2 leads some to conclude that it was the apostles alone upon whom the cloven tongues sat. The fact that the *"cloven tongues like as of fire"* were beheld by some (*"appeared unto them,"* v. 3) may indicate that not all manifested the gift. The fact that *"it sat upon each of them"* does not by itself guarantee a correct interpretation that *"all"* in verse 4 is a reference to *all* present but may refer to *all* the apostles instead. Considering that not all of the 120 would have been Galilaeans and the fact that those speaking in these languages were all identified as Galilaeans (v. 7), would seem to further support this conclusion. In addition, when Peter addressed the crowd in verses 14–15, he seems to point to a much smaller group (*"these"*) than what would have included all of the 120. Indeed, if the 120 were all responsible for the event, chaos would have resulted and it is doubtful that anyone would have been able to hear anything in his own native tongue. This is further supported by the fact that the passage indicates that once it was noised abroad, people came *together*—that is, to a single location to witness the event. Also, note that the languages represented in the passage is a small number not necessitating the 120.

Chapter Nine—The Character: Scriptural Identification

Now as for the model that follows the brief explanation of the events described above, the Bible clearly establishes the form that we are to understand and follow. First, Peter addresses the crowd that had gathered together as word spread about the unusual events described above (see Acts 2:14). Second, the Bible says that many, upon hearing the message of Peter, repented (Acts 2:37–38) and gladly received his word (Acts 2:41). Then, in response to their repentance they were baptized and were *"added unto them."* Finally, these that were added by their baptism continued *"stedfastly in the apostles' doctrine...."*

The issue raised by these events is vitally important to the proper understanding of the New Testament church and the model we are to follow. The identity of these being baptized is not an issue. Rather, the issue at stake is who were these people administering baptism? Just who is implied by the phrase *"added unto them"*? And furthermore, by what authority were they administering the ordinance? Well, the answer is obvious! The group of people identified as *"them"* (plural) has to be the church of Jerusalem that had just previously gathered in the upper room. A further examination of the context underscores this conclusion. In verse 47 the statement is made that *"the Lord added to the church daily such as should be saved."* Since no other *competing* church existed at this point, the reference again has to be to that group that had previously gathered in the upper room. It was by the authority vested in them (the church) by our Lord when He gave them the Great Commission (Matthew 28:18–20), that they were administering this ordinance of baptism. Thus, it was by this baptism that the converts were placed (or *added*) into the local body and where they continued in the doctrine of the apostles and in fellowship with that church.

The Doctrinal Parameters

The challenge in our day—in light of all the competing claims of legitimacy from one Christian group to the next—is to *identify* the New Testament church that Jesus established in the first century. Among all the groups that claim to be "churches," which one is the church that Christ established? And how do we identify that church when the first century church did not have a name over the door?

Furthermore, it would be fruitless to attempt to identify this church historically without first being able to identify the original. It must be kept in mind that in the first century there was no diversity of doctrine among believers. As we have emphasized before, the first century church had no need to identify itself as groups identify themselves today. In the first century there was no competition. Every group of believers—whether in Jerusalem, Antioch, Ephesus, etc.—held to a common faith. That common faith is identified in Acts 2:42 as the doctrine of the apostles. Anyone who challenged this doctrine was rebuffed or excluded!

So, the conclusion of the matter is that the first church must be identified by its doctrinal parameters rather than by a name. Now someone might say that the first century church did have a name—they were called Christians—and they would most certainly be correct (see Acts 11:26). But the term *Christian* was applied to people who were the disciples of Christ. Their commitment to Christ was so very obvious that even their enemies identified them as the followers of Christ. Indeed, rather than identify them one from another, the term actually makes the point that all Christians in the first century had a common faith and practice! Schism, or denominating, was not the norm as it is today.

So what of these doctrinal parameters? How can this church of the first century, the church that Jesus established be identified? If the church can be identified in the New Testament, the same standards will identify it at any time in history, including today. If that first century church exists today with its original form and

Chapter Nine—The Character: Scriptural Identification

format doctrinally speaking, then believers are obligated before God to align themselves with that church and no other. By that, I do not mean to imply that there are "other churches" that have a legitimate claim equal to that of the New Testament church that Jesus built, for none do. The word *church* over a door does not necessarily designate a New Testament church. You have heard it said that "just because a man has athlete's foot does not mean he is an athlete!" The same is true of the claims of so many whose doctrine originates sometime after (most often way after) the first century. Any society of believers whose doctrinal distinctiveness or uniqueness warrants a new classification or denomination cannot possibly be identified as an authentic New Testament church. They are in fact merely man-made institutions with human tradition serving as their doctrinal standard. They full well reject the commandments of God that they might keep their own tradition (Mark 7:9). God is not the author of confusion! Yes, towers have been built and names have been made and all who climb those self-perpetuating monuments to confusion claim to worship God in spirit and in truth. But is it so? That is not to say that the Gospel is not proclaimed in these man-made institutions or that numbers of people have not been saved in these places. God has always blessed the preaching of the Gospel, but the salvation of the lost and the preaching of the Gospel is not the issue here. The *correct identity* and *understanding* of the New Testament church is the matter at hand.

Once again, if the doctrinal parameters of any first century church changed, then it would have ceased to be what it originally was. It would have ceased to be a New Testament church. In fact, some of the churches identified in the New Testament did leave their doctrinal moorings (i.e., Revelation 2) and consequently lost their *light* in the service of the Saviour. Likewise, any church that does not identify with the doctrine of the first century (it removes, supplants, adds to or alters apostolic doctrine) is anything but an authentic New Testament church. A New Testament church is known by its doctrinal parameters.

Let's look then at the claims of Scripture concerning the New Testament church and the doctrinal parameters that mark this institution. There are six parameters that identify this church:

The Body of Christ

> *And he is the head of the body, the church: who is the beginning, the firstborn from the dead; that in all things he might have the preeminence.*—COLOSSIANS 1:18

> *For as we have many members in one body, and all members have not the same office: So we, being many, are one body in Christ, and every one members one of another.*—ROMANS 12:4–5

> *...and gave him to be the head over all things to the church, Which is his body, the fulness of him that filleth all in all.*—EPHESIANS 1:22–23

It is obvious from the foregoing verses of Scripture that a New Testament church is described as the *body of Christ*, of which, Jesus Himself is the head. As we have already discussed, as the head of this church, Jesus is in charge—men are not! The question that arises is how do we define the phrase *body of Christ?* Is this phrase used to identify an invisible entity composed of all the redeemed of all the ages, sometimes referred to as the "one true church," or does the phrase refer to the visible or local New Testament church? This issue has been debated for centuries, and most of Christianity would hold to a mystical or universal church (one true church) position. The reason that so many Christians hold this position is somewhat involved.

Chapter Nine—The Character: Scriptural Identification

This most commonly held position—that the true church is composed of all the redeemed regardless of their doctrinal persuasion—is predominately a Protestant position. It was the position of Luther, Calvin, Zwingli and Knox. These Protestant Reformers had been ejected from the Roman Catholic (universal) Church as troublemakers. Courageously, they had challenged the abuses in their church. They all believed that the Roman Catholic Church was what it claimed, the mother church.[2*] However, they also believed that she had become apostate. They saw themselves as the agents of God to restore the orthodoxy that had been lost in the Catholic Church. Their willingness to take a stand against the abuses that had developed over centuries should not be minimized. Given the power of this state church, they all placed their lives in great jeopardy. However, the truth is, that which began as a reformation effort of the Catholic Church was never a reformation at all because that church never allowed it to gain a foothold.

Upon their removal from the Catholic Church, their mistake was in believing that the New Testament church in its purity had ceased to exist. Although New Testament churches had perpetually existed from the first century forward, the Reformers believed the "mother" church was Roman Catholicism. They further believed

---

[2*]In his commentary on the book of Galatians (Galatians 1:2), Luther writes concerning the church, "Wheresoever the substance of the word and sacraments remaineth, there is the holy church, although Antichrist there reign, who sitteth...in the highest and holiest place of all, namely, in the temple of God. Wherefore, although spiritual tyrants reign, yet there must be a temple of God, and the same must be preserved under them. Therefore...the church is universal throughout the whole world." In essence what Luther was saying is that regardless of the apostasy of the Church of Rome, they still maintained the sacraments and thus maintained their status as the mother church. However, he concluded that any church that maintained the word and the sacraments (i. e., baptism and the Lord's Table) thus retained the grace of God and was thereby legitimized as an agent of the holy church.

that their authority came from their priestly link (ordination) to this church, corrupt though it may have been. Luther and Calvin were well aware of the Waldensian church for example and even acknowledged their purity.[3*]

But rather than seek out such New Testament churches and properly unite with them, they formed new "churches" with doctrines unique to each of them. The result was the Protestant Reformation that we will examine later in more detail. For the sake of our present discussion however, it is important to note that all the Reformers also carried with them unscriptural baggage that they were unwilling or unable to relinquish (i.e., infant baptism).

As their movement began to congeal, they realized that they themselves, as the fathers of the Reformation, did not agree doctrinally. Thus, the difficulty that faced the Reformers concerned not only how to challenge Roman Catholicism, but also how to reconcile the doctrinal differences among themselves. However, their rejection of the doctrines and actions of Roman Catholicism did justify their own exit (howbeit by **excommunication**) from that system. Still (although they could condemn many of the doctrines and polity of the Catholic Church) their exit from Catholicism did not resolve the matter that the Reformers did not agree doctrinally among themselves. These men were not naïve. They knew that the validation of their movement was essential to its success. They understood that God was not the author of confusion and

---

[3*] Indeed Luther, "while being pursued by Pope Leo X, found the only place to hide was among the Picars, a colony of Waldenses who were settled in Bohemia. Luther later reported that after he had more exactly informed himself of their belief, he owned them as brethren and commended them for being faithful Christians. Although he did not agree with them in all things, not being wholly freed from the impurities of the Church of Rome, yet he writes to them with such affection and esteem, as abundantly shews the respect he had for those who for so long a time had opposed the corruptions of the truth." *Allix's Ecclesiastical History*, p. 321–322.

Chapter Nine—The Character: Scriptural Identification

that the Bible had a single thought and message, or did it? If their validation could not come from a unity of beliefs, then perhaps changing the Christian perspective would vindicate their own doctrinal diversity.

The consequence of this thinking was a redefining of the old Catholic doctrine of the church. Remember, these Reformers were all priests or monks at one time. Their immediate frame of reference was the Catholic Church, and only recently had they begun to challenge that church's beliefs and practices in the light of Scripture. The Catholic Church for centuries had defined the church as visible referring to itself, and universal or exclusionary (that is, all competitors were heretics).

The Reformers adjusted this position by saying the true church was invisible and universal, meaning that the church was all inclusive regardless of doctrinal persuasion. Luther defined the church "as the community of believers in the divinity and redeeming passion of Christ."[4] The Augsburg Confession of 1530 was an effort by Reformers to concisely state their doctrines for the emperor, Charles V. This confession became the basis of further confessions among various Protestants in the centuries following the sixteenth century. In point of reference to the doctrine of the church, the Lutheran historian, G.E. Hageman quotes the summary by Dr. Pieper as follows:

DEFINING THE TERMS

Excommunication: *Latin for "out of communion," excommunication represents one of the most severe punishments in the Catholic Church. It deprives the guilty Christian from all participation in "the common blessings of ecclesiastical society." Since divine grace is conveyed via the sacraments in the Catholic Church, the excommunicated are thus excluded from or deprived of divine grace, jeopardizing their eternal state.*

> The Church, in the proper sense of the term, is the aggregate of all believers. All those, and only those, who believe in Christ are members of the Church...Again, the Word of God and the Sacraments, the means of grace, are necessarily connected with the Church and consequently are also the true marks of the same...And bearing in mind that the Church is the aggregate or congregation of all believers, the only means employed in this Church to produce faith in Christ in the hearts of men are the preaching of the Word of God and the correct administration of the Sacraments. Neither can the Church be called visible...The Church universal, the congregation of all believers, is and always remains invisible, for God alone knows those who truly believe.

And in reference to local or particular churches Pieper adds:

> And this Church universal,...is thus not confined to particular orthodox churches or congregations...in which all the articles of the Christian faith are taught in their purity, but it is found throughout the world in those ecclesiastical communities also in which, besides errors, so much of the saving truth is taught that true faith in Christ may be produced.[5]

Thus, they validated their doctrinal diversity and justified their own individual and distinct efforts in the Reformation. So, Luther produced the Lutheran church; Calvin produced the Reformed churches; John Knox produced the Presbyterian church of Scotland; and Henry VIII in England produced the Anglican Church. For the last four centuries the Reformer's definition of the church has been the accepted norm among most Christians. But is it biblical?

It should be realized from the foregoing discussion that the Reformers' doctrinal identity of the church was not derived from Scripture but from the pressure of the moment. The position was born more out of necessity than a sincere and unbiased study of the Scriptures. The Protestant position is therefore suspect at the

Chapter Nine—The Character: Scriptural Identification

very least. Sadly, this unscriptural understanding of the church has been planted deeply within the hearts and minds of the Christian world and it is not easily uprooted. Why? Could it be that it so conveniently justifies diversity and validates every man's claim to legitimacy?

Now back to the *body of Christ*. We have seen previously that the Greek word translated in our English Bible as the word *church* is *ecclesia*. The Greek definition of this word implied certain inherent criteria—location, visibility and organization. These requirements are all physical in nature. But what of the phrase *the body of Christ*? We know that one cannot separate the church from our understanding of the body, for we are clearly told in the Bible that *"he is the head of the body, the church"* and that He is the *"head over all things to the church, which is his body."* The Bible is not speaking of two entities but one! The word *ecclesia* refers to the structural nature of the church and the word *body*, (Greek *soma*) refers to the nature of its function. The New Testament church is a living organism. The Greek word *soma* can refer to any body of matter or material, but the basic meaning of the word refers to someone or something that is able to cast a shadow. In other words, the biblical description of the New Testament church, using both *ecclesia* and *soma*, requires physicality. Thus, it is never proper to refer to the New Testament church in terms that would imply invisibility or mysticism. Nor is it correct to suggest that doctrinal

DEFINING THE TERMS

Mystical: *By mystical we mean that something is mysterious, unexplained or secretive. The facts are unknown or difficult to ascertain. Because the theory of a universal church involves invisibility we refer to the concept as mystical.*

purity is unimportant or irrelevant. The New Testament church is local (visible) and is identified by the purity of its doctrine.

The Scriptures show that the local, visible church was always the thrust of the apostolic position. Perhaps the most often quoted passage in support of a universal, **mystical** church position is found in 1 Corinthians 12. To properly understand this passage, one must realize that this chapter immediately follows the apostle's admonitions concerning the Lord's Table. In that discussion the Apostle Paul establishes the framework in which the memorial is to be celebrated. His statements in 1 Corinthians 11:18, that *"when ye come together in the church"* and in verse 20, *"When ye come together therefore into one place,"* are obvious references to a local church. Indeed, the title of this particular book tells us that the church referred to here is the church at Corinth. It is in this context that the discussion in the following chapter takes place. That is, in every local New Testament church, gifts of the Spirit are *"given to every man to profit withal."* This specific discussion in 1 Corinthians 12:1–11 is immediately followed with a description of the New Testament church (v. 12). The church is described as a body (*soma*). The analogy that is made here compares the human body to a local New Testament church.

> *For as the body is one, and hath many members, and all the members of that one body, being many, are one body: so also is Christ.*—1 CORINTHIANS 12:12

Just as the human body, although composed of many individual parts (members), is still seen as one unit, so it is with a local church. The passage continues saying that it is by the Spirit that we are all baptized into one body. The phrase *"one body"* is not a reference to a mystical invisible body but a local church. The emphasis of Paul is that we are not all individuals doing our own thing, but we are a part of a local church and that we are dependent upon one another. Each believer is gifted by the Spirit to profit *withal,* that is, the local

Chapter Nine—The Character: Scriptural Identification

church. This is born out in the rest of the passage (see vv. 12:15–26). In a local church we have the same care one for another; we suffer with one another, and when one member of the body is honored we all rejoice. Each member of the body is a valued part of the whole. The whole is the local church which functions as a body of which Christ is the head.

The Corinthian church was one example of this analogy. In verse 27, they are described as *"the body of Christ, and members in particular."* Literally, the church *(ecclesia)* at Corinth *(ye:* plural*)* was the physical body *(soma)* of Christ in the city of Corinth, and each person, being baptized into that body, was a member in particular.

Numbers of other examples could be given and without exception the church is always described in terms physical in nature and never invisible. For a further examination consider Ephesians 4:1–16, where unity of the Spirit is emphasized (v. 3) and that there is only *"one body"* (vv. 4–6). The Bible knows of no other body except the local New Testament church, just as it knows of no other Spirit; no other hope of your calling; no other Lord; no other faith; no other baptism; and no other God! The purpose of the apostle in writing these things is to point the reader to the ultimate goal, the *unity of the faith* (vv. 13–15). Tell me, where is there today a cry for a unity of the faith? It does not exist! Rather, we speak of unity as if it applies to "getting along," but that is only possible when there is a unity of the faith. Indeed, *"can two walk together, except they be agreed"* (Amos 3:3)?

According to the Scriptures, it is a sign of immaturity (Ephesians 4:14) to ignore the importance of sound doctrine. There is no maturity evidenced in being tossed to and fro with every wind of doctrine. To forsake truth or to exalt the unscriptural traditions of men over the commandments of God in order to maintain unity among believers is counter-productive and scripturally unjustifiable. So then, the local New Testament church is described and identified as the *body of Christ!*

The Habitation of God

Not only is the New Testament church described as the *body of Christ*, but it is also described as the *habitation of God*. First Corinthians 6:19 clearly teaches that the Spirit of God indwells the individual believer. It is this indwelling presence of God that enables the believer to live the Christian life. Without the Spirit of God, sin, the flesh and the world would soon overcome believers. The believer could not resist the temptations he would face. As he resists the flesh and yields to the Spirit of God, the believer gains the victory in faith and becomes fit for the Master's service.

In the same way, each New Testament church must be endued with Spirit power and victory. Remember, the local New Testament church is described in the Bible as a body. Christ is the head, but the body is composed of sinners redeemed by the power of the Gospel and placed into the local church via scriptural baptism. The Spirit of God indwells the local church in the same way He indwells the individual believer. That is the meaning of 1 Corinthians 3:9 when the Apostle Paul refers to the Corinthian church as "*God's building.*" That is also the point made in 1 Corinthians 3:16.

> *Know ye not that ye are the temple of God, and that the Spirit of God dwelleth in you?*—1 CORINTHIANS 3:16

In the same way that a believer may grieve or quench the Holy Spirit, so the members of the local church can corporately defile the temple. Given the fact that individual believers still possess a sin nature and that sin is like leaven, its nature is to spread. So a local church can be filled with leaven and thereby grieve and quench the Holy Spirit (see 1 Corinthians 5:6–7; Galatians 5:9).

> *If any man defile the temple of God, him shall God destroy; for the temple of God is holy, which temple ye are.*—1 CORINTHIANS 3:17

Chapter Nine—The Character: Scriptural Identification

Perhaps the clearest statement of this fact is found in Ephesians 2:21–22.

> *In whom all the building fitly framed together groweth unto an holy temple in the Lord: In whom ye also are builded together for an habitation of God through the Spirit.*—EPHESIANS 2:21–22

Here, the church is described as a building fitly framed together which is the dwelling place (habitation) for God through the Spirit. The little word *ye* (plural) is to be taken as a reference to the corporate body of believers known as the church at Ephesus. In addition, the little word *also* would imply that this church is not the only church that could claim this privilege. Keep in mind that in the first century when this was written, there were no other churches but New Testament churches. These churches, sometimes separated by hundreds of miles, were nonetheless the same doctrinally and thus qualified as New Testament churches.

The conclusion drawn from this principle is that each New Testament church is indwelt by the presence of God. Institutionally, it is God's place of habitation in this age. This fact is not duplicated elsewhere. There is no scriptural evidence that God indwells so-called **para-church** organizations. God established one institution upon the earth that He would choose to empower as His agency and that was the New Testament church. Man-made institutions may exist and may accomplish many fine things in the name of Christ. But, they are not ordained of God and they are not a replacement for the divine institution of the New Testament church. In a time

---

DEFINING THE TERMS

Para-church: By para-church we mean religious organizations of human origin that come along side the church either in support of or as a replacement to the church.

when most of us gauge God's blessing by either the sincerity of the participants or the success of the product, it would be nice if we would frame our confidence in a ministry by its scriptural integrity. That is not to say that God does not sometimes bless the sincere work of individual believers; He does! And certainly God does empower individual believers as they occupy in the kingdom. But the byproduct of that work—the building of towers and institutions—is not the dwelling place of God. That honor belongs to the New Testament church alone.

The Agent of the Great Commission

Third, the New Testament church is identified in Scripture as the *agent of the Great Commission.* In Matthew 28, our Lord established what has become known to all of us as the Great Commission.

> *And Jesus came and spake unto them, saying, All power is given unto me in heaven and in earth. Go ye therefore, and teach all nations, baptizing them in the name of the Father, and of the Son, and of the Holy Ghost: Teaching them to observe all things whatsoever I have commanded you: and, lo, I am with you alway, even unto the end of the world. Amen.*—MATTHEW 28:18–20

These are some of the last words that Jesus spoke. Many often assume that these words were intended for the individual believer to the exclusion of anything else. It is supposed that the disciples are representative of all believers down through the ages until Jesus returns. Consequently, each believer is to actively participate in the spreading of the Gospel. Certainly, in part, this is true. However, it seems to be a bit shortsighted. As we have said before, if the Commission were given to them as individuals without any ecclesiastical connection, then the obligation to fulfill the Great Commission would have ended with the conclusion of their mortal lives. But if they, as the first members of the original New Testament church were being addressed (1 Corinthians 12:28), then it is the New Testament church to whom Jesus was speaking. It should be obvious that since the disciples were not to live forever here on earth, then only the New Testament church as an institution could qualify as a living entity whereby Jesus could *always* be with it! Thus, the New Testament church is the single agent of the Great Commission! Individual believers are to multiply their effectiveness in the proclamation of the Gospel through a united effort of fellow believers in a body of Christ (a New Testament church). That does not relieve individual responsibility to win souls, but it broadens the corporate responsibility of every local church. By pooling resources and manpower, believers are much more effective worldwide.

The Perpetual Witness

Fourth, the New Testament church is identified in terms of its *perpetuity*. The Scriptures are very clear. The church that Jesus started in the city of Jerusalem in the first century not only faithfully perpetuated the Gospel in their Jerusalem but also went far beyond their native borders. They replicated themselves throughout the world.

When Jesus announced that He would build His church, He said that the gates of Hell would not *"prevail against it."* As we have just seen, He also declared in the Great Commission (Matthew 28:20) that He would be with His church always, even unto the *"end of the world."* That requires the perpetuity of the New Testament church. In Ephesians we read:

> Unto him be glory in the church by Christ Jesus throughout all ages, world without end. Amen.
> —Ephesians 3:21

In other words, if the world never ends, the church that Jesus started will always exist in its original form and format. For the glory of God to be associated with that institution throughout all ages, New Testament churches must always exist. Remember, we are not saying that every institution that calls itself a church is really a New Testament church. The church that Jesus started is defined by its doctrinal parameters. We refer to this set of truths as apostolic doctrine or faith. So, in order for a church to be identified as a New Testament church it must maintain the original form and format doctrinally as set forth by the apostles.

Obviously, down through the ages many changes have occurred. The question then is whether these changes merit the exclusion of those who have advocated and devised such changes from being identified as New Testament churches. It is my conclusion that they do. The church of Jesus Christ must continue until Jesus returns with its original doctrinal parameters, for that is Christ's promise. (If He cannot protect and preserve the institution of His church, why would we think He is able to preserve the saints?)

Do you see that every time some "Johnny come lately" comes on the scene claiming to have rediscovered some lost truth, he is in reality saying that Hell hath prevailed? When he insists that the glory has departed and the New Testament church is no longer what God intended, he is challenging the very integrity of God. My friend, it just does not fit! Anyone who infers that God has failed to maintain His church in its original form and format and left man to his own devises just does not understand the Bible on the subject. Rather than building the church, this man is building a new foundation with himself as the cornerstone! Instead of order we have more confusion, and rather than a savior we have a renegade. And so we conclude that the New Testament church has and must continue to exist without doctrinal change in order to rightfully claim to be "New Testament." In other words, the New Testament church has had a perpetual existence since its beginning in the first century.

Chapter Nine—The Character: Scriptural Identification

The Pillar and Ground of Truth

Fifth, the New Testament church is identified in the Scriptures as the *pillar and ground of the truth*. When the Apostle Paul was instructing his young disciple Timothy, he dealt directly with this issue in 1 Timothy 3:15. He emphasized the importance of conducting oneself in an appropriate fashion as a leader of God's flock. Timothy was to know how he was to *behave* himself in the house of God. There are many today who are conducting the business of God in a rather "wing it as we go" or freelance way. We are reminded that all things are to be done *"decently and in order"* (1 Corinthians 14:40). But, as the apostle challenges young Timothy in the work, he also identifies one of the most important characteristics of the New Testament church. Paul said that the house of God was the pillar and ground of the truth.

> *But if I tarry long, that thou mayest know how thou oughtest to behave thyself in the house of God, which is the church of the living God, the pillar and ground of the truth.*—1 Timothy 3:15

The apostle may have had in mind a reference in 1 Kings 7, where some of the details regarding the building of the first temple by King Solomon are given. Here in verse 21, we are told that as Solomon set up the pillars of the porch before the temple, the King then named these two support pillars. The first pillar to the right he named *Jachin* meaning, "He will establish it." The second pillar placed on the left side of the porch was called *Boaz* meaning, "in it is strength." Paul understood the spiritual principle seen in the building of the temple and extended the principle in connection with the house of God, the *church of the living God* in the New Testament. The truth of God's Word would be established by God Himself and that New Testament truth would be the strength of His church. When men depart from that truth and devise other opinions and vain philosophies, they are doomed to failure, for there is no strength in them. And, no matter how convincing they are that "God has revealed to them" this or that opinion, God is not the author of confusion. He changes not! What they promote has not come from God and will not be established, nor will any be strengthened in it.

So, when one desires to find and hear the truth as it was *"once delivered unto the saints"* (Jude 3), he must seek it in a New Testament church. We are promised that the truth will abide in that place. Upon such time when that ceases to be the case, then that church ceases to be a New Testament church.

The Reflection of God

Finally, the Bible describes the New Testament church as the *reflection of God* in every age. Once again we turn attention to Ephesians 3:21.

> *Unto him be glory in the church by Christ Jesus throughout all ages, world without end. Amen.*
> —EPHESIANS 3:21

The Greek word that is translated *glory* here is a word that speaks of the splendor and beauty of God. It is a revelation of God spoken of or alluded to throughout the Scriptures.

Perhaps the most revealing passage of the glory of God in the Old Testament is found in Exodus 33. Here Moses asked to see the glory of God. The people of Israel had sinned a grave sin in worshipping the golden calf (Exodus 32). Consequently, God commanded that the tabernacle be removed from the midst of the people. The issue is one of holiness. The people of Israel were a stiff-necked people, and God declared that if He remained in their midst, He would consume them in the way (Exodus 33:3, 5). However, Moses found grace in God's sight and at his request, God returned.

Chapter Nine—The Character: Scriptural Identification

Moses, in response to God's grace, asked if he might see the glory of God. God responded in Exodus 33:20, warning that no man could see His face and live. To speak of the glory of God is to speak of the holiness of God. No man can be in the presence of God and live because all men have sinned and come short of that glory. But God, understanding the heart and mind of Moses, made provision for him. God placed Moses in the cleft of a rock that would cover Moses as God passed by, and Moses would see the back parts of God but not His face.

Likewise, the only way any man will see God is under the provision of the Saviour, Jesus the Christ. The point is that the core nature of God is one of holiness. All of God's attributes in relation to man stem from this core. We are told to worship God in the beauty of holiness (Psalm 29:2; 96:9) and that *"Thy testimonies are very sure: holiness becometh thine house, O LORD, for ever"* (Psalm 93:5).

When the Bible declares in Ephesians 3:21 that the glory of God will be connected to the New Testament church throughout all ages, the message to believers ought to be clear. In every age the holiness of God will characterize the local New Testament church. The word translated *glory* is the Greek word *doxa*. This word not only speaks of the physical attributes of the glory that necessitated that Moses later wear a veil, but it also speaks of that which causes the splendor, the holiness of God. The association between the holiness of God and His glory is seen in Isaiah 63:15.

The New Testament church will be a place that will not seek the approval of the world and its whims, but will reflect the nature of God, His holiness. I am not saying that the church will be perfect, but that its desire and efforts will be such as to exalt holiness rather than worldliness. So, the New Testament church will be a reflection of the holiness of God in every age. Even if the world were to never end, Jesus Himself will superintend in this process.

The New Testament church is thus revealed by these parameters, and it is by these we are able to identify true New Testament churches down through the centuries. Once again they are:

The Body of Christ
The Habitation of God
The Agent of the Great Commission
The Perpetual Witness
The Pillar and Ground of Truth
The Reflection of God

Having established the scriptural parameters that identify the New Testament church, we are now ready to delve into the actual history of that church. It is often a very tragic story humanly speaking. Yet, just beneath the surface of the story there is a sense that God has been at work all along. The story of the New Testament church is really one of faith and victory. It is a story that needs to be told if for no other reason than as a sacred memorial to those who lost their lives in defense of New Testament truth.

PART THREE

The Heritage of the New Testament Church

PERSONAL OBSERVATIONS

The Heritage of the New Testament Church

It is not the intent to present to the reader a detailed century by century account of the events and personalities of Christian history. This book has been purposely designed to aid the average person in his understanding of the origin, identity, and now the history of the church that Jesus built. The goal is to give the reader a sense of the historical circumstances that have brought Christianity to this present state in connection with the church that Jesus established in the first century. As previously stated, Christianity is generally in a state of confusion which deepens by the willingness of so many to ignore what the Bible clearly claims and teaches concerning the New Testament church.

This book, therefore, attempts to cross the centuries, stopping at those events, movements, and individuals who have either reinforced first-century Christianity, or who have originated or deepened error. It will be important to note that the church of the New Testament has always existed in its original form and format as

God promised it would. There has never been a time since its origin that it did not exist as a light in the darkness, always faithful to its apostolic roots. While some of their numbers may have stepped outside the boundaries of sound doctrine and practice, that does not negate the real presence of a pure church in every century.

Perhaps the two most significant principles relevant to a historical context are that the New Testament church will be ***perpetual*** in its existence and that it will be the ***pillar and ground of truth***. These two principles track the presence of true New Testament churches throughout the centuries.

CHAPTER TEN

The Primitive Church: Early Christianity

The Early Years

The first church was founded by Jesus in the city of Jerusalem somewhere near AD 28, with the disciples being the first members of that church (1 Corinthians 12:28). We date (using a biblical chronology rather than a Gregorian calendar) the origin of this first of many New Testament churches with the selection of certain disciples identified as the twelve apostles (see Luke 6:12–16 and Acts 1:26) because of the statement by the Apostle Paul in 1 Corinthians 12:28 that, "... *God hath set some in the church, first apostles.*" If these men were the first to be *set in the church*, then the church effectively began with their selection. That is not to say that the church is complete in its spiritual order, polity, or doctrine as yet, but it does indicate its origin. Jesus in Matthew 16:18 declared His intention to establish His church and that the gates of Hell would not prevail against it. This church would be built upon the same profession of faith that Peter made—that Jesus was the Christ (the Saviour), the Son of the living God. Every man or woman, boy or girl who receives Christ as their personal Saviour and is scripturally baptized (Acts 2) could be admitted into that institution, the local New Testament church (1 Corinthians 12).

The day of Pentecost established the advent of global evangelism. That is, the disciples understood and acted upon the command of the Great Commission. Pentecost is not the beginning of the church, for the church already existed. The disciples were gathered with others in an upper room, their total number being about 120. The gift of the Holy Spirit had already been received according to John 20:22. Now, in a demonstration of the power of the Spirit's presence, the Spirit of God fell upon them. The Gospel was preached by the means of a powerful but temporary gift (tongues, see 1 Corinthians 13:8–10) that would validate their message and mission before men. The result was that some three thousand souls were saved, baptized, and added to the church of Jerusalem. These continued steadfastly in the apostles' doctrine. In other words, the disciples made more disciples! As Jesus was sent by the Father, so He sent His disciples into the world (John 20:21).

Moving beyond these events we find that the apostles established local, visible churches in a variety of cities, starting in Samaria. In each case the message of the Gospel was proclaimed, believers were baptized and were then organized into New Testament churches. Each of these New Testament churches was modeled after the same doctrine and polity that characterized the church at Jerusalem. So, each church had a common faith with other New Testament churches. These churches remained under the oversight of the apostles until pastors could be appointed. In this way the apostles were able to maintain the doctrinal integrity of each church in particular, as well as the churches in general. "Each of them was independent in their organic relations, one from another; each of them acknowledged no other head but Jesus

Chapter Ten—The Primitive Church: Early Christianity

and owned no Lawgiver but Him; each was composed of baptized believers only; each administered baptism by immersion only; each denied **sacramental salvation**; each held to the equality of the membership; and each held to the freedom of conscience and to religious freedom."[1] As long as the apostles lived, they contended for and fought to maintain the doctrinal purity of all these churches.

The next church of specific record was the church of Antioch located in Syria. It apparently was established sometime during the decade that followed the day of Pentecost. This New Testament church became the missionary headquarters of the world in the first century. It was from here that the Apostle Paul and others were sent out to the Gentile world. New Testament churches were established in places that most of us are familiar with if we read the New Testament—Corinth, Ephesus, Thessalonica, Colossae, Rome, and in the regions of Galatia, Gaul, Britannia, and Asia. Much of the New Testament was written to these churches established by Paul and his companions in the West. Although much is known of the missionary journeys of the Apostle Paul from the book of Acts, relatively little is known of the twelve. Looking at the traditions that surround the ministries of the twelve, we will gain a better realization of how the Gospel spread in the first century. This fact becomes abundantly clear as you examine closely the accounts found in the book of Acts, chapters 8–21. Please note that the

DEFINING THE TERMS

Sacramental salvation: *Sacramental salvation is a belief that there is some saving merit in the ordinance of baptism, usually a belief that the act of baptism washes away original sin. First century churches never believed that baptism played any part in the salvation of a new convert. The Bible clearly teaches that salvation is not the result of human merit but is solely by God's grace through faith in Jesus Christ alone.*

following is primarily based upon historical tradition from various sources and not upon Scripture alone. The primary source for these historical traditions comes from a book by William McBirnie, *The Search for the Twelve Apostles.*[2]

Andrew, the brother of Peter, before his conversion, lived as a fisherman in the city of Capernaum along with Peter and their two partners, James and John, the sons of Zebedee. He was first introduced to us as a disciple of John the Baptist and then as a soulwinner, bringing his brother to Christ. Tradition has Andrew ministering in Asia Minor and Greece. Some have suggested that Andrew preached in lands as far west as Scotland. Tradition has it that he died in AD 69 after hanging on a cross for three days in the land of Greece, where he ministered in the latter years of his life (Mark 1:14–18, 29; Luke 5:10; John 1:35–42).

Peter, originally named Simon, was surnamed "Rock" (Greek, *Petros*—small stone; Aramaic *Cephas*) or Peter. As the brother of Andrew, he was a fisherman before his conversion. Although Peter was impulsive at times, he became known as the apostle to the Jews, and played a very important role in the early church, but he is never mentioned in the Scripture as being the Bishop of Rome. Some historians believe that he may have been the pastor of the church in Babylon based on his salutation in 1 Peter 5:13. In AD 67, at the age of 70, he was crucified upside down at his own request in the city of Rome. His death followed a nine month internment in the "Tullian Keep," a subterranean pit of torture. His death was anticipated in John 21:18–19; 2 Peter 1:14 (John 1:35–42, 13:6–10; Matthew 16:13–20; Acts 1–5; Luke 5:10–11; Galatians 2:9; 1 Peter 1:1, 5:13).

Philip was from the same city as Andrew and Peter—Bethsaida, on the Sea of Galilee (John 1:44). He too was one of the first men called by Jesus to follow Him and is not to be confused with Philip the evangelist. Philip may have been the other disciple mentioned in connection with Andrew in John 1:35–40. His first act of discipleship was to bring his brother

Chapter Ten—The Primitive Church: Early Christianity

Nathanael to Christ. Philip is said to have ministered for some twenty years in Synthia (southern Russia) before spending the remainder of his life in Asia Minor. Philip was eventually stoned while bound to a cross and was thus crucified in the city of Hierapolis in Asia Minor in about AD 60 (John 1:43–45; 6:5–7; 12:20–33).

Thomas, called Didymus by John, was also a fisherman. He is most often known as "doubting Thomas" because of the few references to his unbelief. Thomas, along with Peter, founded the Eastern Church in ancient Babylon, also known as the Assyrian Church, the Nestorian Church, or the Chaldean Syrian Church in history. By AD 49 Thomas, accompanied by Bartholomew and Jude, had brought the Gospel to Asia, primarily to the land we know as India. By AD 52, he had founded at least seven churches in India after converting three principle kings of that land. Despised by the pagan Brahmins, Thomas, while in prayer, was martyred at their hands by arrows in about AD 60. He was buried in the church he founded in Malabar, a coastal city in southern India (Matthew 10:3; John 11:16; 14:5; 20:24–29).

Jude, also called Thaddeus, was probably the son of James the Great, the brother of the Apostle John. He is believed to have accompanied Thomas and Bartholomew into Central Asia, remaining in ancient Armenia (today, Georgia, Armenia, and Azerbaijan) where he ministered between AD 43–66. His influence there eventually produced the first Christianized nation (majority religion) in history by AD 301. He suffered martyrdom in AD 66 by a javelin (Mark 3:18; Luke 6:16; John 14:22).

Bartholomew, also known in the Scriptures as Nathanael, labored for some time in Arabia, then the south of Persia, and with Thomas in India. He then ministered in Asia Minor with his brother Philip until Philip's death. He later traveled into nearby Armenia in about AD 60 where, after the death of Jude, he continued that labor until his own martyrdom in AD 68. It is said that he was beaten with clubs and then crucified head down and flayed alive in that position (Luke 6:14; John 1:45; Acts 1:13).

Matthew, also known as Levi, was the brother of James the Less, both being the sons of Alphaeus. He was a tax collector and a bureaucrat before coming to Christ. Tradition says that he ministered in many lands, but it seems most plausible that he ministered in ancient Ethiopia. He was later martyred by beheading after being condemned by the Sanhedrin in Alexandria, Egypt, (Mark 2:14; Matthew 9:9–11; 10:1–3).

James the Less, known as the son of Alphaeus, was the brother of Matthew as mentioned above. He is sometimes referred to as James the Less in contrast to James the Great, the brother of John, of the sons of Zebedee. The sons of Alphaeus were native to Capernaum and were both of the tribe of Levi. James the Less is not to be confused with James the author of the book of James who was the half brother of our Lord. James the Less is credited with the founding of the church of Syria (Antioch). It seems that he was clubbed and stoned to death after being thrown from the temple in Jerusalem after preaching Christ, date unknown (Mark 3:18; Luke 6:15).

Simon was known as the Zealot for his political persuasions before his conversion. He is also referred to as Simon the Canaanite. He is said to have ministered in his early years in Egypt, Cyrene, North Africa, and Lybia. He probably was responsible for the establishment of the faith in Carthage. This church became a center for Christian activity in North Africa. Still later, he apparently traveled to Spain and then to ancient Britannia. He first arrived in Britain in AD 44. He left shortly thereafter but returned with Joseph of Arimathea and a band of missionary recruits in AD 60 to evangelize Britain. The effort was made during the Boadicean War, an extremely dangerous and violent time to accomplish the task. Some tradition says that Simon was arrested by the Romans, tried and crucified on May 10, AD 61, in Britain. However, a more credible witness states that after leaving Britain, Simon joined Jude in Mesopotamia and then traveled to Persia where he was crowned with martyrdom by being sawn asunder (Mark 3:18; Luke 6:15; Acts 1:13).

James the Great, one of the sons of Zebedee, along with his brother John and Peter, comprised an inner circle of Christ's disciples. When called of Jesus to be His disciples, both James and John immediately left "all" to follow the Lord. Both James and John were surnamed the "Sons of Thunder" because of their quick resolve. There is some tradition that suggests that James went to Spain for a time where he preached to a colony of Jewish slaves who had been deported from Italy for their "superstitious" beliefs. Thus, James was responsible for introducing the Gospel into Spain. Later, after his return to Jerusalem, James was beheaded by Herod Agrippa in the year AD 44. He became the first of the apostles to be martyred (Matthew 4:18–22; Luke 6:14; Acts 12:1–2).

John, one of the "Sons of Thunder," became known as the disciple whom Jesus loved. He perhaps was the most intimate of the disciples in his relationship with Jesus. Because of this, Christ gave him the charge to care for His mother, Mary, which he faithfully carried out until her death in Ephesus years later. He was the first at the empty tomb. He, James, and Peter are called the "pillars" of the church at Jerusalem. He became the pastor of the church at Ephesus in Asia Minor, shortly before the destruction of the city of Jerusalem in AD 70. He was exiled to Patmos, a penal colony off the coast of Turkey, but was said to have been later given back his freedom after the death of Domitian, who had exiled him.

It was at Patmos that John penned the book of Revelation by inspiration. He is said to have preached to the Parthians (a people on the border between Russia and Iran near the eastern border of Turkey). In his lifetime, John is credited with starting several churches throughout Asia Minor. It is said that at the ripe age of ninety eight, John was so feeble that he was carried to the church services in the arms of his disciples. He died of natural causes. His most famous disciple was Polycarp (John 1:34–40; Matthew 17:1–13; Mark 5:37; 9:38; 10:35; John 19:26–27, 35; 20:2, 8; 21:7, 20; Acts 3:11; 8:14; Galatians 2:9).

Matthias was the disciple chosen by lot in Acts 1. He was numbered with the twelve from that time forward. He was the replacement for Judas. Eusebius suggests that he was one of the seventy sent out by Christ early in His ministry. Of his ministry it is said that he preached in ancient Syria, Armenia, and a land identified in ancient literature as Ethiopia located in Mesopotamia near Armenia. Here it is said he met with cannibals and was blinded by them. The story claims that he was rescued by Andrew. He later returned to Judaea and Jerusalem where he was stoned to death, date unknown (Luke 10:1; Acts 1:20–26; Revelation 21:14).

Paul, the apostle to the Gentiles, was not part of the original twelve, nor was it ever intended that he would be one of the twelve. He, by his own testimony, was *"born out of due season."* Paul himself, by referring to the twelve in 1 Corinthians 15:5, excludes himself from their number. We know Paul desired to go to Spain, and there is good testimony that he did preach the Gospel there. Several sources testify that Paul first came to Rome in AD 56 and upon a successful defense before Nero, was released. This would be the defense that Paul refers to in 2 Timothy. He then departed to Spain spending some two years there. Clement, a disciple of Paul and early pastor of the Church of Rome, states that Paul went to the "extremity of the West."[3] That would have to be Spain or even Britain. There are ancient authorities who did in fact testify that Paul reached Britain. Later, upon his return to Rome, he was arrested and beheaded under Nero's direction in AD 67. Tradition says that this was the same day that Peter was martyred in Rome by crucifixion.

Although authentic New Testament churches were in the majority for nearly five hundred years of Christian history, these churches eventually became the minority after the union of church and state in the fourth century and the fall of Rome in the fifth century. These churches became the persecuted church of the Middle Ages, which lasted one thousand years. The persecuted churches during the Middle Ages, although known by a variety of names in a variety of places, were known corporately by their enemies as *Anabaptists*. The term is derived from the Greek *ana*, meaning "again." Thus, their name comes from the fact that they practiced the re-baptism of all those who desired to enter their congregations from churches they found to be apostate.

The causes and development of apostasy within Christianity in the early centuries resulted in a state church later known as the Roman Catholic Church. But our real interest lies in the development of that church that remained true to its New Testament convictions. We will briefly trace the history of those societies found throughout the ancient world whose faith and practice were New Testament or apostolic in their origin (Acts 7:58; 8:1, 3; 9:1–31; 11:25–26; 13–28; Galatians 2:1–14).

The Roman Persecutions

In an effort to destroy this new sect, the government of Rome officially sanctioned ten distinct persecutions. This began with the order of Nero (AD 64–68) to exterminate every man or woman who professed allegiance to the Christ of Christianity. Some historians believe the Apostle Peter as well as the Apostle Paul suffered martyrdom during this persecution. Some tradition has it that while Peter was being hanged upside down at the top of a small hill, Paul was being beheaded at its base. But these were not the only martyrs. Blood began to flow throughout the empire, but especially at Rome. Many were burned alive! The gardens of the Roman palace were lighted by the burning bodies of Christians mounted on poles after being covered with pitch.

With varying intensities there followed nine more persecutions of Christians under various leaders: Domitian (AD 81–93); Nerva (AD 96); Trajan (AD 116); Marcus Aurelius (AD 161–180); Severus (AD 202–211); Decius (AD 249–251); Valerian (AD 257); Aurelian (AD 270–275); and Diocletian (AD 303–310). In all, almost 250 years of severe persecution were directed toward the early church. Any Christian who lived during these years knew someone—a friend, a father, a mother, grandfather, or grandmother—who had been savagely murdered. The following description from *History of Persecutions* exemplifies the terrible nature of these persecutions:

> ...those who would not blaspheme Christ and offer incense to the gods were publicly whipped; drawn by the heels through the streets of the cities; racked until every bone of their body was disjointed; had their teeth beat out; their noses, hands and ears cut off; sharp-pointed spears run under their nails; they were tortured with melted lead thrown on their naked bodies; had their eyes dug out; their limbs cut off; were condemned to the mines; ground between stones; stoned to death; burnt alive; thrown headlong from high buildings; beheaded; smothered in burning lime-kilns; destroyed with hunger, thirst, and cold; thrown to wild beasts; broiled on gridirons with slow fires; cast by heaps into the sea; crucified; scraped to death with sharp shells; torn to pieces by the boughs of trees; and, in a word, destroyed by all the various methods that the most diabolical subtlety and malice could devise.[4]

From the perspective of ancient Rome, Christianity was seen as a threat to the security and well-being of the empire. Rome had conquered the world. It had effectively absorbed societies that had at one time influenced the world. These peoples conquered by Rome still had their own cultures, languages and customs. But the one thing that was common among all of these peoples (the Egyptians, the Assyrians, the Persians, the Greeks, etc.) was their religious preference for **polytheism**. This common belief in multiple gods was seen as the glue that held the empire together. This pagan belief was the common factor that served to unite people in spite of their diverse cultures, languages, and customs.

Christianity, on the other hand, was **monotheistic**. The belief in and radical commitment to the existence of one God was revolutionary. The Jews, of course, believed in one God also. That is why early Christianity was seen as a sect that had grown out of Judaism. The difference that soon became abundantly clear to Rome was that although the Jews never attempted to spread their message to the world, these Christians were militant in their efforts to spread the Gospel. The more Rome tried to exterminate them, the more they spread!

Despite the hellish efforts of Rome to rid itself of Christianity, it continued to spread throughout the empire, including its furthest outposts. Many within the palace itself had been converted. As Christianity was gaining influence, Rome as a society was floundering. She had become depraved, growing more wicked by the day. By the early part of the fourth century, her armies were losing the will to defend the empire and were being defeated by the rabble of Europe.

DEFINING THE TERMS

Polytheism: Polytheism is a belief in the existence of many gods usually associated in some way with nature.

Monotheism: Monotheism believes in the existence of one God and that polytheism is merely idolatry.

The Rise of Apostasy

In the fourth century, evidence of doctrinal error spread in the church. Certain harmful attitudes among some Christian leaders had crept into the early church. These had not produced their ripened fruit as of yet, but the seeds of error had obviously been sown by the evil one and had gained converts in the soil of Christianity. Pure churches certainly continued to be dominant, but some church leaders began to substitute human ingenuity for New Testament principles.

In some ways, early Christianity adopted certain secular attitudes that had enabled the government of Rome to secure the peace of the empire. Rome ruled all the peoples she conquered with an iron hand, but she also learned to unite the empire with those things her subjects held in common (e.g., religion, commerce, language). Some early Christians adopted and successfully used these techniques to bring about some very important changes in the Christian world. The result was an emerging society that was more secular than Christian.

First, there was a *gradual change in church government.* A crude notion of a universal church evolved during the third century. The first time the term *invisible* was used of record was by *Hegessipus,* a converted Jew and early church historian (AD 120–180). He used the term in the second century as a reference to the universal doctrine held in common by Christians throughout the world.[5] Some leaders began to propagate the belief that since all New Testament churches had one faith in common, they should be viewed as one entity. No matter how these individual bodies (local churches) were separated by physical distance, they were the same. The church came to be viewed by some as one great organic, invisible body—the church. Furthermore, if the church was spiritually one body, then logically there should be an outward structure in order to preserve the integrity of the invisible body as a whole. This was accomplished by two means—first by insuring a common doctrine and second, a common form or practice of the religious faith. This in turn

Chapter Ten—The Primitive Church: Early Christianity

required some sort of corporate control and oversight. So, an effort was made to organize! By the middle of the third century we can see the early development of a centralized hierarchy forming.

According to Orchard, in AD 249 "Emperor Decius 'required all without exception to embrace the pagan worship on pain of death.' Professors (professing Christians) were not in a state to meet sufferings, and apostasy to an alarming extent ensued. The officer formerly known by the name of elder, bishop, or presbyter (terms exactly synonymous in the New Testament) now became distinguished by the elevation of the bishop above his brethren, and each of the above terms was carried out into a distinction of places in the Christian church."[6] The purpose for such distinction was to see that certain decisions and actions were carried out by congregations less influential than the seat of central authority. Thus, some clergy believed the church would be more likely to survive the threat of persecution from without and apostasy from within.

The secularization of Christianity continued to develop in two very important ways. By the fourth century there was the evolution in authority of both bishops and church councils.[7] The two were interconnected. This development was at first innocent and probably seemed wise. As churches were called together to address certain problems and/or errors, bishops of larger metropolitan churches would host such meetings and in general would be in charge. Over time these bishops began to see themselves as overlords of smaller, less populated districts where the churches were smaller and their pastors less influential. A kind of regional oversight was assumed, and a superficial order began to develop. "Associations of ministers and churches, which at first were formed in Greece, became common throughout the empire."[8] Councils were irregular at first but eventually became annual events. The bishop of Rome gained the major influence from these developments. The Council of Nicea (AD 325) recognized the bishops of Alexandria, Antioch, and Rome (Jerusalem received an honorary position) as preeminent in their own areas. "Thus, by AD 325 the policy of the patriarchates, that is, the administration of church affairs by bishops from three or four major cities, was confirmed by conciliar action."[9]

This concept was at odds with the New Testament concept that each local church was autonomous (see Colossians 2:8; 2 Corinthians 8:19, 23). Each New Testament church, regardless of its size, was never to be lorded over by someone outside the body itself. Although the church corporately is best described as an institution, the church should not be viewed as one great invisible body. The only scriptural body in particular that exists, are the bodies of individual local churches under the headship of Christ. Although there was a common faith, that faith derived its authority from Scripture, not from the traditions of man, no matter how popular or reasonable they appear. As to the creation of a common form or practice of ritual, the New Testament says nothing, and in principle denounces such activity (see Colossians 2:8, 18, 20).

This shift in attitude as to the nature of church government eventually led to a hierarchical system that became the source of much evil during the Dark Ages. Early American church planter and Baptist historian J.A. Shackleford (1891) states that, "Some of the churches soon lost their independent character, and blending their organizations together, or perhaps striving to make one organization control a larger area of territory, they combined with the secular powers to stamp out such as would not submit to their will. We thus see the wisdom of God in establishing the independent form of church government. When a church became corrupt, it simply dropped out of line, or coalesced with some other corrupt body, and was no longer regarded as a true church, and other independent churches were not corrupted by its doctrine."[10]

The changes just described were likely prompted by three things. First, and perhaps the most important, was the fear of renewed state-sanctioned persecution. Some believed that if the church was organized as one great universal body, then she would become a

Chapter Ten—The Primitive Church: Early Christianity

force with which Rome would have to reckon. The government would then be less likely to initiate any future persecution.

Second, the more influential bishops feared that congregational liberty would jeopardize the unity sought by them and that an ecclesiastical government could maintain a control over such liberty (self determination).

Third, the fear of a rising number of so-called heretics threatened their control. These "heretics," as we will see later, were generally churches that had rejected such errors as infant baptism and baptismal regeneration. They were not heretics at all! Their doctrines were proven purer than those seeking ecclesiastical control, but that made them a threat to the effort to unite the whole.

Another factor that contributed to the rise of apostasy was a *gradual change in attitude toward the ordinances.* The early centuries were characterized by great ignorance and illiteracy. In an effort to mitigate such ignorance, the two ordinances of baptism and the Lord's Table in some churches were accompanied by ceremony and ritual. Ceremony and ritual served to create an atmosphere of great sacred importance. That is not to say that the ordinances are not important, for they are. But some church leaders in the early centuries saw themselves as competing with the form of pagan worship centers. The ceremony and ritual connected with the ordinances would serve to create an atmosphere with which the pagans would be familiar.

In addition, some of these rituals evolved into teaching tools to illustrate Christian truths. For example, it became popular to bless the waters of baptism before the candidate would enter. Thereby they would drive out any evil in the water that might somehow attach itself to the candidate. The candidate was required to recite certain forms of liturgy, and without those recitations, baptism was not considered complete. Salt would be placed upon his head after his immersion to illustrate that he was now the salt of the earth, and he would be given milk to drink to illustrate the importance of receiving the sincere milk of the Word. None of these rituals are commanded in Scripture of course, but still, such ceremony and ritual became prevalent in many churches in the early centuries. The adding of ritualistic traditions to God's simple commands resulted in making the worship services of these early churches mystical rather than substantive.

Eventually the ordinances were viewed as having sacramental (saving) value. Baptism would wash away sins, or at the very least cleanse the damning spot of original sin. The early church leader Justin Martyr (AD 100–165) is quoted as saying:

> The baptismal is called also illumination, because those who receive it are enlightened in the understanding.[11]

> The candidate for baptism is washed in the Name of the triune God, after having prayed for the forgiveness and the pardon of sins, it transplants into a new existence, and without it there is no salvation.[12]

And from the Shepherd of Hermas (AD 115–140) we have this statement:

> There is no other repentance than this, that we go down into the water and receive forgiveness of our past sins.[13]

It is really quite striking to see these kinds of statements being made by leaders as early as the second century. These kinds of sentiments in turn opened the door to the practice of infant baptism (paedobaptism). Error always leads to more error! By the early fifth century (AD 416) the Council of Mela, establishing by law the practice of infant baptism, decreed, "Also, it is the pleasure of the bishops to order that whoever denies that infants newly born of their mothers are not to be baptized, or says that baptism is administered for the remission of their own sins but not on account of original sin, delivered from Adam, and to be expiated by the laver of regeneration, be accursed."[14]

Chapter Ten—The Primitive Church: Early Christianity

If sins are washed clean by baptism, then what of the many young children who die without the administration of the ordinance? Without the cleansing of original sin are they not lost? The answer, of course, is an emphatic no! Although many children died in infancy or in young childhood, the biblical principle is that the soul of any child is not under any divine threat until they have reached the age of accountability (see 2 Samuel 12:18–23). It was, however, a case of the blind leading the blind. This mystical understanding of baptism caused many to wait to be baptized until just before their deaths, hoping to have all their sins washed clean. It showed a complete ignorance of justification by faith in Christ and Christ alone.

The Lord's Table was also given sacramental value. It came to be believed that the elements of communion could actually keep one saved—that the elements supernaturally became the actual body and blood of Christ (transubstantiation) via the liturgy associated with the communion. Indeed, the adherent would be "saved" afresh each time the elements were administered. This doctrine was eventually defined by Pope Innocent III in 1215, but was common practice for centuries.

The doctrine of purgatory was then imagined out of necessity. What of those who would not follow the "rules" but had been baptized as infants? Original sin had been dealt with, but what of those sins committed during adult life? The answer was purgatory! The Latins called it *Limbus Puerorum*, a *middle-place* whereby the sins of the dead could be atoned. First, by the dead themselves, by punishment or purging in purgatory by fire, and second, by the living through the giving of alms and other good works including saying the rosary on behalf of the departed dead.[15] Pure paganism! It had been first suggested by Clement of Alexandria in the third century and promoted by Augustine in the fourth. The doctrine became official church dogma in 1439, at the Council of Florence.

Thus, it was believed for centuries as a church tradition long before it was officially recognized.

For those who desired to hedge their bets, a doctrine creating the sale of indulgences was eventually introduced. The practice was introduced in 1517 by a man named Tetzel. Tetzel obtained permission from the pope to sell indulgences in Germany to help finance the building of cathedrals. Tetzel figured heavily in Luther's actions in 1519. By the sale of indulgences a man could purchase forgiveness of a sin even before he had committed it. If the sin had already been committed, then a system of confession to a priest was devised whereby forgiveness was given after a payment or penance of some sort. The state churches of the Middle Ages became rich through these false and pagan doctrines. These are just a few examples of deviation from Scriptures.

Then also, there was a *gradual change in attitude toward the Bible*. The desire to train men for the ministry produced centers for learning. These centers soon became the breeding ground for religious and cultural hybridization. As mysticism in worship services became prevalent, the Bible also took on a mystical connection for some. The Bible came to be seen as a book of allegory, the depths of which only the elite and the well trained could possibly understand. Some scholars advocated that the Bible should not be taken literally, believing that God did not say what He meant, nor necessarily mean what He said (allegory). It was up to an elite class of bishops to tell the church what the Bible really said. This resulted in a system of study called scholasticism that continues in many circles to this present day.

Although this system of study came of age in the thirteenth century, the seeds of its corruption were sown as far back as the fourth century. The key center for this mindset was the city of Alexandria, in northern Egypt. It was from here that disciples were trained and sent out to contaminate early Christianity.[16]

Chapter Ten—The Primitive Church: Early Christianity

The allegorical approach to the Scriptures was responsible for producing what scholars today refer to as the Alexandrian Text, a corrupt text transmitted to the present time via Eusebius. It has spawned the many diverse Bible translations in our own day. These modern translations are rooted in the mysticism of the first four centuries of Christianity and are nothing more than a reflection of the pagan traditions of the day. (For a more extensive study on this subject, the reader may want to consult the excellent book by R.B. Ouellette, *A More Sure Word*, from Striving Together Publications.)

Last, and perhaps the most serious factor in the rise of apostasy in the early church, was a *gradual change in attitude toward a church-state relation*. Jesus had said that there was to be a separation of church and state; a man was to render unto Caesar that which belonged to Caesar and unto God that which belonged to God (Matthew 22:21). Institutions established by God such as family, church, or government are not to infringe upon the boundaries of another. In the year AD 312, a general in the Roman army named Constantine became the emperor of the Roman empire. He had taken the throne by force and claimed that the God of the Christians had given him a great victory over his enemies in the face of seemingly insurmountable odds. Claiming to have seen a vision from God and marching to victory under the sign of the cross, Constantine proclaimed himself to be a Christian.

Upon cementing his hold on the empire at the battle of Chalcedon in AD 323, he declared Christianity to be the official state religion of the empire in AD 324. It would be the sanctioned religion of the empire. Many Christians at that time saw this as an answer to prayer. After 250 years of bloody persecution, they believed God had placed Constantine on the throne, and now Rome as well as the entire empire would become Christian. Persecution of Christians would cease, and the kingdom of God would be established upon the earth! So as Constantine lavished temporal benefits upon the

Christian church—including lands, buildings, tax support, and privilege—they were more than willing to support his ascendancy to power.

The question arises as to whether Constantine was genuinely a Christian at all. One must realize that Christianity had by this time become a fairly dominant influence in society, howbeit still unlawful. Constantine was the consummate politician. He could see the handwriting on the wall. It was a shrewd political move to profess to be a Christian. He no doubt believed he would gain the support of Christians throughout the empire. However, we seriously doubt his profession. First, one is not saved by seeing a vision or claiming a victory at the hand of God. Second, it is a known fact that Constantine waited until just days before his death to be baptized, believing that his sins would be washed clean and guarantee his redemption before God. Third, the previous point should not be taken lightly given the fact that he secured the throne by removing any threat from members of his own family by murdering them and their children.

Constantine had good reason to hope his bloody hands could be cleansed of their wicked deeds. No, it does not seem to me that Constantine was a child of God. Rather, as Jesus said of the Pharisees, I think his spiritual father was a murderer from the beginning. Still, many Christians were willing to join the parade despite what should have been understood as an obvious political charade.

Baptist historian Thomas Armitage states in his book *A History of the Baptists*, "The condition of things at that moment is well set forth by Niebuhr in the following words: 'The religion which he (Constantine) had in his head must have been a strange compound indeed. The man who had on his coins the inscription, "Sol, invictus," who worshipped pagan deities, consulted the auspices (diviners), and indulged in a number of pagan superstitions, and interfered in the Council of Nice, must have been a repulsive phenomenon, and was certainly not a Christian. He was a superstitious man, and mixed

Chapter Ten—The Primitive Church: Early Christianity

up his Christian religion with all kinds of absurd superstitions and opinions; when, therefore, certain Oriental writers call him equal to an apostle, they know not what they are saying; and to speak of him as a saint is a profanation of the word.'"[17]

Understanding how the citizens of Rome had come to view their emperors provides us with some interesting and important context for changes that evolved in the polity of many Christian churches. The citizens of Rome came to revere their emperors, believing that they held the position of vicar on earth on behalf of the gods. They believed that the emperor was placed on the throne by the gods and was to direct the affairs of the empire according to their (gods') whims. Over time, the Caesars of Rome came to be viewed as divine themselves, and the emperors relished this view and no doubt even fostered its belief.

As vicar of the gods, the emperor was duty-bound to be the head and protector of the state religion that had been, up until Constantine, polytheistic. Although Constantine rejected the polytheism of the past and elevated Christianity, he continued the tradition of viewing himself as the head and protector of the state religion. What many churches failed to realize in their exuberance to crown the new "Christian" emperor was that as Caesar he would be the head and protector now of the Christian faith. This effectively supplanted Christ as the head of any church that aligned itself with the throne. The church at Rome was at the forefront of this compromise. In turn, she was rewarded and exalted to a place of superiority above her peers.

These churches that had formed a superficial alliance with the rise of Constantine now formed a genuine alliance, and a new state church was formed. Up to this point (AD 323), although there were real matters of concern both in doctrine and practice, generally the churches throughout the empire could still be considered New Testament churches. At least we are willing to give them the benefit of any doubt. But upon the recognition of Constantine as their head and protector, any doubt is removed. Any church that joined this unholy alliance with the state could no longer be considered a New Testament church. We thus see the creation of a new "church" society that we will simply refer to as the "state affiliated churches," but they will eventually evolve into what we know today as the Roman Catholic Church.

At this point, the decay was rapid! Armitage observes that, "it seems scarcely necessary here to state how soon every sort of superstition and heathen ceremony was mixed with this state's Christianity. So far from attempting to disguise these things by pious lying, it is their delight to make them known. Take, for example, Cardinal Baronius, who says with delicious openness: 'It is allowable for the church to transfer to pious uses those ceremonies which the pagans employed impiously to superstitious worship, after they have been purified by consecration; for the devil is the more mortified to see those things turned to the service of Jesus Christ, which were instituted for his own.'"[18] Polidore Virgil says, "The church has borrowed several customs from the religion of the Romans and other heathens, but that they have improved them and put them to a better use."[19]

Guillaume du Choul sums up the whole case in these words: "If we examine narrowly we shall discover that several institutions of our religion have been transferred from the Egyptian and other Gentile ceremonies. Such as the tunics and surplices, the crowns or tonsures, of our priests, bowing around the altar; the sacrificial pomp, church music, adorations, prayers, supplications, processions, litanies and several other things which our priests use in their mysteries; offering up to our only God, Jesus Christ, what the ignorance of the Gentiles, with their false religion and foolish presumption, offered to their false deities and to mortal men of their own deifying."[20] Eusebius, the contemporary of Constantine states, "This Emperor, to make the Christian religion more plausible

Chapter Ten—The Primitive Church: Early Christianity

to the Gentiles, adopted into it the exterior ornaments which they used in their religion."[21]

Let me be very clear at this point. This church was not merely a division of the original but a new denomination springing forth from the old. Rather, it was a brand new society with a man as its head rather than Christ. It is Christian in name only, and we are commanded in such situations to come out and have no fellowship with such as deny the faith. Over the next 550 years, various church councils were held to determine the official doctrinal position of "the church" (state church). The official dates of celebration for the birth and resurrection of Christ were set, heretics would be condemned, orders were dictated, and much more. All of these councils were called and overseen by the Emperor himself until the fall of Rome in AD 476. After the fall of Rome, the "vicar" of Christ, the pope, was considered the head and protector of the church in the West. Jesus is declared in the Scriptures to be the "head" of the body, that is, of each New Testament body, each local church. If Jesus is removed as the head, you no longer have the same body. Yes, Christ had been supplanted, and He would never again shepherd this crowd.

The changes described previously were not as subtle as one might think. Relatively little time was necessary for both church and government to codify these changes. Emperor Theodosius, for example, in the year AD 380, just a few years after the death of Constantine, declared the following:

> It is our will that all the peoples we rule shall practice that religion which the divine Peter the apostle transmitted to the Romans....We shall command that those persons who follow this rule shall embrace the name Catholic Christians. The rest, however, whom we adjudge demented and insane, shall sustain the infamy of heretical dogmas; their meeting places shall not receive the name churches, and they shall be smitten first by divine vengeance and secondly by the retribution of

our own initiative, which we shall assume in accordance with divine judgment.[22]

This declaration by the Emperor set the stage for a tremendous wave of persecution that lasted beyond the Middle Ages. The churches that aligned themselves with the state were all too eager to participate in this effort in order to more fully secure their position and thereby remove any threat to their new-found power and influence!

It may be difficult to understand how Christians could so compromise the clear teaching of the Scripture in such matters. How could God's people be so easily duped by what seems so obvious an error? One might ask the same question today. How are so many Christians so easily duped to accept doctrines and worldly practices in the worship centers across our land? Who would ever have believed that certain worldly music forms would become the vehicle of "Christian worship" as they have today? It is not right—it is pagan! Indeed, many have lost the ability to discern the holy from the unholy; that which is fleshly is now seen as holy, and that which has been holy for centuries is now seen as irrelevant because it's not "cool" enough. May God forgive us!

To summarize briefly why so many Christians of that generation were so easily duped: first, there had been over 250 years of persecution, and these events would mean their deliverance. It was easy to suggest that God had brought about these events as an answer to their prayers. Second, the claim of the Emperor that he became "one of them" was no doubt met with great relief and even excitement. Third, certain doctrinal errors had already crept into the Christian church, causing a failure of discernment in spiritual matters for some. Finally, there was the exaltation and empowerment of those bishops who would cooperate.

The declaration that Christianity was to be the state religion of the empire infuriated many in the Roman senate, and in part prompted Constantine to leave the western capital, Rome, and

Chapter Ten—The Primitive Church: Early Christianity

seek a location more centrally located in the empire. Having spent much time directing military campaigns in western Europe, Constantine knew that it was simply a matter of time before the roving hoards of Goths and Vandals to the north of Rome would strike at Rome itself.

As we have mentioned, the armies of Rome were becoming less and less willing to protect the empire. So, Constantine sought out a city that could be easily protected from attack and found such a city in Byzantium, modern day Istanbul. He renamed the city Constantinople and set up shop. We now had a capital in the West and one in the East, and this created a bitter rivalry between the church at Rome and the church in Byzantium that has continued to this day.

Not all New Testament churches aligned themselves with the state, nor followed in lockstep with their peers. How substantial this treachery was cannot be ascertained. However, it was a large enough shift to bring about a condemnation and persecution of fellow believers who did not participate in the compromise. Many bishops and their churches saw the flagrant violations of Scriptures being advocated by the "liberals" of their day, and refused to participate, regardless of the consequences. These faithful followers of Christ disassociated themselves from the state affiliated churches and refused to receive the baptism of those societies. Throughout the early centuries there had been groups of believers that challenged the subtle changes taking place in the Christian community. So it should not surprise us that in this dark day, the light of truth still burned in certain quarters.

Early Dissidents

As the direction of some churches in the early centuries moved ever closer to a state far different from that described in the New Testament, there were groups or societies that saw these trends for what they were and refused to participate. Certainly, there were heretical groups in these early centuries, but it is a mistake to assume that every society referred to as *dissident* in Christian or secular histories should be taken to be a reference to a renegade or heretical movement. The majority of these societies are identified as dissenters simply because they stood in opposition to what eventually became the majority movement (Roman Catholic). That made them the enemies of those who would write their histories.

Indeed, often the only information we have about these groups comes from statements by their enemies. We would not necessarily agree with every position they may have held, but they did stand for the truth as they best understood it in a time when the Bible was not readily accessible. This is not to imply that they were corrupt doctrinally, but simply to acknowledge that we are forced to consider the accusations of their enemies concerning their specific beliefs. Often their own writings were destroyed as they were persecuted, leaving us with some question as to what these societies actually believed. However, these dissident groups are the historical link to the apostolic or primitive church of the first century. They demonstrate that there were societies from the earliest centuries that opposed the license that some of their peers had taken in relation to New Testament principles.

There were three notable societies that challenged the liberalism of their day and each of them was composed of many local churches of like faith and practice. The first of these groups is first seen in the region of eastern Asia Minor. They are called the **Montanists,** named for the leader of this group of dissidents. They are dated from AD 170. By AD 177, they are found throughout southern Europe as well as northern Egypt. It was in Alexandria, Egypt, that their impact was most realized. The Montanist movement was a reaction to the increasing ceremony and ritualistic nature of worship in many churches of their day.[23*] As you may recall, it was in Alexandria that questions arose concerning the appropriate

Chapter Ten—The Primitive Church: Early Christianity

way to approach the study of Scripture. The Montanists were fully committed to a literal interpretation of the Bible and rejected the notion that only the ecclesiastical elite should be given the right to interpret the Bible. They challenged the elitist class of scholars and called upon all churches to return to their simple apostolic roots. They rejected the idea that the clergy had a monopoly on the Gospel, and placed great significance on the work of the Holy Spirit in the lives of individual believers. They insisted that those who had "lapsed" from the true faith should be re-baptized, because they had denied Christ and ought to be baptized anew. On this account they were termed "Anabaptists," and some of their principles reappeared in Anabaptism.[24]

The most well known of their converts was a man named Tertullian (AD 160–230) who was from Carthage, in northern Africa. Born of pagan parents, Tertullian was well educated in the law. His learning exceeded most of that day, and his writing gained him the respect of all. He is known as the first of the Latin Fathers. According to Orchard, Tertullian "withdrew from one society on account of its corruptions, and united with another on the grounds of purity of communion."[25] For the remainder of his life, he ably advocated the views of the Montanists and no doubt planted the spiritual seed that later produced the Donatist movement in North Africa. The Montanists were deeply rooted in the faith, and their opponents admitted that they received the entire Scriptures of the Old and the New Testaments, and they were sound in their views of the Father, and of the Son, and of the Holy Spirit.[26]

---

[23]"The Montanists maintained that theirs was not a new form of Christianity but a recovery of the old, the primitive church set over against the obvious corruptions of the current Christianity. The old church had demanded purity; the new church had struck a bargain with the world, and had arranged itself comfortably with it, and they (the Montanists) would therefore, break with it. (Moeller, Montanism. Schaff-Herzog Encyclopedia, Vol. 3. 1562).

In the year AD 252 another group arose on the scene in Rome itself. They are called the **Novatianists**, once again after the name of their dissident leader. This was during the time of Roman persecution by Emperor Decius (AD 249–251). During that particular persecution, a certain bishop named Cornelius recanted his faith in order to save his life. After that round of persecution ended, Cornelius was placed in candidacy for the position of bishop of the church of Rome. Apparently, a man named Novatian was also under consideration but was unsuccessful, given the popularity of Cornelius. Supported by both Cyprian the Bishop of Carthage, and by Dionysius the bishop of Alexandria, Cornelius was placed into the position of bishop or pastor of the church of Rome. Novatian was outraged that someone who had denied the Christian faith would serve in such an influential position and in such an influential church. Novatian became the leader of the stricter party and was selected as their Bishop.[27] Cornelius was certainly not the only Christian to compromise. Many other bishops had also recanted their faith or surrendered copies of the Bible to be burned. It was not long before Novatian's actions were taken up by others whose pastors or church members had compromised the faith but without repercussions. The division extended throughout the empire, and along with individuals, entire congregations joined the movement.

The purity and integrity of the local church was the issue in the minds of the Novatianists. If thousands of Christians had sacrificed their lives for the cause of Christ, how could they expect any less from all believers? The unwillingness to die for the faith as well as the unwillingness to administer church discipline to those who had recanted their faith was seen as an indicator of the spiritual decay of the early church. Because they practiced re-baptism of all who came to their societies from the Catholics, they were accused of Anabaptism:

> The Novatians were the earliest Anabaptists; refusing to recognize as valid the ministry and sacraments of

Chapter Ten—The Primitive Church: Early Christianity

their opponents and claiming to be the true church they were logically compelled to rebaptize who came to them from the Catholic church. The party gained great strength in Asia Minor where many Montanists joined it, and, in spite of the persecution, the Novatians survived to the 6th or 7th century.[28]

Given the early date of these events (AD 252), the churches that aligned themselves with the *stricter* or *purer* party saw themselves as the orthodox and historic link to the New Testament church. Their churches had not originated with the movement itself nor did they come from the church in Rome, for the church of Rome as we know it today did not exist at that time. Instead, their churches had existed previous to the issues that had brought about their separation. Thus they saw themselves as the true New Testament church. They were condemned with the imposition of the death penalty by the fourth Lateran Council.

Dr. Robinson, author of *Ecclesiastical Researches*, traces a continuation of that movement up to the Reformation and the rise of the Anabaptist movement. "Great numbers followed his, i.e., Novatian's example, and all over the empire Puritan churches were constituted and flourished through two hundred succeeding years. Afterwards, when penal laws obliged them to lurk in corners and worship God in private, they were distinguished by a variety of names and a succession of them continued until the Reformation."[29] Although they were identified as Novatians by their enemies, churches aligned with the movement preferred the term the *Cathari* or pure ones. They eventually became identified with the people known as the Waldenses.

Then there were the **Donatists** (AD 311) of North Africa. According to Thomas Armitage, the Catholic societies by this time had developed the notion that unity was of more consequence than purity. The Donatists had concluded that a spiritual regeneration was the prime qualification for membership in the churches of

133

Christ. The Catholic societies did not agree but believed that the tares should exist with wheat in the kingdom (they believed the church was the kingdom, see Matthew 13). Thus the Donatists had come to charge the Catholic with being a fallen church because it had become lax in its morals, tolerating open and notorious sin, and regarding visible unity as a higher attribute of church-life than personal purity.[30]

During the last of the Roman persecutions (Diocletian AD 303–310), and perhaps one of the most severe, a situation arose similar to the one described above in Carthage of North Africa. In AD 311, Caecilianus was elected as the Bishop of Carthage in a somewhat irregular manner. Caecilianus had been hastily ordained by certain bishops, and among them was a bishop named Felix, Bishop of Aptunga. Felix had been charged with surrendering a copy of the Holy Bible to be burned by the authorities during the persecutions of Diocletian. There is some indication that the surrendered text at issue was one of the last remaining copies of the Bible in North Africa. Because of his connection with Felix, the election of Caecilianus displeased many in Carthage. A bishop named Donatist was among those who believed that the whole affair was improper and led a group of like-minded churches to break fellowship with the dominant party. This movement grew very quickly as others joined their ranks, and many churches of that type were founded throughout the empire.

As the movement continued to grow, churches that were busy aligning themselves with Constantine brought political pressure to bear upon Donatist as the leader of this "rebellion." The Donatists then made a crucial error. In an effort to avoid a conflict with their peers, they appealed to the Emperor to redress their grievances. The end result is that the Donatists were condemned in church councils instigated by Constantine in AD 313 and in AD 314. As enemies of the state, Constantine deprived the Donatists of their churches, confiscated their properties and banished their bishops which numbered near four hundred.[31] Donatist was eventually summoned by the Emperor himself to come and give an account as to why he would not submit to the headship of the Emperor. The response of Donatist is very telling. It shows that Donatist had adjusted his understanding of the true headship of Christ's church. He refused to go to Rome and give answer to the Emperor but did send this response: "What has the church to do with the emperor and what has the emperor to do with the church of God?" The response of Constantine was to send an armed troop to destroy them.

Thus the Donatists came to understand that the union of church and state was an evil with far-reaching consequences for all believers. The Donatists survived the attempts by their enemies to eradicate them and were given their liberty in AD 367. The Donatists continued as a Gospel light in North Africa for at least two hundred years, and their numbers equaled those of the Catholics. Societies continued to be identified as Donatists by their enemies into the eighth century in various parts of Europe. The Donatists, like the Novatianists, were accused by their enemies of practicing *Anabaptism.*

This brief description of certain dissident groups in very ancient times serves as a window into the Christian past. Through these groups one can see an evolution of change not prompted by God or His Word, but by men and circumstance. Very early, when apostolic simplicity was threatened by ritual and ceremony, some were bold enough to stand their ground. When the purity and integrity of the local church body was in jeopardy, others were willing to dissolve ancient alliances and form new ones while maintaining their own individual autonomy. When some would unite the church with the secular state under the guise of the greater good, there were Christians who properly understood the significance of the autonomy of the local church. They revered and sustained the headship of Christ alone!

These groups saw themselves as true New Testament churches. Their origins did not coincide with their dissent, for they had existed as New Testament churches long before the issues arose that prompted their actions. Others had lowered the banner of truth. The stricter societies thus rejected those who had compromised. They saw them as illegitimate and refused fellowship with them. In addition, they refused to receive their baptisms, re-baptizing all those who came over to their societies from those churches they deemed tainted with compromise (Anabaptism).

The Fall of Rome

The fall of Rome took place in AD 476. The roving hoards of the Huns and Vandals in the no man's land of Europe had finally seized upon their opportunity to attack Rome. By this time, the Emperor in the East had little interest or concern for the citizens of the city of Rome. Emperor Romulus Augustulus in the West, was politically anemic. The garrisons of Rome were weak in men and will. Few were willing to give their lives for the glory of the empire.

The character of Rome in the West at this time was indeed far different than that found in the days of their former glory. In fact in AD 452, it had been Pope Leo I, not the emperor, who faced Attila the Hun and persuaded him to withdraw his army as the Huns invaded northern Italy. Again in AD 455, the city of Rome would have been decimated if it had not been for the efforts of Pope Leo I. He confronted Gaiseric the Vandal outside the walls of Rome. By his intervention, the total destruction and looting of the city by the invaders was thwarted. The pope was seen as a savior. In the absence of any real secular order, the church at Rome was able to fill the vacuum. Although the city finally fell in AD 476, the church of Rome had in large part secured herself as heir to Roman imperialistic authority and prestige.

Rome politically was now gone, but the church of Rome (the Roman Catholic Church) had clearly positioned herself as the supreme ruler of Christianity. The bishop of Rome was now seen as the pope, the vicar of Christ on the earth. The church now began to be legislative rather than executive in her assumed authority over others. Blatant errors began to be sanctioned under the authority of tradition as opposed to the authority of a literal interpretation of the Bible.

It was during the fifth century that baptismal regeneration and infant baptism was officially sanctioned by this church. Infant baptism had been introduced in AD 250 in North Africa during a great famine. By AD 416, it was sanctioned regionally in southern Europe and still later became a common practice throughout Europe. In AD 300, prayers for the dead and making the sign of the cross were instituted. The use of images as well as the veneration of angels and saints was sanctioned in AD 375. Mariolatry was sanctioned in AD 431 and the doctrines of **Extreme Unction** (AD 526) and Purgatory (AD 593) were officially sanctioned.

The list continues down through the centuries (see appendix). Any churches that did not accept these beliefs and practices were considered enemies of both the church and the state. Conclusions reached by church councils were deemed supreme and became the law of the land. Those who were condemned by them were severely persecuted. Church worship in the state churches became more

DEFINING THE TERMS

Extreme Unction: The Catholic doctrine of Extreme Unction refers to the spiritual aid and comfort given to Catholics by a priest when they are seriously ill or their lives are in jeopardy. The Catholic Church claims that the practice provides for perfect spiritual health, including if need be, the remission of sins, as well as the restoration of bodily health.

and more elaborate, and the new birth ceased to be a requirement for entrance into that church.

With the fall of Rome the world was ushered into the Dark Ages, a period of little advancement by almost any measure. Superstition and poverty were common. In this environment the church at Rome continued to consolidate its power and influence over the masses. The rivalry between the church of Rome and churches remaining faithful to New Testament principles also continued. Rising to prominence were such societies as the Paulicians, the Albigenses and the Waldenses, each claiming apostolic origins for their churches and each becoming the objects of hatred and scorn by the dominant party. Eventually Anabaptism emerged as more than just a practice by various dissident groups but as a movement itself.

CHAPTER ELEVEN

The Medieval Church: Anabaptism

It should be clear from the foregoing examination of the lives and ministries of the apostles that the Gospel spread very quickly around the known world. These men truly became the fishers of men Jesus intended them to be. Without at least a brief accounting of their ministries, one may be left with the opinion that outside the Apostle Paul, the twelve did very little to spread the Gospel. This is just not true.

In addition, it is important to note that beyond their life spans, the Gospel continued to spread into ever increasing segments of the ancient world. Obviously, not only were the apostles fishers of men, but they were also effective in discipling others to carry on the work after their passing. These in turn discipled others, and all of this was accomplished through the ministry of local New Testament churches. Polycarp was the pastor of the church at Smyrna in AD 81 just fourteen years before the Apostle John was banished to the isle of Patmos in AD 95. Polycarp had been the disciple of the Apostle John and was trained and instructed by him. Polycarp gives us a direct connection to the teachings of Christ via a second generation of disciples. He continued in the pastorate at Smyrna for eighty-five years until his death by burning in the year AD 166. Nothing more is known of this church except that in AD 180 there was a bishop named Irenaeus, a Greek, pastoring in the church at Lyons, France (ancient Gaul) who has a connection.

Irenaeus, before serving in this church, had been a member of the church at Smyrna where Polycarp was pastor. Irenaeus apparently received his instruction and training under the spiritual tutelage of Polycarp. He continued as the pastor of the church at Lyons until AD 200, when he was martyred. This church at Lyons was one of the earliest churches to resist the claims of supremacy by the bishop of Rome. In the same year that Irenaeus suffered martyrdom, Justin Martyr and others were beheaded under the reign of Marcus Aurelius.

Along with Polycarp, other men were discipled by the Apostle John. These disciples became men of important influence in the early church. For example, Ignatius (AD 37–117) was the pastor of the church at Antioch; Papias (AD 120) was the bishop or pastor of the church of Hierapolis; and Hermas (AD 140) pastored in the church of Rome.

J.A. Shackelford records, "About AD 215 at the latest, we find a church in existence at Carthage, Africa, which continued to exist as a single church for a period of two hundred years, or until AD 400."[1] It was here at Carthage that the principles of the dissident group, the *Montanists,* took deep root. Indeed, the church at Carthage seems to have been established by those of the Montanist persuasion. Agrippinus was the first pastor of this church, and he was later assisted in his labor by the famed Tertullian, who became an able defender of their principles after disassociating himself from the dominant party of Carthage that later became the Catholic Church. His separation from that church was over the matter of baptism and to whom it should be administered. Tertullian along

Chapter Eleven—The Medieval Church: Anabaptism

with the Montanists believed that many churches had "too hastily administered" the ordinance in order to gain numbers for their churches. The Montanists maintained that there should be a proper examination of a candidate's profession of faith before receiving him or her into a church body. Furthermore, they held that no child should be admitted to baptism that was unable to understand its significance.

It was here at Carthage that the Donatists arose in the early fourth century. No doubt the seed sown by the Montanists of North Africa in the third century produced the Donatists of the fourth century. The Donatists continued as a viable society well into the eighth century.

As much of Christianity in the early fourth century began to apostatize, movements among Christians in a variety of areas began to evolve. These movements were generally provoked by the compromise of church leaders who saw expediency as a virtue rather than a vice. They had become loyal to position and prestige, and thereby compromised their loyalty to the Saviour. Indeed, they saw themselves as the saviors of the faith to the exclusion of Christ as the head! The movements that arose in opposition to such compromise were deemed divisive by their antagonists, who were the dominant party by this time. These movements became very large and threatening to the state-aligned churches, which did everything within their power to bring about their extermination. Three such groups were perhaps the most successful at perpetuating the New Testament faith in the face of horrendous persecution by their enemies.

The Paulicians

The Paulicians were a society of churches that claimed apostolic origin; that is, they claimed that someone in the first century brought the Gospel to their people. They inhabited the ancient land of Armenia. This area today is composed of three countries: Georgia,

Chapter Eleven—The Medieval Church: Anabaptism

Armenia, and Azerbaijan, and is located just south of the Caucasus mountains that separate Central Asia from ancient Russia.

Remember, Jude as well as other apostles invested all or a part of their ministries in Armenia. Tradition says the Apostle Thomas initiated this contact and introduced the Gospel here before moving on to the East (India). The result of such apostolic evangelism was that Armenia became the first Christianized country on earth.

In the early centuries, as various dissident groups such as the Montanists, Novatianists, and Donatists were persecuted, they spread throughout the empire. Some of them may have found fertile ground in Armenia to continue the spread of the Gospel. These groups often lost their individual identities as they were assimilated into Christian bodies in regions where they migrated, including in ancient Armenia.

This ancient Christian society became especially loyal to the writings of the Apostle Paul and thus their name, the Paulicians. Baptist historian John T. Christian, identifying their ancient roots, quotes from *The Greek and Eastern Churches* by Adney: "Therefore, it is quite arguable that they should be regarded as representing the survival of a most primitive type of Christianity."[2]

In addition, Dr. Newman in his book *A Manual of Church History* quotes Conybeare, author of *Key of Truth*, saying:

> The Paulicians Church was not the national church of a particular race, but an old form of the apostolic church, and that it included within itself Syrians, Greeks, Armenians, Africans, Latins, and various other races. Finding refuge in southeastern Armenia, when it was nearly extirpated in the Roman empire, it there nursed its forces in comparative security under the protection of the Persians and Arabs, and prepared itself for a magnificent career of missionary enterprise in the Greek world, which the sources relate with so much bitterness.[3]

Because of their opposition to the state church, they eventually became an outlaw society. Although apostolic in their origin, an antagonistic relationship arose between the Paulicians, under the leadership of a man named Constantine (also called Silvanus, AD 630–687), and the Roman authorities (Constantinople) in the seventh century.

After receiving a copy of the four Gospels from a friend, Constantine was saved and joined himself with other believers in his area. Previous to this, Constantine was associated with **Manichaeism**, and Paulicians are sometimes incorrectly called Manichaeists by their enemies because of Constantine's former association.

An ancient Paulician document discovered in 1891 in Armenia called "The Key of Truth" is evidence of their New Testament purity.[4] Many were saved because of the preaching ministry of Constantine and his associates, whose influence lasted nearly thirty years. Under order of Emperor Pogonatus in AD 684, Constantine was betrayed and murdered by his adopted son, Justus. The antagonistic relationship between the Paulicians and the authorities, including the Catholic Church, lasted for years, and the bloodletting was horrific.

As we have mentioned above, because of their biblical purity, the Paulicians suffered the threats and condemnation of both the state church and the state itself. They were driven underground

DEFINING THE TERMS

Manichaeism: *Manichaeism was one of the major Gnostic religions of the early centuries. Its founder, Mani (AD 210–276), was born in Babylon. Manichaeism thrived between the third and seventh centuries and became a significant religious force. Its theology was dualistic—it believed in two equal and opposite powers, one good and one bad. Augustine (AD 354–430) was converted from Manichaeism and became one of its most severe critics.*

Chapter Eleven—The Medieval Church: Anabaptism

more than once by persecution, but as water bubbles up through rock by the pressure beneath, the Paulicians always returned, more zealous than ever.

In AD 845, the armies of the Empress Theodora attempted to extirpate them from the land. The effort continued for almost twenty-five years under the Empress and her son, Michael III. G.H. Orchard writes, "After confiscating the goods and property of a hundred thousand of these people, the owners to that number were put to death in the most barbarous manner, and made to expire slowly under a variety of the most exquisite tortures."[5] But the Paulicians organized their own army and eventually drove their enemies back in retreat. After losing over one hundred thousand of their own in their struggle for freedom, the people of Armenia then established the first free state—a place where any man could worship God according to his own conscience without fear of reprisal by the state.[6] This freedom allowed for the migration of others into Armenia whose doctrines were not as pure as the Paulicians.

The Paulicians are sometimes accused of believing things that were not characteristic of them as a whole. The freedom of worship and religion became a hallmark of "Anabaptism," and is still held precious by their spiritual descendants (Baptists) to this very day.

The Paulicians were obviously diverse and numerous, but their churches all had two things in common. First, the Paulicians were known for their evangelism. They are given credit for spreading the Gospel among the "Synthians," the ancient inhabitants of the land of Russia, as well as into Poland, Moesia, and some believe as far away as ancient Gaul (southern France).

Second, they all practiced "Anabaptism," so-called because of the practice of re-baptizing any who came over to their societies from churches they believed to be in violation of New Testament principles. That is not to say that the recipient of such baptism was required of this society to be baptized twice, for they believed that the administration of the first was unlawful and they were simply administering a scriptural and therefore legitimate baptism. Scriptural baptism was required for membership into their churches and was seen as the means to maintain the purity of the body.

The Albigenses

The Albigenses were a people located in southern France. They were probably named for an ancient city in southern France called "Albi." This society of New Testament churches also claimed to be apostolic in their origin.[7]

Some tradition suggests that Philip was sent by churches in Galatia to ancient Gaul to introduce the Gospel there,[8*] and there is also some dubious tradition that Joseph of Arimathea, along with his friends Lazarus, Mary, and Martha, came here after the fall of Jerusalem in AD 70. The Paulicians are also credited by some historians as the planters of the Gospel in this ancient land. The Albigenses were primarily located in the region known as Lanquedoc where the city of Albi was located. They were severely hounded by the Catholic Church for their unwillingness to submit to her authority. This persecution continued down through the period known as the Dark Ages.

In 1119, the Albigenses were condemned at Toulouse for their rejection of infant baptism. Again in 1165, they were condemned at Albi for the same position. In both 1139 and 1163, two different Catholic Church councils, the Lateran Council and the Council at Tours condemned the Albigenses as heretics.

In 1209, a forty-day crusade was initiated by Pope Innocent III in order to destroy them.[9*] It was a brutal period. It ultimately lasted some sixty years and effectively eradicated them from southern France. According to Jones, historian and author of *The History of the Christian Church*, "the armies employed by Pope Innocent III destroyed about two hundred thousand of them in the short space of a few months."[10] "In order to better seduce the superstitious

Chapter Eleven—The Medieval Church: Anabaptism

Catholics into their army, the Pope granted plenary indulgence to sin, with the promise of the joys of heaven, as a reward for murdering the saints of God. So great was their enthusiasm against the Albigenses that 'the legate Milo's army, was found to consist of about three hundred thousand fighting men.'"[11] The prisons of Europe were virtually emptied as men volunteered for the devilish effort. From the initial slaughter, the conflict continued for several years, howbeit with a smaller army.

Again, according to Jones, "…in which time it has been computed that a million persons bearing that name [Albigenses] were put to death, had occasioned many of them to cross the Pyrenees, and seek shelter from the storm in the Spanish provinces of Arragon and Catalonia."[12] It became the common practice during this extended persecution to strike terror into any would-be converts by cutting off the index fingers, thumbs, big toes, ears, the upper lip, and noses of any villagers who were deemed in sympathy with their beliefs. Eyes were gouged out and holes were burned into their cheeks in order to identify them as heretics. Entire villages were razed and thousands died, all at the order of the pope.

A description of their sufferings has been handed down to us from one, Everwin of Steinfeld. He says, "We live a hard and

---

[8*]Mr. McBirnie (*The Search*, pp. 126–7) briefly outlines the evidence for this statement citing the writing of Isidore, the Archbishop of Seville (AD 600–636) in which he states that "Philip preached Christ to the Gauls (ancient France), and brought barbarous and neighboring nations seated in darkness…to the light of knowledge and port of faith." (Isidore, *De ortu et obitu Patrum, Cap LXXIII 131*). Bede, born in AD 673, according to Usher (*Antiquities, Cap 2*) assigns Gaul to Phillip in his work *Collections and Flowers*.

[9*]A full and detailed account of these events is given by many authors but perhaps the most detailed comes from Peter Allix, *The Ecclesiastical History of the Ancient Churches of the Piedmont and of the Albigenses*, Chap. XXI. 1692.

wandering life. We flee from city to city like sheep in the midst of wolves. We suffer persecution like the apostles and martyrs because our life is holy and austere. It is passed away amidst prayer, abstinences, and labors, but everything is made easy for us because we are not of this world."[13]

Eventually, the effort to exterminate the Albigenses was delivered into the hands of the Dominicans and the Inquisition. However, the persecution designed to destroy them actually brought about the spread of their beliefs. Those who survived the wrath of Rome were forced to leave their ancient homeland and migrate north. They were responsible for the spread of the Gospel into northern France, Germany, and even Poland during the Dark Ages; and as they were faithful to spread the Gospel in other lands, they eventually lost their own unique identity, being absorbed by other Anabaptist societies in the lands to which they migrated.

The Albigenses eventually became so numerous and varied in Europe that they became known as the *Cathari,* meaning, the "pure ones."[14] The Albigenses or the Cathari were accused of being Anabaptist by their enemies throughout the Dark Ages.

The Waldenses

Perhaps the most aggressive and well-documented society of Anabaptists during the Middle Ages was a people known as the Waldenses. Some historians believe them to be the same people known as the Albigenses, but found in northern Italy rather than in the southern provinces of France. If they were not the same people, they at the very least knew of one another and even migrated across the mountain range separating their two locations, seeking relief during times of persecution.

The Waldenses dwelt in the Alpine valleys of the Piedmont region of southeastern France and northeastern Italy in an area known as the *Vaudois* (valleys). Their name is derived from the

Latin word *Vallis* and thus *Valdenses*. Some have tried to date their existence from the time of Peter Waldus (1170), an able defender of their beliefs and practices.[15*] But the evidence contradicts this assumption, and the claim of the Waldenses that they were apostolic in origin is more likely.

The Novatians, mentioned previously, arose in the mid-third century and were severely persecuted by Constantine during the fourth century after the union of state and church. Numbers of these persecuted Novatians left Italy proper for the valleys of the Piedmont at different times from about the year 325 to 425, and these wandering Novatians were in later times called Waldenses.[16]

Respected Church of England historian, Dr. Peter Allix, in his *History of the Churches of the Piedmont* (1690), gives the following account, "That, for three hundred years or more, the Bishop of Rome attempted to subjugate the Church of Milan under his jurisdiction; and at the last the interest of Rome grew too potent for the Church of Milan, planted by one of the disciples; insomuch that the bishop and the people, rather than own their jurisdiction, retired to the valleys of Lucerne and Angrona, and thence were called Vallences, Waldenses or people of the valley."[17] Thus, instead of being reformed by the popery, the ancient Waldenses claimed to be the bride of Christ that fled into the wilderness from the face of the dragon (Revelation 12:13–17).

[15*]From Jones' History we are told that Reinerius Saccho, an inquisitor who lived only eighty years after the time of Waldo, admits that the Waldenses flourished five hundred years before that preacher (Jones' History, p. 232). Allix continues to quote Saccho, "among all the sects that either are, or have been, there is none more dangerous to the Church than that of the Leonists (Waldenses), and that for three reasons: The first is, because it is the sect that is the longest standing of any; for some say it hath been continued down ever since the time of Pope Sylvester (AD 325), and others since that of the apostles. The second is, because it is the most general of all sects; for scarcely is there any country to be found where this sect hath not spread itself." (Allix, *Ecclesiastical History*, p. 192).

Furthermore, the original name of the old Latin text of Scripture (second century) is derived from this northeastern district of Italy (the *Italic* district) referred to above and reveals that these people were responsible for preserving in their native tongue the Holy Scriptures (using the **Byzantine Text**), long before the twelfth century. By their own testimony recounted to us in the preface of the French Bible, we are told that "they have always had the full enjoyment of that heavenly truth contained in the Scriptures, ever since they were enriched with the same by the apostles themselves, having in fair manuscripts, preserved the entire Bible in their native tongue, from generation to generation."[18] Other documents such as the *Noble Lesson* that rehearsed the history of the Waldenses written about 1120, would further support this position.

From a petition submitted by their leaders to the Duke of Savoy (Italy) requesting their liberty to worship God according to their conscience without molestation, Jones states in *The History of the Christian Church*: "They implored his highness to consider that their religious profession was not a thing of yesterday, as their adversaries falsely reported; but had been the profession of their fathers, grandfathers, and great grandfathers; yea, of their predecessors of still more ancient times, even of the martyrs, confessors, apostles, and prophets; and they called upon their adversaries to prove the contrary, if they were able."[19]

DEFINING THE TERMS

Byzantine Text: Byzantine Text is a reference to those Greek manuscripts deposited at the city of Constantinople, formerly known as Byzantium, during the early period of the Dark Ages. It was here that many manuscripts were preserved until their removal to the Christian West when the Byzantine East was threatened by the Ottoman Turks in 1453. They form the core of the Majority and Received Text from which the King James Version is translated.

Theodore Beza, the successor of Calvin in the late sixteenth century wrote, "As for the Waldenses, I may be permitted to call them the very seed of the primitive and purer Christian church, since they are those that have been upheld, as is abundantly manifest, by the wonderful providence of God, so that neither those endless storms and tempests by which the whole Christian world has been shaken for so many succeeding ages, and the western part at length, so miserably oppressed by the Bishop of Rome falsely so called, nor those horrible persecutions which have been expressly raised against them, were ever able so far to prevail as to make them bend, or yield a voluntary subjection to the Roman tyranny and idolatry."[20]

In 1644, a Waldensian named Commenius published a document entitled, *Discipline of the Churches of Bohemia*. One of his assertions is that in 1457, a company of Bohemian Hussites separated themselves from certain *false* Hussites. In order to procure a legitimate ministry, they sent deputies to a group of Waldenses who had been recently forced out of France for their beliefs and had settled in Austria. Upon properly ordaining three of the Hussite pastors, it was claimed by the Waldenses that their own legitimacy rested in the fact that the Waldenses had "lawful bishops among them, and a lawful and uninterrupted succession from the apostles themselves."[21]

In 1655, this statement is recorded in their own words in a Waldensian Confession of Faith: "That God has gathered together a church in this world for the salvation of mankind; but she has but one head and foundation, which is Jesus Christ."[22] But also in article twenty-six of the same confession we read, "That this church cannot fail, or be quite destroyed; but that it will always remain."[23] For this reason the Waldenses were often called the "*Acephali*" or headless because they acknowledged no earthly head.

These ancient peoples were hated and hounded by the Catholic Church for centuries. In fact, it was the Waldenses that dated the beginning and consequent apostasy of the church of Rome (Catholic Church) with the assent of Constantine, while Sylvester served as bishop of that church. "From the church of Rome they distinguished themselves by reducing, as they supposed, the ancient Roman doctrine to practice, by rejecting the Pope, the prelates, and all the religious orders, by renouncing councils, fathers, and all traditions, and adhering to Scripture alone as the rule of faith, and by refusing all papal ceremonies of baptism, the Lord's Supper, penance, orders, and so on. They distinguished themselves from the latter Vaudois, and from the reformed churches, by not using liturgy; by not compelling faith; by not taking oaths; by allowing every person, even women, to teach; by not practicing infant baptism; by not admitting god-fathers; by rejecting all sacerdotal habits; by not bearing arms; and by their abhorrence of every species of persecution."[24]

They were often condemned to death by their enemies for such practices as memorizing the Scriptures at great length. It was said that many of the ancient Waldenses had memorized the entire New Testament. An eminent Catholic historian is quoted by Mr. Jones: "They can all read and write. They know French sufficiently for the understanding of the Bible and the singing of psalms. You can scarcely find a boy among them who cannot give you an intelligent account of the faith which they profess."[25]

They were condemned for translating the Scriptures into their native tongue and propagating those Scriptures to the masses. From one of their own pastors, a man named Vignaux, who pastored among them for forty years, we read the following: "That the Holy Scriptures contain all that is necessary to our salvation, and that we are called to believe only what they teach, without any regard to the authority of man; that nothing else ought to be received by us except what God hath commanded."[26]

They were condemned for preaching without training and without official sanction by the "church" (Romanists); for refusing to baptize their babies and small children; for practicing Anabaptism;[27*] for never using inappropriate language or losing their tempers (said to be a sign of demonic control); for wearing

Chapter Eleven—The Medieval Church: Anabaptism

apparel that was simple, modest, and out of date; and for never attending social places of entertainment such as the theater.

Much more could be given to illustrate the godly character and lives of these simple people, but certainly none of their beliefs or practices made them worthy of condemnation or death. Yet, they did die, and by the millions—men, women and children.

For some 1,260 years these innocent Christians were persecuted. The ancient writers often describe them as the "woman of the book of Revelation driven into the wilderness by the Papal dragon." Indeed, the Waldenses described themselves in those terms. In 1159, a group of thirty Waldenses were apprehended in England where they sought refuge from persecution in France. In Gascoyne they were described by the Catholic historian, William of Newburg, as being "as numerous as the sands of the sea." Upon examination it was found that they rejected purgatory, prayers for the dead, and the invocation of saints, along with other differences with the Roman church. Upon refusing to recant these beliefs, they were turned over to the secular arm for punishment.

The King (Henry II) was encouraged by the clergy to treat them harshly, which he did. The King commanded them to be branded with a red-hot iron on the forehead; to be whipped through the streets of Oxford; and, having their clothes cut short to their girdles, to be turned into the open fields, all persons being forbidden to afford them any shelter or relief under the severest penalties. This cruel

---

[27*]In 1554 the Waldenses drafted a Confession of Faith for the King of France that among other things, addresses their practice of receiving individuals into their membership. "We believe that in the ordinance of baptism the water is the visible and external sign, which represents to us that which, by virtue of God's invisible operation, is within us, the renovation of our minds, and the mortification of our members through (the faith of) Jesus Christ. And by this ordinance we are received into the holy congregation of God's people, previously professing our faith and the changed of life. (J.T. Christian, *A History*, p. 78. quote: Sleiden, *The General History of the Reformation*, London, 1689. p. 347).

sentence was executed in its utmost rigor; and, it being the depth of winter, all these unhappy persons perished with cold and hunger.[28]

In 1194, the King of Arragon of Spain issued the following edict against the Waldenses: "Whosoever, therefore, from this day forward, shall presume to receive the said Waldenses or any other heretics of whatsoever profession, into their houses, or to be present at their pernicious sermons, or to afford them meat, or any other favor, shall thereby incur the indignation of Almighty God, as well as ours, and have his goods confiscated without remedy of an appeal, and be punished as if he were actually guilty of high treason."[29]

Severe persecution of the Waldenses also commenced with the excommunication of Peter Waldo in 1183 by Pope Lucius III. Waldo was a leader among the Waldenses of that time. In 1212, some five hundred of their number were taken prisoner in Strassburg, and eighty of them were burned. Beginning in 1380 and lasting thirteen years, several hundred more were put to death by burning at the order of Pope Clement VII. About the year 1400, the Waldensian inhabitants of the valley of Pragela (Italy) were surprised by Catholic soldiers. The attack was made upon them in December, when the mountains were covered with snow. As the work of slaughter and death went on in the valley, the remnant of the inhabitants that escaped the fury of the soldiers perished in the mountain snows.[30] Jones describes the event in horrifying terms:

> They fled to one of the highest mountains of the Alps, with their wives and children, the unhappy mothers carrying the cradle in one hand, and with the other leading such of their offspring as were able to walk. Their human invaders, whose feet were swift to shed blood, pursued them in their flight until night came on, and slew great numbers of them before they could reach the mountains. Those that escaped were, however, reserved to experience a fate not more enviable. Overtaken by shades of night, they wandered up and down the mountains, covered with snow, destitute of the means of shelter from the inclemencies of the weather. Benumbed

with the cold, they fell an easy prey to the severity of the climate, and, when the night had passed away, there were found in their cradles, or lying upon the snow, four score of their infants deprived of life, many of their mothers also lying dead by their sides, and others just at the point of expiring.[31]

In 1486, Pope Innocent VIII ordered their extermination after organizing an armed troop of eighteen thousand men for that cause. In the valley of Loyse, a part of the inhabitants had apparently taken refuge in the caves in the mountains. When the Catholic general discovered their places of retreat, he ordered large fires to be built at the mouths of the caves. Large numbers were suffocated as a result and among them, four hundred children.[32]

In 1561 as "*heretics,*" they were granted the freedom to worship as they pleased in the region of Piedmont. But in 1655 all Waldenses living outside their traditional homeland were ordered to return to those valleys under penalty of death. With little time given them to relocate their families and belongings, many were caught by the authorities and massacred on a winter's day. Thousands died that day, and the massacre is remembered as "Bloody Easter."[33]

The event brought this historic society to the attention of all Europe. Upon hearing of the attempt by Catholics to eradicate the Waldenses, Oliver Cromwell, *Lord Protector* of England, announced a national day of prayer and fasting on May 30, 1655. Writing to the Swiss Cantons, Cromwell said, "Next to the help of God, it seems to devolve on you to provide that the most ancient stock of pure religion may not be destroyed in this remnant of its ancient faithful professors, whose safety, reduced as it is now is to the extremity of hazard, if you neglect, beware that the next lot do not speedily fall upon yourselves."[34]

Cromwell was so intent on rescuing the ancient Waldenses that he launched a public appeal for funds to aid the Waldensian communities of northern Italy. The monies raised for the relief totaled some $5,000,000 in current dollars. His foreign secretary, the famed poet John Milton, drafted official letters declaring the injustice of the massacre and later stated in his own unique way:

> Avenge, O Lord, thy slaughtered saints, whose bones
> Lie scattered on the Alpine mountains cold,...
> Forget not: in thy book record their groans
> Who were thy sheep and in their ancient fold
> Slain by the bloody Piedmontese that rolled
> Mother and infant down the rocks.
> Their moans the vales redoubled to the hills,
> And they to heaven.
> Their martyred blood and ashes sow
> O'er all th' Italian fields where still doth sway
> The tripled tyrant, that from these may grow
> A hundred fold, who, having learned thy way,
> Early may fly the Babylonian woe.

The English fleet was dispatched to the Mediterranean to bring a halt to all sea-going commerce off the coast of Savoy. The Duke of Savoy, whose region of control included the Piedmont, was forced to enter into an agreement with England to stop the heartless massacre of Waldensian society. Although this did not end the persecution of these societies, it did ensure their existence into modern times. All of this and more serve to emphasize the purity of the ancient Waldensian sect and to demonstrate that it preceded the origins of Roman Catholicism by logic and necessity.

The final blow came in the form of an edict by the Duke of Savoy (northeastern Italy), Victor Amadeus II, in January of the year 1686. The edict forbade the exercise of the Protestant religion by all his subjects upon pain of death. From the survivors we are given the following: "The armies of France and Savoy, having inhumanly butchered a multitude of the Waldenses, committed more than twelve thousand of them to prison, and dispersed two thousand of

Chapter Eleven—The Medieval Church: Anabaptism

their children among the Catholics; concluding that their work was accomplished, they caused all their property to be confiscated."[35]

After the Swiss expressed their outrage in September of that same year, the Duke of Savoy ordered the release of those who were still alive. In October they began the release from several prisons. "…the ground was covered with snow and ice; the victims of cruelty were almost universally emaciated through poverty and disease, and very unfit for the projected journey. Only a very few survived the ordeal. Those who survived the journey arrived in Geneva, about the middle of December, but in such an exhausted state that several expired between the two gates of the city, 'finding the end of their lives in the beginning of their liberty.' Others were so benumbed with cold that they had no power to speak; many staggered from faintness and disease; while others, having lost the use of their limbs, were unable to lift up their hands to receive the assistance that was tendered to them. 'And thus were the valleys of the Piedmont depopulated of their ancient inhabitants, and the light of the glorious Gospel extinguished in a country where, for many preceding centuries, it had shone with resplendent luster.'" At Geneva they experienced that kind and hospitable reception which was due to them as their fellow-creatures, and more especially as their persecuted Christian brethren.[36]

To understand such persecution is to understand the depravity of man. D.B. Ray summarizes it this way: "The first step toward persecution among professed Christians, was the gradual introduction of a change from the simple brotherly compact of religious equality established by Jesus Christ, for the hierarchy in the third century. As long as the principles of religious equality are observed, there can be no persecution. Any religious system which gives one person ecclesiastical authority over another, contains the seeds of persecution."[37]

So revered were the Waldensian people that when the Reformers, Luther and Calvin, determined to translate the Bible into the common vernacular of their own people, they sought out the ancient works of the Waldenses to edit their own translations, believing the texts of the Waldenses to be pure and untainted in contrast to the Catholic Vulgate. Indeed, one of the accusations made by the Catholic priests at inquisition was that these peoples used a Bible different from that of the priests themselves.

The Waldenses used a Byzantine Text (Textus Receptus) of the Scriptures, whereas the Catholic priests used the Vulgate, a predominately Alexandrian Text. Furthermore, Catholic priests and monks were so ignorant of Scripture, it is reported that they were sometimes shocked to find out that there even was a New Testament. Make no mistake, it is to the ancient Waldensian people that we owe the credit and honor for humanly preserving the pure text of the Scriptures for generations of believers to follow.

The Waldenses were known to be the most evangelistic society that existed during the Dark Ages, although the accounting for this could simply be that more is known about this particular sect than other groups. They were eventually driven out of their ancient homeland and forced to flee into the regions north of Italy. But once again, as they fled from persecution with their families, they carried the Gospel further into Europe, France, Germany, the Balkans, and Poland. Even the far away Netherlands felt their impact. They are often referred to in church councils in terms of hatred and condemnation. In the eyes of the Catholic Church, they were heretics. Their influence for the faith as was once delivered to the saints was steady and immeasurable for well over a thousand years. Unfortunately, the Waldenses eventually succumbed to the relentless pressure of their enemies, and by the eighteenth century adopted the doctrines of certain Protestant sects such as the French Huguenots (Calvinists) in southern France, and Arminianists elsewhere in Europe. In addition, they became paedobaptists (infant baptizers) after 1532. Sadly, we would not consider the modern Waldensian church today as a New Testament church.

CHAPTER ELEVEN—THE MEDIEVAL CHURCH: ANABAPTISM

Anabaptism

Numerous groups throughout the Middle Ages had practiced Anabaptism such as the Waldenses, the Arnoldists, the Poor of Lyons, the Petrobrusians, the Henricians, the Hussites, and the Lollards. During the Dark Ages, they were often forced to secret themselves because of their enemies' efforts to destroy them. However, the Reformation (1520) afforded them some semblance of freedom, at least for a time. They seemed to spring up in many countries all at once. They are far too numerous to cite each group or society, but the better known were called by such names as the *Bogomils* (beloved of God), the *Paterines* (the suffering ones), the *Picards* (the holy ones), the *Cathari* (the pure ones), the **Separatists**, the *Rottengeister* (the agitators), the *Winkler* (corner preacher), the *Stabler* (staff bearers), the *Humiliati* (the humble), the *Sabots* (the wooden shoed), the *Inzabatati* (the Sabbath men), and the *Sacramentarians* (grace through faith ones).

Most often these names were contrived in the minds of their enemies. Without exception, they were terms meant to be derogatory; they were terms of contempt. The term *Anabaptist* is still used today as a term of derision toward those living in places like Germany and Austria, who continue to practice the preaching and baptism of the Anabaptist. "But all these names, and many more, were given to persons in Italy, France, Germany, Spain, and Flanders (for they were found in all of these countries) whose

DEFINING THE TERMS

Separatist: *The term separatist refers to certain religious societies that during the latter part of the sixteenth century rejected the authority of the Church of England as well as the union of church-state that often resulted in the persecution of dissenting groups. The Separatists usually consisted of Brownists or Congregational societies as well as Baptist churches.*

religious views and practices were substantially the same. We say substantially, because it is not to be supposed that they agreed with each other in every specific particular. The freedom which they claimed from the Roman Church was still further indulged among themselves. They would call no man master. But the diversities of opinion which might prevail among them were perfectly consistent with unity in regard to the essential truths of the Gospel."[38]

People who aligned themselves with these societies numbered into the hundreds of thousands by the time of the Reformation and existed throughout Europe. Their numbers became so vast and the people of those societies so diversified by culture, borders, and language, that the one term that expressed their doctrinal distinction from the state churches was the ancient term *Anabaptists*.

No one is able to say where they first appeared, and it does not appear that they had any special connection with each other from one place to another. No one leader existed under which they were all united as a body. They simply appear to be a continuation of an ancient faith bubbling up to the surface.

All of these groups identified generally as the Anabaptists in the days of the Reformation were the spiritual offspring of the Paulicians, Albigenses, and primarily, the Waldenses of the Dark Ages. The practice of Anabaptism linked them together. Driven from their homes and leaving behind the corpses of friends and loved ones, their work was paid for in blood. I am reminded of what God says in Hebrews that almost all things are sanctified by blood. Although they preferred to be designated as *Baptists*, they were identified by the authorities as *re-baptizers*. By that designation they had the legal means to destroy them, with the full blessing of both the Catholic Church and eventually, those state churches of the Reformation. Had it not been for the providence of God, these faithful followers of Christ surely would have perished, so determined were their enemies.

Historian J.T. Christian states that "many Roman Catholic historians and officials, in some instances, eyewitnesses, testify

Chapter Eleven—The Medieval Church: Anabaptism

that the Waldenses and other ancient communions were the same as the Anabaptists in the days of the Reformers." He references the following: the Augustinian Bartholomaeus von Usingen, set forth in the year 1529, that the "Anabaptists, or Catabaptists, have gone forth from Picardism;" the Mandate of Speier, April 1529, declares that the "Anabaptists were hundreds of years old and had often been condemned;" Cardinal Baronius, the most learned historian of the Catholic Church says, "The Waldenses were Anabaptists."[39] Where Waldenses flourished, there the Baptists set deep root; where Waldenses were found during the Medieval times, Baptists were found in the days of the Reformation.[40]

The author of a letter, "Successio Ana-baptistica" dated 1521, a communication between the Swiss brethren and the Anabaptists of the Netherlands, states the following concerning the origins of the Anabaptists: "I am dealing with the Mennonites or Anabaptists, who pride themselves as having the apostolic succession, that is the mission and the extraction from the apostles. Who claim the true church is found nowhere, except among themselves alone and their congregations, since with them alone remains the true understanding of the Scriptures. If one charges them with the newness of their sect, they claim that the 'true church' during the time of the dominion of the Catholic Church, was hidden in her."[41] So we see that as early as 1521, as Protestantism was being initiated, the Anabaptists claimed an ancient history with apostolic authority.

J.T. Christian quotes J.J. Van Oosterzee, Dutch Protestant preacher and theologian, who claimed that "they [the Anabaptists] are peculiar to the Netherlands and are older than the Reformation, and must, therefore, by no means be confounded with the Protestanism of the sixteenth century, for they can be shown that the origin of the Baptists reaches further back and is more venerable."[42]

The most flagrant issue that epitomized the great division between those who would be true to the Bible and those who would place their loyalty in tradition was the issue of infant baptism. Societies that practice any form of infant baptism (baptismal regeneration) were seen by the Anabaptists everywhere as apostate and illegitimate. Thus, any baptism administered by such societies was also deemed illegitimate and needed correction by a legitimate body when once the candidate had genuinely received Christ. This action was seen by apostate societies as an attack on their credibility, and so it was! This in turn positioned the Anabaptists everywhere to experience the wrath of the state churches (both Catholic and Reformed) in conjunction with their allies, the governments of most European countries. A quote from the following text is eerily familiar:

> Some were racked and drawn asunder; others were burnt to ashes and dust; some were roasted on pillars or torn with red-hot pinchers....Others were hanged on trees, beheaded with the sword, or thrown into the water. ...Some were starved or rotted in darksome prisons.... Some who were deemed too young for execution were whipped with rods and many lay for years in dungeons.... Numbers had holes burned into their cheeks. ...The rest were hunted from one country and place to another. Like owls and ravens, which durst not fly by day, they were often compelled to hide in rocks and clefts, in wild forests or in caves and pits.[43] Kautsky, 1897

Eventually, Europe became sickened with the bloodshed. The injustices of the Inquisition, for example, had taken their toll on the consciences of the people of Europe. The governments of Europe had grown weary of using their resources to punish those at odds with the Catholic Church and wanted their own freedom from the tyranny of Rome.

The Dark Ages finally came to a close with the invention of the printing press by Guttenberg in 1450. The Roman Catholic Church had controlled almost all of Europe in a church-state relationship. It is estimated that some fifty million Anabaptist people were butchered under the watchful eye of the Catholic Church during the horrible one thousand years of the Middle Ages.

Remember, from the first century until the Protestant Reformation, no churches existed except those two societies we have identified—the New Testament church (having become known historically to us as the Anabaptists), and the Roman Catholic Church system. Yes, there were groups that arose on the scene from time to time that claimed to be legitimate, but their doctrines betray them as heretical rather than biblical. Their impact was relatively short-lived and not widespread. The issue of tracking the New Testament church down through the centuries, then, is really a very simple matter, and the persecuted church of the Middle Ages is easily identified.

During the early days of the Reformation, the Anabaptists found their best opportunities to preach in Switzerland, the Rhineland, and the Netherlands. Although the Anabaptists hoped for some degree of freedom in Switzerland at first, in 1525 the tide turned against them. Two leaders of the Reform movement there under Ulrich Zwingli, Conrad Grebel and Felix Manz, became convinced of Anabaptist principles. In the fall of 1524, Grebel's wife gave birth to a son. After refusing to baptize their infant son, the authorities threatened them with banishment from Zurich on January 17, 1525. On January 21, Grebel and his wife gathered together with others at the Manz home where Grebel was baptized. Manz, Grebel and others of their group soon removed themselves to a small village outside of Zurich called Zollikon, where they formed the first Anabaptist congregation of Switzerland.

In March of 1526, the council of Zurich decided that anyone practicing re-baptism would be put to death. Within a year, on January 5, 1527, Felix Manz was apprehended and drowned in the Limmat River which flowed through Zurich. Manz thus became the first Anabaptist martyr of the Reformation. Within four years the movement had been eradicated from Zurich.

Many of the Swiss Anabaptists were then forced to move to Austria and into Germany along the Rhine. However, in 1529, the imperial Diet of Spieyer proclaimed Anabaptism a heresy, punishable by death. In the years to come, some four to five thousand Anabaptists were executed by fire, water and the sword. Once again the Anabaptists were obliged to move further north.

"The Waldenses had entered Holland in 1182 and by 1233 Flanders was full of them," according to Armitage. Armitage continues with the opinion of the Dutch historians, Ypeg and Dermout who were of the opinion that, "The Waldenses scattered in the Netherlands might be called their salt, so correct were their views and devout their lives. The Mennonites sprang from among them."[44] In several Dutch towns it was estimated that two-thirds of the population were Anabaptists.[45] Emperor Charles V of Spain did everything he could to rid Holland and the Netherlands of Protestants and Anabaptist influence. Some fifty thousand persons were hanged, beheaded, buried alive, or burned in the Netherlands alone. A large portion of those were Baptists. In 1535, a decree was issued calling for the death of all Baptists. Even if they recanted, they were to die by the sword instead of fire.[46] In 1550, Charles issued this decree:

> ...We forbid all lay persons to converse or dispute concerning the Holy Scriptures, openly or secretly...or to read, teach, or expound the Scriptures, unless they have duly studied theology, or have been approved by some renowned university...or to entertain any of the opinions of the above mentioned heretics...on pain of death...punished as follows...the men [to be beheaded] with the sword, and the women to be buried alive if they do not persist in their errors...if they persist in them they are to be executed with fire; all their property in both cases to be confiscated to the Crown.[47]

Religious freedom was not realized in the Netherlands until Emperor Charles V died in 1558. His son, Philip II, had inherited Holland from his father, but his control was short lived. After organizing various Protestant and **non-conformist** groups, including Baptists, William of Orange defeated Catholic Spain in a series of conflicts that eventually led to the full independence of Holland. While yet a Catholic, William wrote, "I have neither the will or the means to help the Inquisition, or execute the placards. If peace is to be preserved in this land, liberty of worship must be guaranteed to every inhabitant. There must be a halt in persecution until an appeal can be made to the King."[48] In 1568, freedom was granted to the people of Holland. No country was more thoroughly soaked with the blood of the saints than Holland.

In 1579, Article XIII of the Union of Utrecht compact declared, "Every one shall be free in the practice of his religious belief, and that, in accordance with the peace of Ghent, no one shall be held or examined on account of matters of religion." Finally, it became legal for a people called the Baptists to meet in the open in the Netherlands. It was here for the first time that Anabaptists had the freedom to meet in a public structure, and place their name over the door. But rather than call themselves Anabaptists, which they believed to be a misnomer, they identified themselves simply as Baptists; and from that day to this, it is the name which people holding to certain biblical distinctives have called themselves.

Verduin in his book *The Reformers and Their Stepchildren* observes, "The sources (historians) single out no man as the originator of sixteenth century re-baptism. In the words of Josef

DEFINING THE TERMS

Non-conformist: *"Non-conformists" refers to a movement within the Church of England to purify the Church of England of Papal influence and rituals. Non-conformists were loyal to the church but demanded a purification of it. These dissidents were known as the Puritans, but they never advocated Separatism.*

Beck, 'From whom the idea of re-baptism issued, of this the sources say not a word.' This requires an explanation. To re-baptize is to do an extremely radical thing...How so radical a practice sprung up anonymously is passing strange, if it is assumed, as the vogue is, that Anabaptism was simply the product of the sixteenth century. But this silence as to who must be credited with the idea becomes wholly explicable once it is realized that what was known as Anabaptism in the Reformation times was in no sense a new thing. Neither the name or the practice was new...The Anabaptists did not initiate a new school of thought; they merely restated an ancient ideology, in idiom of the sixteenth century to be sure, but ancient nevertheless. No one is credited with having invented the Anabaptism of the sixteenth century for the sufficient reason that no one did."[49]

The doctrinal distinctives of the Anabaptists, regardless of their origin, their location or their period in history, are identified as follows:

1. The autonomy (self-determination) of each local church under the headship of Christ.
2. The Scriptures alone as the sole rule of faith and practice.
3. The finished work of Christ.
4. A regenerate church membership.
5. Believer's baptism only.
6. Purity in life and conduct.
7. The priesthood of every believer (that every believer is a priest before God, and thus any mediator other than Christ is unnecessary).
8. Liberty of conscience (the freedom to worship God according to individual conscience without fear of condemnation by any human authority).

It is our contention that the above represent the substance of the New Testament faith. These distinctions are apostolic in origin and nature. Churches that have held to these distinctives down through the centuries are properly identified as the New Testament church, that is, the church that Jesus built and that He promised He would preserve until He returned. It is not a mystical church; rather, it consists of local assemblies identified by the purity of their doctrines. It is a church that is apostolic in its doctrine and thereby derives its authority. It was never intended or commissioned by our Lord to rest upon the traditions of men. It is the institution for which Christ Himself died, and He alone is the head of each representative body of that institution, the local New Testament church!

CHAPTER TWELVE

The Protestant Reformation: The Reformers

The Scripture wisely warns that *"only by pride cometh contention…"* (Proverbs 13:10). As the author of this book, it is very important to me on a personal level to honestly examine the work of the Reformers. After much study, I have come to the conclusion that these men and many of their associates were anything but ordinary men. In a historical context, we might even say they were great men. Indeed, some paid for their convictions with their lives. Others were hunted and hounded for years. Who would not admire their boldness and their courage? Their actions led many to align themselves with the Reformers that had been the objects of persecution during the Dark Ages.

The Reformers lived in very dark and dangerous times and it is difficult for us today to understand and fully appreciate all that they risked while they stood for the truth as they understood it. It is certainly not my desire to cradle a contentious spirit but rather to be honest and respectful in regards to their movement. I realize that there will be some who may read this book who are coming from a Protestant background and understanding. As sincerely as I can I want to encourage the reader to consider the framework of our historical reference, the Bible alone, without the imposition and contradiction of human traditions. Proverbs 13:10, continues *"...but with the well advised is wisdom."*

Although there were many men who participated in the movement referred to as the Protestant Reformation, we are most interested in those who by conviction positioned themselves in opposition to the Catholic Church. Even in this number, there are many more men of lesser degree of influence that we will not take the time to examine, but they did exist.

The men upon whom we will focus are generally accepted as the stalwarts of the movement itself. Among these men are Martin Luther, John Calvin, and John Knox. We will also detail the turn of events involving King Henry VIII. He is listed among these men not because of any personal conviction on his part but simply because certain events in his life precipitated a withdrawal from Rome and the control that popery exhibited over England at that time. However, it must also be said that although the personal character and conviction of Henry may disqualify him from being allied with the work of the Reformers directly, there were certainly men of influence in Henry's court that agreed in principle with the Reformers.

Martin Luther, 1483–1546

The Catholic Church had been seething in its own depravity for almost fifteen hundred years. There was little debate by reasonable men, even in the Catholic Church, that this "church" had been responsible for horrendous crimes. Not only was she guilty of abusing so-called heretics, but her doctrines had also gone far afield of the New Testament.

Chapter Twelve—The Protestant Reformation: The Reformers

In the early part of the sixteenth century, some began to challenge the corruption of the Catholic Church. The most prominent of these was Martin Luther. Luther, who was a Catholic priest living in Germany, had become very disillusioned with the church and its many abuses. Luther also began to examine the Scriptures and discovered a truth that changed his life and became the doctrinal wedge between himself and the Catholic Church. The truth that forever changed Luther and the other Reformers was the statement by the Apostle Paul in the book of Romans, *"The just shall live by faith"* (Romans 1:17). This became the battle cry of the Reformation.

With his new understanding, Luther set about to correct the abuses within the Catholic Church. He believed that a general reform was needed to bring the church back into a New Testament framework. Other men eventually joined Luther such as John Calvin, a French Reformer who had similar views and concerns.

The Protestant Reformation refers to this effort to reform the Roman Catholic Church from within. Although the church had for many centuries advocated certain beliefs that could not be substantiated by Scripture, the doctrinal problems were not the main focus of the Reformers. The Reformers were more concerned with abuses such as the selling of indulgences, the worship and selling of relics, the immorality and drunkenness of the clergy, and the widespread persecution of dissenting groups. The Reformation effort was a miserable failure, in that the Catholic Church was not reformed, and resulted in the excommunication of all those who challenged the supreme authority of the Catholic Church. Luther, Calvin, and others who protested the political, moral, and doctrinal abuses of the church were compelled to start their own movements, believing their efforts would restore orthodoxy to Christianity.

Luther's specific demands to reform the Catholic Church were enumerated in a document that he posted on the doors of a Catholic church in Wittenberg, Germany on October 31, 1517. The document contained ninety-five items that required redress in the mind of Luther. In the view of some scholars, this act marks the official beginning of the Protestant Reformation. After his subsequent excommunication from the church in 1520, Luther eventually organized his own church in 1526 after a series of political events. However, Luther maintained some of the old baggage from his former association with Roman Catholicism.

Although Luther pleaded for the supremacy of the Scriptures as the rule of faith and practice, he violated the Scriptures in at least three very important areas. First, Luther established a church-state relationship for his "church." This later set the stage for the persecution of any who opposed his positions. Anabaptist societies of Germany consequently became outlaws.

Second, he maintained the practice of infant baptism, although he at first rejected its legitimacy. Luther eventually justified the practice by saying that infant baptism secured grace for the adherent through the parent sponsorship, that a child's regeneration takes place at his baptism because of the faith of the parents. "Baptism is not simply water, but water comprehended in God's command and connected with God's Word, and it has a saving effect produced by the Word of God."[1]

In reality, Luther had come to realize that after a thousand years of darkness and ignorance, women in Catholic Germany were not about to risk their children's eternal fate by doing away with a practice that they had come to believe would wash away the damning effect of original sin. And so, after due consideration, Luther, as well as other Reformers, maintained the practice of baptizing infants and small children.

Third, Luther devised a doctrine of "Consubstantiation," a belief that rather than the elements of the Lord's Table actually becoming the body and blood of Christ (as the Catholic Church had taught), he taught that Christ was merely present in, with, and under the elements. "The notion that a priest, by the incantation of

Chapter Twelve—The Protestant Reformation: The Reformers

his words, can change bread into Christ seemed to Luther absurd and blasphemous; nevertheless, he argued, Christ of His own will comes down from Heaven to be present consubstantially with the bread and wine of the sacrament."[2]

Remember that both of the ordinances of baptism and the Lord's Table had taken on sacramental or saving value by this time, something the Bible does not teach. The Scriptures teach that these ordinances were simply pictures of the death, burial, and resurrection of Christ, and that only by placing one's faith in the saving efficacy of the shed blood of Christ is one saved from the penalty of his sins. Consubstantiation is not a biblical concept any more than the Catholic concept of transubstantiation is. Both positions are of human origin.

Finally, Luther also identified the church as an *invisible* Catholic (universal) Church in contrast to the Catholic position that the church was *visible* and Catholic. This was not necessarily a new concept. Others had described the church in the same way down through the centuries. But as the father of the Reformation, Luther opened the door to the multitude of denominations that exist in our own day as we shall see.

Eventually, Luther secured the existence and success of his new "church" from any Catholic threat by joining his movement in northern Germany with certain governments. During the time of Luther, government was largely associated with small city-state regions that were ruled by princes who were appointed or sanctioned by the King. These local governments were more than happy to accommodate Luther, as it would provide the opportunity to vanquish Rome and its control over Germany's resources. All that was left was to drive Catholicism out of Germany. In July of 1522, after certain bishops attempted to silence Luther, he responded by writing "Against the Falsely Called Spiritual Order of the Pope and the Bishops." In it he declared that all Germans should drive them out as wolves by force.

> It were better that every bishop were murdered, every foundation or Cloister rooted out, than that one soul should be destroyed, let alone that all souls should be lost for the sake of their worthless trumpery and idolatry. Of what use are they who thus live in lust, nourished by the sweat and labor of others? But if they will not hear God's Word, but rage and rave with bannings and burnings, killings and every evil, what do they better deserve than a strong uprising which will sweep them from the earth? And we would smile did it happen. All who contribute body, goods, and honor that the rule of the bishops may be destroyed are God's dear children and true Christians.[3]

Although the Anabaptists saw a glimmer of hope in this reform movement at first, they soon realized that Luther and others were addicted to certain errors that would place the Anabaptists at odds with the Reformation. Indeed, according to Verduin,

> The Reformation did not begin on the night of October 31, 1517 (Luther's 95 Thesis). Luther's brave deed of that night no doubt encouraged and inspired all who already had reformation in their banner; but Luther found followers before he made any, followers who later, when they saw where Luther was going, peeled off again.[4]

Persecutions against the Waldenses of France and Italy had driven many of their societies into Germany. The respected Lutheran historian, Johann von Mosheim (1694–1755) said,

> Before the rise of Luther and Calvin, there lay concealed, in almost all the countries of Europe, particularly in Bohemia, Moravia, Switzerland, and Germany, many persons, who adhered tenaciously to the following doctrine, which the Waldenses, Wickliffites, the Hussites, had maintained, some in a more disguised, and others in a more open and public manner…[5]

As tradesmen and artisans, their numbers in Germany were ever increasing. W.A. Jarrell writes, "...so widely had the sect been scattered that it was said a traveler from Antwerp to Rome could sleep every night in the house of one of their brethren."[6]

Luther saw the Anabaptists as a threat to his "church" and determined to drive the Anabaptists from Germany as heretics. Luther himself wrote, "In our times the doctrine of the Gospel, reestablished and cleansed, has drawn to it and gained many who in earlier times had been suppressed by the tyranny of Antichrist, the Pope; however there have forthwith gone out from us Wiedertaufer, Sacramentschwarmer and Rottengeister...for they were not of us even though for a while they walked with us."[7] Luther who in 1528 counseled leniency, later advised "the use of the sword" against them as "not only blasphemers but highly seditious."[8]

The death penalty was decreed for the Anabaptists in 1529 at the Diet of Spieyer. In 1536, Luther signed a memorandum written by his comrade, Melancthon, approving the death of Anabaptists. The first martyrs of the German Reformation were three Catholic monks: Henry Voes, John Esch, and Lambert Thorn, who had adopted reformation views. They were sent to the stake at Brussels as the first Protestant martyrs.[9] Although these men were not Anabaptists, many Anabaptists reacted to this event by migrating further north into the Netherlands and Flanders where their numbers continued to grow, and over time produced a relatively sympathetic population where freedom of religion became the dominant attitude.

King Henry VIII of England, 1491–1547

Henry, heir to the Tudor throne, had been forced into an arranged marriage at the tender age of twelve by his father, Henry VII, the King of England. Henry married Catherine of Spain, a woman eight years his senior. Catherine had formerly been married to Henry's brother, Arthur, who died shortly after his marriage to Catherine.

The marriage to Henry was of course a political arrangement designed to create a more amiable relationship between Spain and England. A special dispensation for the marriage was granted by Pope Julius (1443–1513) to Henry VII. Several years later, after Henry had ascended to the throne, he determined to divorce Catherine and marry Ann Boleyn, with whom he had apparently carried on an affair. Catherine had born seven children to Henry, but six of the seven had died and the seventh was a girl (Mary), leaving Henry without a male heir.

England at the time was a Catholic state, and the only way Henry could secure a divorce from Catherine was to petition the pope, who was not in the habit of issuing decrees of divorce for anyone. After petitioning the pope in 1527 for a ruling to invalidate his marriage, his request was eventually denied by the pope, and Henry found himself in a dilemma—married to Catherine, a good Catholic girl, but carrying on an illegitimate relationship with Ann Boleyn.

In the summer of 1530, Henry was advised by Thomas Cranmer, a doctor of divinity at Cambridge and an anti-Catholic Protestant, to poll the major universities in Europe as to whether the pope should have ever sanctioned Henry's marriage to his brother's wife. Henry's agents then scattered bribes about Europe in an effort to influence the vote. The agents of the Emperor did the same on behalf of the pope. After all the gamesmanship, only Oxford and Cambridge fell into agreement with Henry (as might be expected).[10] You can imagine how elated Henry was at finding support for any action he might take to resolve the situation. It gave Henry the excuse he needed to establish his own national church and, by placing himself as the "head" of that church, the validity of his marriage to Catherine could be resolved. It would not only deliver him from his personal woe, but at the same time

Chapter Twelve—The Protestant Reformation: The Reformers

would deliver a blow against the pope, which he well deserved for not issuing a decree of divorcement in the first place.

In February of 1531, after certain political maneuvers, Henry demanded that the Catholic clergy acknowledge him as the "protector and only supreme head of the church and the clergy of England."[11] His intentions were becoming clearer. Henry would create his own national "church." He soon ordered all Catholic priests to either leave the country or become the official priests of this newly created church. After winning over a majority of the clergy by intimidation, in 1532 England officially separated from the Roman See. In February of 1533, Parliament enacted the "Statute of Appeals" by which all litigation that had formerly been sent for judgment to Rome was henceforth to be decided "in spiritual and temporal courts within the Realm...."[12]

In May of 1533, Henry's former marriage to Catherine was declared invalid by the new Archbishop of Canterbury, Thomas Cranmer. Cranmer had convened a court in April to officially question the legitimacy of Henry's marriage to Catherine. The court found in favor of Henry of course, and Catherine was placed in prison. She was later released and sent back to Spain. By this time however, Henry had already secretly married Anne Boleyn, now four months pregnant. Pope Clement responded in 1534 by decreeing the marriage of Henry to Anne Boleyn invalid, and ordered Henry to restore Catherine to the throne or suffer excommunication. The King refused and was excommunicated by Clement. Many of the Catholic priests, in jeopardy of their lives, chose to back Henry, and consequently, the Church of England was born in 1534. Henry was the "head" and the pope had been supplanted in England.

In that same year, the English Parliament passed the "Act of Supremacy" which stated, "The King our sovereign lord, his heirs and successors, kings of this realm, shall be taken, accepted, and reputed the only supreme head on earth of the Church of England...."[13] The church basically maintained all of the practices of the Catholic Church, including infant baptism, and Henry persecuted all those who would not submit, as did all those who followed him on the throne of England for years to come.

The Anabaptists of England, known as *Separatists or Nonconformists,* were thus persecuted for their rejection of the monarch as head of the church and their refusal to accept the practice of infant baptism in England. Others too were identified by these terms (i.e., Congregationalists, Presbyterians) but only the Anabaptists held a position that excluded infant baptism and maintained the biblical position on immersion.

It is from this Anglican Church (Church of England) that many evangelical Protestant churches in America, with which we are familiar, derive their origin and much of their church polity.

John Calvin, 1509–1564

Often called the Swiss Reformer, John Calvin originally served the Catholic Church as a priest in France. He studied for the priesthood at the University of Paris where he became influenced by the writings of Martin Luther. Later, while studying law at Orleans, Calvin was greatly influenced by his cousin, the Waldensian, Peter Olivetan. Calvin was converted to Christ at the age of twenty three in 1532, and from that point he immersed himself in the study of the Scriptures. But like Luther, Calvin at first refused to break with the Catholic Church. He was eventually forced to leave France or be imprisoned for his reform views, and he consequently fled from Paris in 1534, marking his official break with the Catholic Church.

Whereas Luther was a man of shear will and determination, Calvin was a man of tremendous intellect. He is often credited with reviving and popularizing the old beliefs of Augustine from the fourth century concerning predestination. This reform theology of Calvin has proved to be a very destructive doctrine for many, including Baptists.

Chapter Twelve—The Protestant Reformation: The Reformers

Calvinism is probably best known by the acrostic, spelling the word TULIP that summarizes its positions. It stands for the "Total Depravity of Man," that is, the total inability of the lost to choose Christ without the grace of God enabling one to make that decision; the "Unconditional Election of Man," that the elect are chosen in Christ before the foundation of the world; a "Limited Atonement," that Christ died only for the elect or chosen (predestination); an "Irresistible Grace," that the grace of God cannot be resisted by the elect; and the "Perseverance of the Saints," that the elect will persevere unto the end as a mark of being among the chosen (elect).

We have stressed before that any doctrine that is not first century doctrine is at the very least suspect. Let me caution the reader to be very careful of adopting a belief system that may not have originated in the first century. There is good evidence that the Catholic scholar Augustine first originated this thinking in the fourth century. John Calvin, of course, further developed it during the sixteenth century. Remember, orthodox doctrine does not evolve; traditions evolve! A New Testament church is identified by its doctrinal parameters. To change or alter the doctrine of a New Testament church is to sacrifice its identity and thus its legitimacy.

Having been exposed as a Reformer in France, Calvin sought sanctuary in a place that might be sympathetic to his beliefs. He found such a place in Switzerland. It was a place where centuries earlier the Anabaptists under Arnold had made a great impact on the thinking of the citizens of this country. Once again, many of the Anabaptists who had been previously persecuted in France and Italy had made their way to Switzerland during the Middle Ages. In fact, Ulrich Zwingli, the contemporary of both Luther and Calvin living in Switzerland before Calvin, is quoted as saying:

> The institution of Anabaptism is no novelty, but for thirteen hundred years has caused great disturbance in the church (Catholic), and has acquired such strength

that the attempt in this age to contend with it appears futile for a time.[14]

Thus Zwingli dated the presence of these ancient peoples to the year AD 225. His statement apparently related to the Montanists. In 1525, an edict of the city of Zurich was written by Zwingli himself against the Anabaptists saying:

> You know without a doubt, and have heard from many, that for a very long time, some peculiar men, who imagine that they are learned…have preached, and without the permission and consent of the church, have proclaimed that infant baptism did not proceed from God, but from the devil…[15]

In Switzerland, Calvin published his "Institutes of the Christian Religion," (1536) which was a systematic defense of Reformation doctrine. The final edition of this work, published in 1559, soon became the most influential systematic theology in Christendom to that date, and perhaps since that date. However, many important points are of human origin, including the false doctrine of predestination, justification for the practice of baptizing infants and small children, and an unscriptural view of Lord's Table. It thus does not represent the true and complete teaching of the New Testament.

Calvin had arrived in Geneva in 1536. Calvin, along with William Farel, a Reformer who had preceded Calvin in Switzerland by a few short years, organized the Genevan church. After being forced out of Geneva in 1538, Calvin returned in 1541 at the request of the city's council. Although not holding an elected position, he was allowed to set the political tone of the city by dictating all laws and the methods to enforce them. He literally ran the city like a church, believing that it was proper for the state to be subservient to the church. He believed the duty of the city council was to uphold the will of the church.

Chapter Twelve—The Protestant Reformation: The Reformers

According to Hageman, "Intolerance against those who differed from his views was one of the chief faults of Calvin's career as a reformer." He continues, "the chief victim of his intolerance being Servetus who had accused Calvin of tyrannical and unchristian conduct. The burning of Servetus (October 27, 1553) for heresy is a sad, ineffaceable blot on the character of Calvin."[16] Michael Servetus' convictions generally resided with the Anabaptists.

Calvin later wrote of the punishment of Servetus, "Whoever shall maintain that wrong is done to heretics and blasphemers in punishing them makes himself an accomplice in their crime and guilty as they are. There is no question here of man's authority; it is God who speaks and clear it is what law he will have kept in the church, even to the end of the world. Wherefore does he demand of us so extreme severity, if not to show us that due honor is not paid him, so long as we set not his service above every human consideration, so that we spare not kin, nor blood of any, and forget all humanity when the matter is to combat for his glory."[17]

Anabaptists became marked targets in Calvin's Switzerland. Although at first sanctioned by Calvin, the Anabaptists stood in opposition to the practice of baptizing infants. They were not a threat to him personally or to his reform movement, but their numbers made him uneasy.[18*] He used the power of the state to either execute them or drive them from the region. Calvin is quoted as saying in a letter to King Edward VI of England that "Anabaptists and reactionists should alike be put to death."[19] After

---

[18*]Mr. Calvin clearly understood that the primitive church practiced baptism by immersion. In his comments on Acts 8:38, He says, "They went down into the water. Here we see the rite used among the men of old time in baptism; for they put all the body into the water. Now the use is this, that the minister doth sprinkle the body or the head." He continues, "It is certain that we want (lack) nothing which maketh to the substance of baptism. Wherefore the church did grant liberty to herself since the beginning to change the rites somewhat excepting the substance." (Baptist Doctrines, C. Jenkins. Quote: Calvin's comments on Acts 8:38).

several debates with representatives of the Anabaptists, Calvin "…soon decided that the only efficient argument against it was the fagot [burning by a wood fire] or the sword."[20]

The Reformed churches of both Switzerland and France were the result of Calvin's efforts. His influence was also exercised in the Reformation movements of England and the Netherlands, from whence it was eventually carried to America. John Calvin died in 1564, and Theodore Beza continued the Swiss Reformation.

John Knox, 1505–1572

Another significant reform movement that resulted in the establishment of yet another Protestant church was that of John Knox. Knox was born in Scotland of peasant parents in 1505. He eventually trained for the priesthood and was ordained into the priesthood in 1532. Scotland was a Catholic country at this time and its priests and monks were as vicious and worthless here as anywhere in Europe.[21] Politically, Scotland was aligned with France and had won its independence from England under the leadership of Robert the Bruce. One hundred years before, both the Lollards and the Hussites were responsible for planting the seeds of the Gospel in the British Isles during the Middle Ages. "In 1407 the Lollard preacher, John Resby, and in 1432 the Hussite Bohemian, Paul Crawer, were burned in Scotland for disseminating their anti-papal views. From this time onward a strong, but for the most part suppressed, sentiment in favor of reform prevailed in Scotland among all classes."[22]

Although Knox was trained as a Catholic priest, he was influenced to move toward the Protestant cause after witnessing the burning of the Reformer, George Wishart, who had been strangled and burned in 1543 for expounding reform beliefs. Knox described himself later as an "ardent disciple and fearless bodyguard of George Wishart."[23] Knox became a leader among a band of Protestants and

Chapter Twelve—The Protestant Reformation: The Reformers

was later captured and imprisoned by the French in 1547. He was then forced to serve as a galley slave for some nineteen months.

After being released from slavery in 1549, Knox settled in England and helped direct the English Reformation. He also served as the chaplain to the King of England at this time, Edward VI. When Queen Mary, a loyal Catholic, ascended the throne of England in 1554, Knox was compelled to seek refuge in Geneva, where he came under the influence of Calvin and the Swiss Reformation. Knox later described Geneva under Calvin as "the most perfect school of Christ that ever was on the earth since the days of the apostles."[24]

Knox remained in Europe for five years, returning to Scotland once in 1555, and then again in 1560 to remain. The result of his time with Calvin was that Knox adopted the doctrinal persuasions of Calvin and brought them back to his homeland where he directed the Protestant cause. Here, after various political events with which Knox was heavily involved, the Parliament declared the Reformed church to be the "only true and holy kirk (church) of Jesus Christ within the realm."[25]

Knox died in 1572. After another thirty years of contention between the church and the state, the Presbyterian Church was formed officially as the Church of Scotland in 1592. The Presbyterian Church maintained the practice of infant baptism as did Calvin and Luther in their Reformation churches. This in turn placed those who disagreed with the practice of paedobaptism at odds with the state church in Scotland. Persecution of these dissidents it seems was inevitable.

Albert Newman in his *Manual of Church History* says, "Like all other branches of the Reformation, except the Anabaptists and **Socinian**, Scottish Protestantism was exceedingly intolerant. Knox and his followers, like Calvin, believed that heresy ought to be promptly and violently suppressed, and so great was their energy of conviction that their practice was generally conformed to their theory."[26] The Presbyterians continued their intolerance well into the seventeenth century, speaking of the tolerance of other societies and religious sects as a great "error."[27]

DEFINING THE TERMS

Socinian: *Socinian is a reference to the teachings of Faustus Socinius (1539–1604). Socinius was both anti-trinitarian and anti-paedobaptist. Socinians rejected Calvinism, believed the Lord's Table was simply a memorial to be partaken by baptized believers only, and that baptism is to be by immersion after an affirmation of belief. Thus he rejected infant baptism. However, Socinius rejected the position that baptism was a perpetual ordinance. He is not considered an Anabaptist although his views were similar in some aspects. His greatest influence was among the Mennonites.*

CHAPTER THIRTEEN

Reformation Consequences: Evangelicalism

Luther, Zwingli, and Knox all held the same position as Calvin in the matters of salvation by faith, predestination, and the church, but their doctrinal views differed from there.[1] Originally (and by many today) Protestantism was seen as a church as opposed to a movement. Indeed Luther suggested that it be called evangelical. He originally advocated an ecclesiastical democracy, in which each congregation would select its own minister and determine its own ritual and creed, but ever increasing dependence on the princes compelled him to surrender these prerogatives to commissions appointed by, and responsible to, the state.[2] Keep in mind that the princes were obliged not only to keep their subjects happy but also to maintain their sovereign control over them. They were familiar with a certain amount of oversight in the affairs of religion. Thus, in order to keep the people happy, paedobaptism was maintained, and rather than local church autonomy, a state

185

church was established and a hierarchy set in place. This was not only true of Luther but of all the Reformers.

The founders of the Reformation undoubtedly advanced the Gospel in their day. No doubt many souls were saved as a result of their preaching ministries, but to what were these converts added? It was not to the New Testament church, but to their own churches respectively.

Because the Reformers failed to deal with the issue of paedobaptism—to which the people had become accustomed, as well as their willingness to establish a popish system of oversight—it is my opinion that most of the work of the Reformers over time, has become relatively fruitless. Indeed, using the Bible as our standard, these movements were doomed from the start.

I am reminded of an event that preceded the crucifixion (Matthew 21:18–21). The Bible says that Jesus hungered and sought fruit on a fig tree on His way from Bethany to Jerusalem. After approaching the tree, Jesus found that the tree had leaves but no fruit. Upon seeing that the tree had no fruit, Jesus cursed the tree and immediately it began to wither. The apostles were astonished to see the tree wither. The tree becomes a type of Israel. Israel had the promise of fruit (leaves) but never produced what it should have produced. One could easily make the case that Israel bore no fruit because she surrendered the commands of God for the traditions of men. The nation's predisposition for human tradition constantly brought them into conflict with Christ and His teachings. Their allegiance to their traditions was responsible for their own blindness when it came to the truth of Scripture. It is interesting to note that when the disciples pointed out the following day that the tree had completely withered (see Mark 11), Jesus responded saying, *"have faith in God."* You see every time someone alters the design of God, it demonstrates a lack of faith or confidence in God' plan. God cannot bless unbelief. The nation had the promise of fruit but realized a curse.

Chapter Thirteen—Reformation Consequences: Evangelicalism

We have a very similar situation with the Protestant Reformation. The fault of the Reformers was two-fold. First they failed to organize their churches after the New Testament model. For example, rather than create an order of autonomy (self-rule) among their churches where Jesus was the head, they insisted on a human hierarchy. They also created a perception that membership in their churches was considered a national heritage (being born into a religious system) rather than a personal decision. Second, and perhaps most importantly, they devised doctrines that more closely resembled those of Rome than that of the New Testament church of the Bible. We have already pointed out their loyalty to the baptism of infants and small children too young to understand the significance of the ordinance. And, what of the distortion of the Lord's Table by both Calvin and Luther? Yes, there were principles for which they stood that were rooted in Bible truth and these principles proved to drive a wedge between themselves and their previous union with the Roman church. That was a good thing! But, a close examination of these matters will only serve to demonstrate their practice did not always line up with their theology. The Reformers' commitment to salvation by grace through faith certainly seems to be a contradiction of principle when one contemplates their view of infant baptism. And, what about the principle of "sola scriptura"? Can someone truly believe in the authority of Scripture and then reject its authority when it may hinder the "movement"?

We must be careful not to measure the Protestant Reformation of the sixteenth century by our experience with the more moderate and even "baptistic" positions of evangelicals in our own day. Much of Protestantism has been Americanized and no longer reflects the attitudes and actions of the original Reformers at least in America. However, the evangelical movement of today is a direct byproduct of the Protestant Reformation. How? The answer to this must come from an honest evaluation of the reform movement. The Protestant Reformation contained the leaven of human tradition and as it spread in the loaf, the movement ceased producing fruit that would remain. Although it has continued to exist in its various forms for the past five hundred years, it continues to wither. Evangelicalism is the evidence of this conclusion. In the eighteenth century the Reformation gave birth to evangelicalism via the Church of England as a direct result of that church's allegiance to human tradition. The irony of this is that evangelicalism has continued on the same path.

A passage in John 15 that we are all familiar with may be very pertinent to our discussion. It is clear from this passage that unless the disciple (*"branch"*) abides in Christ, he will not bear fruit that remains. The key according to John 15:7, is to abide in His Word (*"keep my commandments"* v. 10). By inference, the branch (in Christ, v. 2) that does not abide in the Word is taken away (15:2) and is *"cast forth…and is withered"* (15:6).

So the debate is not whether the disciple is saved but whether he abides in the *Word*. Remember, a little leaven will infect the whole! The destructive effects of such leaven will become even more clear as time goes on.

Quoting D.B. Ray in his book *Baptist Succession*, "…various branches have gone out from these three leading Protestant churches [Lutheran, Reformed, and Anglican], which originated in the sixteenth century. And, besides all the other disqualifications, these churches want about fifteen hundred years of being old enough to claim to be the church that Jesus Christ established; they all came out of the Church of Rome; their ordinances came from Antichrist; they have all persecuted the Baptists for the sake of conscience, and they are all state churches, in every land where it is possible for them to establish themselves. And, while many good men belong to these denominations, we must conclude that they are not the churches of the Lord Jesus Christ."[3]

The mark of any false system of belief is that of regeneration by personal merit as opposed to regeneration by the grace of God

Chapter Thirteen—Reformation Consequences: Evangelicalism

alone! Over time, the churches of the Reformers have been generally characterized by a belief in personal merit. Ironically, although each of the Reformers was correct in his understanding that salvation is by grace through faith, by allowing certain remnants of their old Catholicism (i.e., a sacramental view of the ordinances) to be added to their theological format, the leaven of personal merit has generally captured the thinking of their disciples.

The point is, any religion that suggests a man may approach God via his own righteousness is not in agreement with what the Bible teaches on the subject. The Bible clearly teaches that salvation is, *"Not by works of righteousness which we have done…"* (Titus 3:5). You see, once a system of human merit has been introduced into the theological mix, those works of the flesh always lead to a confidence in the flesh. Over time, rather than a simple faith in the redemptive plan of God alone (2 Timothy 1:9), men begin to count on their own righteousness to save them. Each of the original Protestant churches has thus wasted away under the decay of their own human traditions because they quite naturally spawned a confidence in the flesh.

Consequently, the theology of each of the Reformers can be examined under the light of God's grace and be found wanting. At the very core of this decay of personal merit is the matter of baptismal regeneration. It stands as a monument to the useless traditions of men. What it breeds is destruction, and it is an evident token of the fact that the movement was not wrought in God. God established one church with one baptism and one faith. Diversity does not produce unity but instead chaos and confusion, and so it is in our own day.

The irony of it all is that the Reformers created an environment that they would not have purposely designed and yet one they demanded for themselves. Each of the Reformers demanded the freedom of their convictions. But once they had achieved their goal with the aid of the secular arm, they practiced the same intolerance toward others with whom they disagreed as was formerly directed at them by the Catholics. However, it would be a mistake to underestimate the psychological value of the Reformation. While history records that the Reformers actually persecuted the Baptists, the freedom they won from Rome ultimately paved the way for Baptists and other non-conformists.

Without meaning to do so, the Reformers created an environment that suggested that the possibility existed that men might someday live in free societies—a place where every man might worship God according to his own conscience without fear of reprisal from a competing religious society. It would be many years before this became a reality, but the success of the Reformation as a movement gave hope to others.

The Reformers without question were great men. They were men of tremendous courage at a time when courage meant something. It could be said that God used them, but I think they fell short of divine intention. How different would the Christian world be today if the Reformers had identified the New Testament church correctly and yielded totally to the tenants of New Testament Christianity!

The church that Luther began almost five hundred years ago has proven to be a dead movement. The church created by Henry VIII to indulge his wicked behavior has proven to be impotent. The church started by John Calvin was anemic from the beginning, and given its predisposition toward making God a respecter of persons, would have failed miserably had it not been for the aid of a state-church relationship. Knox's Presbyterian church, although still with us in many forms, like the Reformed churches, still makes God a respecter of persons by virtue of its position on "election." For this and other doctrinal reasons (i.e., paedobaptism), it must be rejected as illegitimate.

Furthermore, the Reformation connection to Roman Catholicism cannot be lost in the discussion. The Protestant

Chapter Thirteen—Reformation Consequences: Evangelicalism

movement and the churches it has produced are the offspring of the Roman Catholic Church.[4*] Although this church was once a New Testament church, it very soon became apostate and thus illegitimate. She was unfaithful to the Saviour and ceased to be worthy of His precious name. All those who derive their origin from her womb are as illegitimate as she is, and have no right to claim to be the heirs of the kingdom. They are not the church that Jesus built. They are the churches that Rome built.

Just as Henry VIII fathered an illegitimate heir and covered it up by exchanging one false faith for another, so the Protestant Reformation is the byproduct of Roman corruption. It is important that we realize these facts.

Certainly, Protestantism was not as corrupt as its mother church (Roman Catholicism) in the beginning, but as Jesus said, *"wisdom is justified of her children"* (Matthew 11:19). Time has not justified or vindicated the Reformers. Truth has not been exalted but it lies in the street (Isaiah 59:14). The Reformation simply served to create more confusion. It added to the doctrinal mix!

Perhaps the most significant consequence of Protestantism is modern evangelicalism, and this brings us to John Wesley.

John Wesley, 1703–1791

The matter that remains to be dealt with is the legitimacy of so-called evangelical churches that most of us have become accustomed to seeing. If the fathers of the Protestant Reformation were the offspring of Roman Catholicism, then the churches known to us

---

[4*]The ancient Waldenses consistently identified the Roman Catholic Church with the Great Whore of Revelation 17 throughout the Middle Ages. The Reformers also referred to the Roman Catholic Church as the Great Harlot, "...altogether polluted with all kinds of spiritual fornication." (Durant, p. 611. quote: Knox, History Vol. 2 p. 18).

generally as evangelical are the stepchildren. As we examine the life and ministry of John Wesley, it should become quite clear that from him came much of modern evangelicalism.

Both John and Charles Wesley were exceptional men. There is no doubt that they loved the Lord and wanted to accomplish great things for the cause of Christ in their day. But our frame of reference is the New Testament church. The issue has to do with the legitimacy of the church they established in the mid-eighteenth century.

John and Charles Wesley were both seminarians at Oxford University, studying in preparation to become ministers in the Anglican Church. John Wesley had preceded his brother at Oxford, receiving a master's degree in 1724. He was ordained into the priesthood (as a presbyter or elder) of the Anglican Church in 1728.

While Charles attended Oxford, he was compelled with others to conduct voluntary student Bible studies. Charles Wesley could see that there was generally very little spiritual life in the membership of the Anglican Church. Yet, there was an obvious desire on the part of some of his peers to understand the Scriptures. About this time John Wesley returned to Oxford and became the leader of this fledgling movement (November, 1729).

These Bible studies began to spill over into the population at large and before long became a very popular movement within the Church of England. At first, the movement was simply known as the Union Society. Eventually it became known as *"Methodism"* because of its emphasis on a strict observance of religion, especially holiness. In the years to come this would prove to be the outstanding characteristic of the movement. The Wesleys were often accused by the leadership of the Anglican Church as being divisive, but to their credit, they did their best to bring to light the Scriptures among their fellow seminarians. The problem was that at this time, neither man was saved!

Upon graduation, they felt called of God to travel to America to minister among the native Indians in America. They came to

Chapter Thirteen—Reformation Consequences: Evangelicalism

Georgia in 1735 by ship—Charles as secretary to General Oglethorpe and John as a missionary to the Indians.

Within a few short months, Charles was dismissed from the work (1736). Two years later, John was also asked to leave the mission because he too was not equipped for the task (1738). Years later, John himself would acknowledge that he was ill-prepared spiritually for the ministry. He said, "I went to America to convert the Indians, but, oh, who shall convert me?"[5] Wesley clearly understood his lost condition at this time. He honestly declared, "This, then, I have learned, at the ends of the earth, that I am fallen short of the glory of God, and that my whole heart is altogether corrupt and abominable. I am a child of wrath and an heir of hell....I, who went to America to convert others, was never myself converted."[6]

On their initial trip to America aboard ship, a great storm arose that threatened the ship and all aboard. As John Wesley trembled in fear at the thought of losing his life and of what would become of him if he did, he saw a group of Christians gathered together by their pastor, Peter Bohler. In contrast to the other passengers aboard ship, these people were singing hymns, seemingly unmoved by the storm and at complete rest with whatever might befall them.

The storm eventually passed and all were safe, but Wesley was determined to find out how, in the face of such danger, some could be singing. He approached the leader of this small group and found that they were a Moravian sect of believers. Upon asking the reason for their confidence during the storm, the pastor began to share with Wesley that their confidence lay in a personal relationship with Christ, and whether they lived or died they were secure in that knowledge. This was something Wesley had never heard or understood in his own church.

After leaving America and upon his return to England in 1738, Wesley began attending the meetings of a Moravian society in London. During one these meetings on the evening of May 29, 1738, he received Christ into his heart and life. "In that moment," says

Methodist J.M. Buckley, "evangelical Methodism was born."[7] Who were these Moravians to whom Wesley owed his understanding of the Gospel and the salvation of his own soul? The Moravians were Anabaptists from Moravia.

It is interesting to note that Wesley's first society of converts was brought together under a Moravian congregation in Fetter Lane, London, but was later removed because of certain doctrinal differences between Wesley and the Moravians. According to Phelan, the first official Methodist Society was then organized in London in 1740, in an abandoned government building known as the Foundry. This building became the headquarters of Methodism for many years.[8]

John Wesley was convinced, however, that the Church of England was the true church, that it had replaced the Catholic Church, which he considered apostate. When certain bishops advised him to withdraw from the Anglican Church, John Wesley responded, "I live and die a member of the Church of England."[9]

So, John and Charles Wesley continued in the Anglican Church as ordained ministers for the remainder of their lives despite the fact that the Anglican Church continued in many unscriptural beliefs and practices, including the most offensive, infant baptism. Indeed, John Wesley advocated the practice, believing that it was an initial step of grace. For example, in Wesley's notes on Acts 22:16, he uses this language: "Baptism administered to real penitents, is both the means and the seal of pardon. Nor did God ordinarily in the primitive church bestow this on any, unless through this means."

On Romans 6:3, he comments as follows: "In baptism we, through faith, are engrafted into Christ, as we draw new spiritual life from this root through His Spirit...." And perhaps most shockingly, the following taken from a Methodist discipline for young ministers: "Baptism introduces the adult believer into the covenant of grace, and the church of Christ. It secures, too, the gift of the Holy Spirit in those secret influences, by which the actual

Chapter Thirteen—Reformation Consequences: Evangelicalism

regeneration of those children who die in infancy is affected; and which are a seed of life in those who are spared to prepare them for instruction in the Word of God."[10]

J.A. Shackelford's (1892) comments on Wesley's theology are thought provoking: "Certainly no one will dispute the fact that baptismal regeneration is taught in Methodist theology. This is easily accounted for when we consider that this church is one of the branches of the Catholic Church. The corrupt foundation of Romanism has divided its turbid water into hundreds of streams to spread itself over the earth, like the flood cast out of the mouth of the serpent (Revelation 12:15), to drown the true faith." "If the principles of infant baptism as inculcated by the branches of the church of Rome were universally practiced, the world would soon swallow the true churches. Then where would be the bride of Christ!"[11]

The movement that originated with the Wesleys while in training at Oxford continued to be a force within the Anglican Church, and was often referred to as the Methodist Connection. By 1743, Methodism had spread to northern England and still later to Scotland. Eventually this movement was exported to America, not as a church but rather as a movement within the Anglican Church. Remember, America at this time was a British colony. The first American Methodist society was formed in 1760.

By the time of John Wesley's death, the movement had grown to include some 2,000 societies boasting some 85,000 members in England. Believing that the Anglican Church would never legitimize the Methodist Connection within its ecclesiastical framework, Wesley instituted measures in 1784, to prevent the dissolution of his societies. Wesley issued an order instituting the *Deed of Declaration*. The declaration established an annual conference (General Conference), independent of Anglican Church authority, and also allowed for the securing of properties held by societies. It was not until after Wesley's death (1791), however, that Methodism in England was organized into a new church calling itself the Wesleyan Methodist Connection.

While at Oxford, the Wesleys adopted a doctrinal position that is very important to our understanding of evangelicalism in America. In the early seventeenth century, a man arose on the scene in Holland named Jacobus Arminius (1560–1609). After holding a pastorate in Amsterdam for some fifteen years, he eventually became a professor of theology at Leyden University. Still later, he studied at Geneva under Beza, Calvin's hand-picked successor. His beliefs soon fell into contention with the Calvinists. Most of what is known of him comes from his disciples.

Perhaps the biggest point of contention of the doctrine of Arminianism is a belief that someone, after receiving Christ as his Saviour, can lose that salvation by willful acts of sin.[12] The Catholic Church had positioned itself doctrinally centuries before in a similar way. If someone was barred from the Mass (i.e., excommunicated), then grace was no longer extended and a man's soul would be in jeopardy.

In other words, salvation as a result of personal merit was at issue, and so it was with the position of Arminius. Once again, salvation becomes a matter of personal merit or works as opposed to grace and grace alone. Jacobus Arminius died before he could have a full hearing in 1609, but his disciples are later found at Cambridge and Oxford Universities. Here at Oxford, the Wesleys became contaminated with this "Johnny come lately" doctrine. Although the doctrine was *methodized* by Wesley, it retained its central theme of "falling from grace." Remember, while attending Oxford University, both Wesleys were unsaved.

As Methodism continued to grow in the Anglican Church in America, Wesley found it necessary to assign two men to oversee the movement. In 1771, two laymen, Richard Wright and Francis Asbury, were sent to America and given the responsibility of overseers. Wesley later sent Thomas Rankin who joined Wright and Asbury

CHAPTER THIRTEEN—REFORMATION CONSEQUENCES: EVANGELICALISM

as "superintendent." As superintendent, Rankin presided over the first American Methodist "conference" held in Philadelphia in 1773. The conference acknowledged the authority of Wesley and the British Conference and resolved that the preachers should strictly avoid administering the sacraments, since none of them had been ordained.[13] Rankin left the country shortly before the outbreak of war as a loyalist, leaving only Asbury to continue the work.

The Revolutionary War had indirectly created a problem for the Methodists. The issue involved the sacraments in the Church of England. Since the Anglican clergy had returned to England before the war for obvious reasons, the Methodist societies, as members of the Church of England, had to go to the Presbyterians or Episcopalians to receive the sacraments. After the war, the Anglican Church in America came to its end as a state church. This change caused Wesley to rethink his position concerning ordaining men in the Methodist society. The Church of England had refused to ordain men with any connection to Methodism, especially those in America. Leadership within the Anglican Church feared the creation of a church within a church. However, Wesley feared the eventual dissolution of the American movement without the administration of the sacraments.

Wesley began to move quickly. According to A.B. Hyde, a Methodist historian (1887), here are the details. Although John Wesley was ordained as a presbyter or elder in the Church of England, he assumed the office of bishop (without Anglican Church authority). On September 1, 1784, he along with other elders, ordained Richard Whatcoat and Thomas Vassey as deacons, and the next day as presbyters. They in turn ordained Thomas Coke as bishop or general superintendent of the American societies (following the Anglican Church system of order). After arriving in America six weeks later, Coke summoned all the preachers to meet him in Baltimore on December 24. With the *Deed of Declaration* now officially separating their loyalties from the Church of England, the conference created the Methodist Episcopal Church of America. Thomas Coke and Francis Asbury were selected as superintendents. Asbury, who had merely been an overseer, was ordained a deacon, then a presbyter, and then consecrated as superintendent (bishop), all in the same day. Thus formed, Coke and Asbury were given the authority to baptize and serve the Lord's Table. The conference also reaffirmed its allegiance to Wesley during his life, as his sons in the Gospel, obeying him in all matters of church government.[14]

Francis Asbury (1745–1816) eventually became the more dominant influence on Methodism in America. He traveled thousands of miles on horseback in his efforts, and ushered in the age of "circuit riding preachers." "Coke especially, went everywhere baptizing children."[15] Before the formation of the Methodist Episcopal Church in 1784, on more than one occasion, both Coke and Asbury requested that Wesley ordain them as ministers, but that request was denied by Wesley until his death. Wesley strongly believed that there could only be one "true" church and that that church was the Anglican Church of England. He feared that Coke and Asbury might yield to the temptation to establish their own church in America, given the fact that an ocean separated them from Wesley's immediate control. But, as we have seen, necessity is often the mother of invention.

Was this church not created out of circumstances that were seen by its founder as a threat? Does not reason conclude that Wesley and Wesley alone, was the founder of that church? If Wesley was the founder, while a member and priest of the Anglican Church, then what of the legitimacy of this new church? And, what of the measures taken to secure its future, starting with Wesley's assuming the position of bishop to enable the quick ordination of others? If we question the legitimacy of Methodism, then should we not raise a question concerning the legitimacy of all those who have denominated out of Methodism?

CHAPTER THIRTEEN—REFORMATION CONSEQUENCES: EVANGELICALISM

It is from this Methodist Episcopal Church that many evangelical churches in America denominate (multiply), including other Methodist groups (i.e., United Methodists, 1907, 1932 and 1968). Churches that originated with their roots in Methodism generally

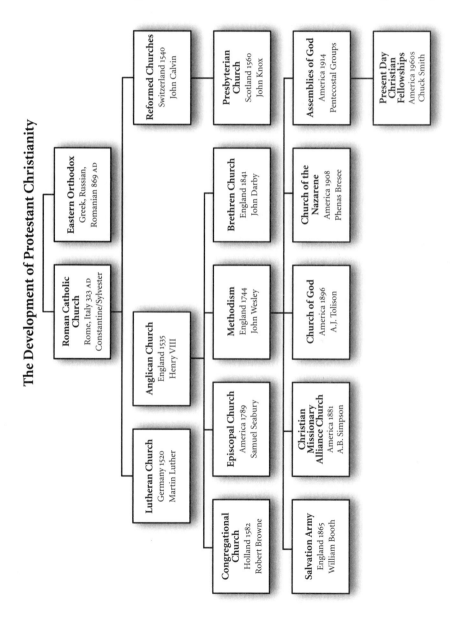

emphasize, in one way or another, the entire sanctification of the believer as a single event rather than a progressive work of grace. They also tend to be Arminian in their view of salvation, believing someone can be saved today and lose it tomorrow by willful acts of sin.

This brief history of the Church of England may seem somewhat irrelevant to labor over, but without a basic understanding of the pieces of this puzzle, one is tempted to exalt evangelical churches in America to a position that is not due them.

This chart delineates several of the most well known evangelical churches and their founders, as well as the dates they were founded. Without meaning to seem unkind to the brethren, given the history of the Anglican Church and the circumstances that produced most of the evangelical churches in America via Methodism, we must conclude that most evangelical churches cannot legitimately claim what they claim. They are not New Testament churches.

Someone might be saying to himself right about now that I am concluding that he, or some friend or relative, is not or could not be saved in such churches. Read carefully. I am not saying that at all! A person is saved because he places his trust in the death, burial and resurrection of Jesus Christ and His substitution in his stead. The salvation of any man's soul can take place anywhere the Gospel is preached in its purity regardless of the name over the door of a building. I am dealing with the claim of so many today that things can be different and still be the same—that things may not be equal to each other and still be equal to the same thing. My friend, unapologetically, this isn't so.

Jesus built one church—the New Testament church. The reason one church bears a name over its door that is different than the one down the street is because of the difference in doctrine. Again, God is not the author of confusion! God did not ordain that we have the diversity of doctrine we have today. Many have

Chapter Thirteen—Reformation Consequences: Evangelicalism

obviously built movements (denominations of churches) that are tradition based, not Bible based.

Now someone might say that this is a matter of interpretation, but God is the same yesterday, today, and tomorrow. God said what He meant and meant what He said when He said it. The faith was *"once delivered unto the saints"* (Jude 3) and is called a *"common faith"* (Titus 1:4). To believe that God is the author of doctrinal diversity makes Him the author of doctrinal confusion! To believe that God encourages men to be the determinant judges of Scripture through some warped and unscriptural view of interpretation, makes God out to be something less than ALMIGHTY, for *"no prophecy of the scripture is of any private interpretation"* (2 Peter 1:20).

The only justification for any other conclusion is to believe the Reformation doctrine of the *invisibility* of the church. This tradition, of human origin, teaches that all believers, regardless of their doctrinal persuasion, are a part of one great mystical universal church. We have shown that this kind of thinking flies in the face of what the Bible actually teaches on the subject. It requires that one abandon the Bible doctrine of the local church, and that one's personal experience or opinion be substituted for sound doctrine.

Once someone holds to a position that the church is mystical, then doctrine ceases to be an issue, and that is exactly why the Reformers and their offspring hold to this position. They cannot justify the tremendous diversity in their beliefs outside of saying that it does not matter, but it does matter. The soundness of a man's doctrine will determine in large part how he lives before God and man in this life. "What you believe" is important! It is important whether what you believe is of God or is of human origin and tradition. Yes, all believers are united by genuine faith in Christ Jesus. We have identified this "universal" union in Christ as the family of God, the household of faith, the saints of the living God; but these terms do not reference the New Testament church!

So, the Reformation movement eventually produced the evangelical movement via John and Charles Wesley. We have jumped ahead of ourselves a bit for the sake of continuity in order to make this historical connection in the eighteenth century.

In chapter 11 we found Baptists living in the Netherlands enjoying the freedom afforded them in that land. But now, we want to trace their movements from the continent into England and eventually to America. Along the way, we will correct some historical errors that have been perpetuated by some, either ignorantly or on purpose, and have led many to certain false conclusions. Regardless of the motive, the record needs to be corrected.

CHAPTER FOURTEEN

Migration to Freedom: The Baptists

The case has now been made that down through the centuries, the church that Jesus built has continued to exist in its original form and format, with its doctrinal integrity intact. These peoples and the societies of which they were a part were found in all the countries of Europe, speaking different languages and with differing cultures, but were corporately identified by their enemies as the Anabaptists. Their common label was the result of a unanimity of core convictions and beliefs.

Furthermore, we have briefly examined the movement of these peoples as they migrated across borders and entered regions of Europe previously unknown to them. They were forced to flee from their own countries to save their lives and the lives of their little ones. As they moved across Europe, ever seeking a place where peace with their neighbors could be found, they ardently carried their faith with them. They shared the true Gospel with all who would listen. Thousands listened to their message, and over time the Anabaptists became so numerous that nations feared their humble yet determined presence in their lands. What the governments of Europe feared then is what people in America take for granted today—religious freedom!

As already noted, there were some regions that had become sick of the bloodshed, and weary of the ever watchful eye of the Catholic Church over the decisions of their governments. The first of the European nations to consider religious freedom was the Netherlands. The Waldenses had entered Holland in 1182. Here the Anabaptists found a degree of freedom under William of Orange (1554), also known as William the Silent. This freedom eventually blossomed into the full freedom of their faith in 1568. William initiated an eighty-year war with Spain over the independence of Holland which was achieved in 1648. When permitted to freely identify themselves, the choice of their identity revealed an age old struggle over the issue of scriptural baptism.

The Anabaptists had always resented the implications involved in being called *Anabaptists,* given the fact that they never considered the proper administration of scriptural baptism a "re-do" of any original action. The prefix *ana,* meaning "again," placed before the word *baptist,* implied that they were simply practicing a second baptism of the candidate. The Anabaptists did not consider the first administration of the ordinance proper if the church performing the baptism was apostate. The issue was the presence of proper authority. The practice that most often identified an apostate church throughout the Middle Ages (although other issues were also involved), was that of baptizing infants. So when Anabaptists were able to publicly identify their societies (Netherlands, 1568), they chose to use the word *Baptists,* as it expressed their true convictions on the matter. However, it is a mistake to believe that this date identifies the origin of Baptist societies.

Baptists in England

A question that remains is how the Baptists moved from the continent of Europe to Britain and then to America. It is most often put forth that John Smyth was the first Baptist in England, so a brief history of Mr. Smyth and his followers is in order at this point.

Mr. John Smyth was an ordained minister in the Church of England. In 1606, Mr. Smyth along with Mr. Thomas Helwys led a group of Brownists, better known today as Congregationalists[1*] (a Separatist movement within the Anglican Church), from England to Amsterdam, Holland, where large numbers of non-conformists and Separatists had established congregations during the early years of the reign of James I. This was at a time when James I (1603–1625) was vigorously making good his threat regarding sectaries in England. "I will make them conform, or I will harry them out of the land." Persecution became so violent that these Separatists despaired of maintaining themselves in England.[2]

In Holland they united with an English church of Brownists pastored by a man named Henry Ainsworth. Smyth was likely first introduced to the theology of Arminius here in Holland as well as the Mennonite[3*] view of the New Testament church and that its membership should consist of believers only. By 1608, Smyth began to question the legitimacy of infant baptism, the mode and authority of their baptism, as well as their church order.

[1*]The Congregationalists were originally organized as Brownists under the teachings of Mr. Robert Browne about 1578. Browne had become convinced that both the Presbyterian and Episcopal forms of church government were unscriptural. He taught that each church should be independent one of another and that each church should practice a pure democracy. Because he believed that each church should be under the headship of Christ alone, their churches withdrew from the Church of England as Separatists. This prompted their persecution by the state. Although holding to many Anabaptist principles, the Congregationalists retained the practice of paedobaptism.

[3*]Mennonites was the name given to certain Anabaptists who organized themselves under the leadership of Menno Simons (1492–1559) from about 1536 onward, primarily in the Netherlands. They are in agreement with Baptists in rejecting infant baptism but allow baptism by affusion (pouring). They are presbyterial in church order rather than congregational. They are usually identified as Anabaptists historically but this is certainly debatable.

Smyth's group was eventually excluded from the Ainsworth group over the issue of infant baptism. The Smyth party believed that the Ainsworth group was in violation of the Scripture because they practiced paedobaptism. Smyth, Helwys, and thirty-six others set about to form a New Testament church. The problem was that none of them had a scriptural baptism. Smyth, in an effort to establish correct New Testament principles, baptized himself by affusion and then baptized the remainder of their number. Consequently, Smyth became their pastor. They soon after issued a Confession of Faith, Arminian in its theology, but distinct in its claims that a church should be composed only of baptized believers, and that only such should "taste of the Lord's Supper."[4]

Still later, a division arose between Smyth and other leaders of his company when Smyth became convinced that his baptism was invalid. Smyth, in opposition to Helwys, concluded that they should have sought out a proper authority to administer the ordinance of baptism. Smyth and twenty-four others were thus excluded from their own church. Smyth then repudiated his pseudo-baptism (se-baptism, "self") and joined a Mennonite church in Amsterdam. Smyth died in 1610 with an unscriptural Mennonite baptism administered by sprinkling.[5]

Mr. Thomas Helwys, the former associate of Smyth, returned to England with the remnant of Smyth's original company in 1611 or 1612. The remainder of the original group in Amsterdam united with a Mennonite church in 1615. Mr. Helwys established a General Baptist church (general atonement, Arminian) in London, and thus the credit for establishing the first Baptist church in England is often given to John Smyth as the original leader of this group.

However, this is most certainly not the case. Smyth never received "Baptist" baptism (immersion) nor did he ever return to England.[6]

The origin of Baptists in England can be traced further back in time than the seventeenth century. J.A. Shackelford in his book on

Chapter Fourteen—Migration to Freedom: The Baptists

Baptist history (1892) gives a very good illustration of the perpetuity of Baptist societies:

> Consider a railroad track two thousand miles long. A train of cars is seen to start on the farther end of the track with coaches unlike any other coaches. These are freighted with passengers who speak a dialect unlike any other dialect spoken. We follow the train for a distance of four hundred miles when it disappears into a tunnel and is seen no more for a distance of one thousand miles when it again appears and proceeds to the end of the track. The cars which come out of the tunnel, are identical in every feature with those which entered on the other side, and the passengers speak the same dialect spoken by those who were known to have occupied the cars until they disappeared from sight. Further testimony shows that subsequent explorers find at every eyelet (opening) in the tunnel evidences upon the walls, a dialect which has been spoken only by the persons occupying these coaches. Who will say that the cars did not pass through?[7]

The history of Baptists has often been a history of concealment. Their very survival required it. However, although there may be times during the dark days of popery when New Testament churches seem to fail and disappear from sight, it does not mean they ceased to exist. The fact that we find the very same people holding the very same doctrines later in history speaks of their perpetuation during the whole time.

The ancient roots of Christianity in the British Isles can be traced back to the first century as we have previously suggested (Simon the apostle). An author of English history, B. Evans, makes the following observation:

> The true origin of the sect which acquired the denomination of Anabaptists by their administering anew the rite of baptism to those who came over to

their communion...is hid in the remote depths of antiquity, and is, of consequence, extremely difficult to be ascertained. No one conversant with records of the past doubt this. The whole facts of history place the truth beyond dispute. I have seen enough to convince me that the present English dissenters, contending for the sufficiency of Scripture, and for primitive Christian liberality to judge of its meaning, may be traced back in authentic manuscripts to the Nonconformists, to the Puritans, to the Lollards, to the Vallenses, to the Albigenses, and I suspect, through the Paulicians and others, to the Apostles. Dissidents from the popular church in the early ages, compelled to leave it from the growing corruption of its doctrines and morals, were found everywhere. Men of the apostolic life and doctrine contended for the simplicity of the church and the liberty of Christ's flock, in the midst of great danger. What the pen failed to do, the sword of the magistrate effected. The Novatians, the Donatists, and others that followed them are examples. They contended for the independence of the church; they exalted the divine Word as the only standard of faith; they maintained the essential purity of the church, and the necessity of a holy life springing from a renewed heart. Extinguished by the sword, not of the Spirit, their churches broken and scattered, after years of patient suffering from the dominant sect (Catholic) the seed which they scattered sprung up in other lands. Truth never dies! Its vitality is imperishable....Over Europe they were scattered, and their converts were very numerous, long before the Reformation shed its light in the darkness of Europe.[8]

Without debate, the first churches planted in Britain were Baptist churches. The Roman Catholic historian, Lingard, was compelled to admit that in apostolic times "the Christian doctrines were silently disseminated among the natives" (Britains).[9] Thomas Crosby (1738) remarks in his book *History of the English Baptists*,

Chapter Fourteen—Migration to Freedom: The Baptists

"The true Christian doctrine, and form of worship, as delivered by the apostles, was maintained in England, and the Romish government and ceremonies, [were] zealously withstood, till the Saxons entered into Britain, about the year 448."[10] We know that Christians existed in Britain before Austin's visit in AD 597, for they resisted his control and expelled him. The laws of Northumbria in AD 950, demanded "every infant be baptized within nine days...."[11] The very fact that such a law was imposed upon the citizens by the Catholic Church would indicate a religious struggle in process.

After the year 1000, the Paulicians began to make their appearance in England. In 1154, a body of Germans migrated into England driven into exile by persecution on the continent. A portion of them settled in Oxford. Six years later another company of Paulicians entered Oxford and Henry II ordered their cruel mistreatment.[12] We have previously referred to the horrendous details of this matter.

In 1315, a man named Walter Lollard migrated to England from Germany when King Edward II was king of England. Walter Lollard was a preacher of great renown among the Waldenses in Germany. The disciples of Mr. Lollard came to be called the "Lollards." The Lollard Tower, a holding pen and place of torture, was so named because of the efforts of the Catholic Church to exterminate the Lollard preachers from England. One chronicler described England within a few years of their appearance as being one-half Lollard.[13] Lollard was captured and burned in 1320, but his followers and their influence continued for years, and the movement eventually merged into that of the Anabaptists. Bishop Burnet wrote, "at this time (1549), there were many Anabaptists in several parts of England. They were generally Germans, whom the revolutions there had forced to change their seats" [this is long before the arrival of John Smyth in 1601].[14] The Lollards, although they preceded Wycliff, were later identified with the work of John Wycliff as itinerate preachers.

A Baptist church was located at Hill Cliffe, near Warrington, in Cheshire county. English Baptists constantly mention this church as having its origin long before the Reformation.[15] It was spoken of as flourishing in the year 1522. The church is said to be at least five hundred years old and that Oliver Cromwell worshipped at this church. In fact, one of his officers occupied the pulpit there.[16] Describing the church, Goadby says in *Bye-paths in Baptist History* that it "has existed for several centuries in a secluded spot of Cheshire...removed from all public roads, enclosed by a dense wood, affording ready access into two counties. The ancient chapel built upon this spot was so constructed that the surprised worshippers had half a dozen secret ways of escaping from it and long proved a meeting place suited to the varying fortunes of a hated and hunted people."

He continues, "there is some probability for the tradition that the chapel itself was built by the Lollards who were of Baptist opinions. One of the dates on the tombstones is 1357. Hill Cliffe is undoubtedly one of the oldest (and most secret) Baptist churches in England. The extant deeds of the property describe the property as being 'for the Anabaptists.'"[17] The church extended mission works out in every direction that it designated as "quarters." Contributions came to Hill Cliffe from Liverpoole, Chester, Bickerton, Nampwick, and Newton, all of these churches being mission works (quarters) out of Hill Cliffe.

Shackelford stated that in 1891 he was in touch with the current pastor of Hill Cliffe church, a Reverend A. Kenworthy, who informed Mr. Shackelford that, "not only he, but his father, grandfather and even his great grandfather had pastored the church in previous times."[18]

As already discussed, the Church of England was created by Henry VIII in 1535. In 1538, Henry issued a proclamation against the Anabaptists, and in that same year, Archbishop Cranmer proceeded to burn their books and to deliver the obstinate over to the secular

Chapter Fourteen—Migration to Freedom: The Baptists

arm for punishment. The famed Erasmus wrote in 1528 that "The heresy of the Anabaptists is much more widely diffused than anyone suspects."[19] Ammonius, in 1531, writing to Erasmus of the great numbers of Anabaptists in England said, "It is not astonishing that wood is so dear and scarce, the heretics cause so many holocausts, and yet their numbers grow." Erasmus responded that Ammonius, "has every reason to be angry with the heretics for increasing the price of fuel for the coming winter."[20] These are obviously cruel references to the burning of Anabaptists.

Thomas Fuller, historian for the Church of England, tells us that in 1538, "Dutchmen flocked into England and they were Anabaptist of the 'Donatist' type."[21] These Dutchmen came to England because the lucrative shipping business there provided them jobs at the docks.

By 1550 the Baptists had steadily increased in their numbers. They were found in the court as well as among the common people in both town and country. They had churches meeting both publicly and privately in London as well as many other areas. Those who chose to meet publicly were often short lived, compelling most to meet secretly. Bishop John Hooper wrote the following to Henry Bullinger in 1549, "The Anabaptists flock to this place (London) and give me much trouble."[22] Bishop Fowler Short says, "Complaints had been brought to the Council of the prevalence of the Anabaptists...." "To check the progress of these opinions, a Commission was appointed."[23]

When Mary Tudor came to the throne in 1553, according to Crosby, "Baptists were very numerous...and no doubt many of the martyrs in Queen Mary's days were such, though historians seem to be silent with respect to the opinions of the martyrs about baptism...." Crosby's instincts were correct. According to Ivimey in his *History of the Baptists*, "the Baptists came in for their full share of suffering, and that many of the martyrs were of that denomination, which was then numerous."[24]

In the day of Elizabeth I (1533–1603), the Baptists were treated with the greatest of cruelties. Although Elizabeth showed leniency to the Catholics who often plotted against her, she hated the Anabaptists without cause. During her reign, Anabaptists were sometimes referred to as Baptists by government officials. Elizabeth's Secretary of State, Sir William Cecil, once wrote to the Queen of the imperfections of the country saying:

> The next imperfections are here at home, which be these: The state of religion many ways weakened by boldness to the true service of God; by increase of the number and courage of the Baptists, and the deriders of religion;[25]

J.T. Christian, quoting the opinion of Marsden, a Puritan living in these times, remarked, "But the Baptists were the most numerous, and for some time by far the most formidable opponents to the church. They are said to have existed since the days of the Lollards, but their chief strength was more abroad."[26] The reason for the evident increase in the number of Baptists during Elizabeth's reign was more than just evangelism. Elizabeth had given protection to Dutch and French refugees who had been displaced by conflicts with Spain. These refugees were allowed to establish worship sites according to their own views. Of course none of these were Baptist churches; however, it is possible that many Baptists came into England, taking advantage of the policies of the Queen. No doubt many hoped that England's openness toward refugees might mean they could find religious freedom there. Also, this open policy toward foreigners may have encouraged those Baptists secreted in England itself to become more obvious and open about their principles and practice. Regardless, there certainly seems to be an increase in their numbers during Elizabeth's reign, howbeit, often in secret.

By the reign of James I (1603–1625), many believed that the Baptists had all but become extinct. The persecution by both state and church had taken a horrible toll. But they did still exist and in great numbers. In 1615, they took a bold step. They addressed the

Chapter Fourteen—Migration to Freedom: The Baptists

King concerning their earthly plight. The title of their address was "Persecution for Religion Judged and Condemned." In it we read the following:

> Yet our most humble desire of our Lord the King is that he would not give his power to force his faithful subjects to dissemble to believe as he believes, in the least measure of persecution; though it is no small persecution to live many years in filthy prisons, in hunger, cold, idleness, divided from wife, family, calling, left in continual miseries and temptations, so as death would be to many less persecution; seeing that his majesty confesseth, that to change the mind must be the work of God. And of the lord bishops we desire, that they would a little leave off persecuting those that cannot believe as they, till they have proved that God is well pleased therewith, and the souls of such as submit are in safety from condemnation; let them prove this, and we protest that we will forever submit to them, and so will thousands; and therefore if there be any spark of grace in them, let them set themselves to give satisfaction by word or writing, or both. But if they will not, but continue their cruel courses as they have done, let them remember that they must come to judgment, and have the abominations set in order before them.

The appeal is signed by "Christ's unworthy witnesses, his majesty's faithful subjects, commonly (but most falsely) called Anabaptists."[27]

In 1633, a number of those who practiced infant baptism in London became convinced of the correctness of Baptist principles. However, they were concerned about the correctness of obtaining valid baptism. Because Elizabeth had exiled all dissenting ministers from England and because they did not feel comfortable with any religious societies in England, they sent one of their number, a Mr. Richard Blount, to Holland (Amsterdam), where a church was known to exist in regular succession from the ancient Waldenses.

Blount, who spoke Dutch, was baptized by immersion by the pastor of that church, Pastor John Batte. Upon his return to London, Blount baptized Mr. Samuel Blacklock, their minister, and they two, the remaining members (fifty three) by immersion.[28] This church then constitutes the first regularly (properly) organized Baptist church in England that can be verified by record. It was Calvinistic in its doctrine and is properly identified as a Particular Baptist church (a reference to the chosen or elect). But, as before, it is a mistake to believe that the establishment of this church constitutes the historical origin of Baptists. As we have demonstrated, their origins date to the earliest of times in church history.

The question as to why no regularly organized Baptist churches existed previous to 1633 is answered simply by understanding that it was illegal to promote and hold to Baptist principles in England. Both the Catholic Church and the Church of England sought to exterminate such people. Each of these state churches practiced infant baptism and baptism by sprinkling by this time, rather than immersion. Most likely, people holding to Baptist principles existed throughout the history of the English people, but under threat of harm, were not often organized publicly.

Again, Mr. Shackelford offers proof of this very fact by supplying us with a list of twenty-six regular Baptist churches supplied to him before 1891 by Mr. Davis, the eminent English historian of his time. Each of these churches was organized before the year 1640, and existed in 1891 according to Mr. Shackelford. The Baptists in America have thus been shown to have descended, in regular succession (proper ordination and baptism), from the English and Welsh Baptists during the seventeenth and eighteenth centuries.[29]

Baptists in America

So how did Baptists come to America? Millet, who wrote *A History of the Baptists in Maine*, says, "There is no certainty that any of the

Chapter Fourteen—Migration to Freedom: The Baptists

Pilgrim Fathers were Baptist."[30] However, it is also obvious that their influence was there. It is not unlikely that some of the pilgrims who identified themselves as "Separatists" held Anabaptist beliefs, for Cotton Mather, a Congregationalist, states that "many of the first settlers of Massachusetts were Baptists, and that they were as holy and faithful and heavenly people as any, perhaps in the world."[31]

Some mistaken ideas about where Baptists got their start in America need to be corrected. Roger Williams, who is often credited with being the founder of the first Baptist church in America, came to New England in 1631. When Williams arrived in Boston, he was already a resolute non-conformist (Puritan). In England he was mentored by Sam Howe, a Baptist minister in London.[32] After arriving in New England, Williams co-pastored a Congregational church in Salem, Massachusetts for a brief time. He was soon relieved of his position for doctrinal differences with the church that apparently involved Anabaptist beliefs (primarily the issues of religious freedom and proper communion). He also held that government could not give a citizen title to any land unless it was first purchased from the Indians. After his dismissal from the church in Salem, Williams spent two years in Plymouth as assistant to Pastor Ralph Smith. In 1633, he was invited to return to his former church in Salem as assistant to Mr. Skelton. However, Williams was eventually driven from the Massachusetts Bay colony in the winter of 1635 after writing a book that agitated certain magistrates. The treatise disclosed his strongly held beliefs and religious principles.[33]

After being banished from Massachusetts Bay colony, Williams took refuge among the Narragansett Indians and then settled in Providence, Rhode Island. Here he formed a society with those ten or twelve who accompanied him from the Salem church. According to the famed Cotton Mather, "The church came to nothing."[34] The details will prove to be very enlightening. In Providence in March of 1639, Williams was baptized by Ezekiel Holliman, a layman appointed to the task by the society. Williams then proceeded to baptize Holliman and about ten others in an effort to restore New Testament baptism to the little group.[35] Four months later, after having concerns about the legitimacy of their actions, Williams repudiated his own baptism and that of the others, believing it to be illegitimate because it was not done by an apostle.[36] He left the society with two or three others and became a "**seeker**," believing that no true church existed upon the earth. Shortly after the dissolution of William's society, Thomas Olney reorganized it in the same year. The church met in private homes over the next sixty years.

By virtue of the actions described above, Roger Williams is often credited with starting the first Baptist church in America. Williams is said to be its founder, and 1639 is given as the date of its inception. However, the church had no official creed or covenant until 1700. Furthermore, there were no records kept until 1775, and many of those records are known to be mistaken in detail.

As mentioned above, it is known that Thomas Olney followed Williams in shepherding the society after reorganizing it. Olney died in 1682, but the church continued until 1718. In 1652 or 1653, a division took place in the Olney society over the issue of "laying on of hands." From this division, a new society was formed under the leadership of three men named William Wickenden, Gregory Dexter, and Chad Browne. This society became known as the "six-principle" church, while Olney's group was known as a "five-

---

DEFINING THE TERMS

Seeker: *During the seventeenth century a "seeker" was one who believed that the true church would be organized under the authority of an apostle. Since none were to be found, it usually meant that the seeker never united with any society of believers.*

Chapter Fourteen—Migration to Freedom: The Baptists

principle" church. It was the six-principle church that started as a split in 1652–1653 that is identified today as the First Baptist Church of Providence, Rhode Island. The Thomas Olney church continued with no records of itself until 1718, and then disbanded and disappeared without a trace.

Given these facts, it is certainly questionable as to whether or not Roger Williams should be considered the founder of the Baptist societies in America. If he is not to be considered their source, then neither can we conclude that the First Baptist Church of Providence, Rhode Island is actually the "first" Baptist church in America. The history of this church itself is certainly dubious having started not in 1639 with William's baptism, as is claimed by some, but in 1652–1653 as a split. No doubt the small group of believers who associated themselves with Williams were sincere. Williams was attempting to establish a legitimate New Testament church according to the reasoning of his day. However, the method utilized to establish the church (se-baptism) was biblically incorrect. We dare not base the legitimacy of the work of God upon the sincerity of believers alone but upon their practice.

However, it remains that Williams played a very important part in securing religious freedom in this country. Quoting Mr. James Bryce, a distinguished Ambassador to the United States from Great Britain, "Roger Williams was the founder of Rhode Island in a clearer and ampler sense than any other single man—scarcely excepting William Penn—was the founder of any other American colony; for he gave it a set of principles which, so far as the New World was concerned, were peculiarly his own…he and his community deserved to be honored by those who hold that one of the chief services which the United States has rendered to the world consists in the example set there of a complete disjunction of religious worship and belief from the machinery of civil government."[37]

A more reliable investigation of the history of Baptists in America focuses on the history of the First Baptist Church of

Newport, Rhode Island.[38] The founder of this church was a man named John Clarke. Clarke was born in Bedfordshire, England in 1609. He was baptized and ordained in Elder Stillwell's Baptist church in London, England. In 1637, Clarke, a medical doctor, came to Massachusetts to preach the Gospel, where he was imprisoned for preaching purer doctrines than those of the state church (Congregational) in violation of the law. Fleeing persecution in Massachusetts, he eventually arrived in Rhode Island in the spring of 1638. Shortly after coming to Rhode Island, Clarke organized a Baptist church in Newport. With the help of Williams, land was purchased from the Indians in March, upon which a meeting place was erected. From its very beginning, Clarke's church and government was better organized and more populated than the society under Williams. In fact, at this time, the society under Williams had not yet been organized into a church.

Dr. Clarke served as the first pastor of the church at Newport. An inscription on Clarke's tombstone confirms the founding date of the Newport church. The stone reads, "...He [John Clarke], with his associates, came to this Island from Mass., in March, 1638, O. S., and on the 24th of the same month obtained a deed thereof from the Indians. He shortly gathered the Church aforesaid, and became its pastor...."[39] The date of the church's beginning is further confirmed by the minutes of the Philadelphia Association in 1738. On the occasion of the annual meeting of that Baptist Association, the minutes include the statement, "When the first church in Newport, Rhode Island was one hundred years old in 1738, Mr. John Callender, their minister, delivered and published a sermon on the occasion."[40] This church has continued in perpetuity to the present time with its original constitution intact. Thus, the origin of the first Baptist church in America is not that of Williams in Providence, but that of John Clarke in Newport, Rhode Island. The Newport church was established in 1638, predating William's

Chapter Fourteen—Migration to Freedom: The Baptists

church in Providence by one year, although William's society had existed without organization for about two years before.

It is interesting to note the words of Williams himself in a letter dated November 10, 1649, to Mr. John Winthrop. In defense of Dr. Clarke's evangelistic efforts at Seekonk, Williams says, "At Seekonk a great many have lately concurred with Dr. John Clarke and our Providence men about the point of new baptism, and the manner by dipping (immersion) and Mr. John Clarke hath been there lately, (and Mr. Lucar) and hath dipped them. I believe their practice comes nearer the first practice of the great Founder Jesus Christ, than any other practices of religion do."[41]

In 1644, the churches of Providence and Newport being established, the governments of both Massachusetts and Connecticut passed laws that "no persons, except members of the established churches should be admitted freemen, within their jurisdiction."[42] Massachusetts was so fearful that Anabaptist principles would spread into their colony, that they passed a law in November stating "that if any person or persons should within their colony openly condemn or oppose infant baptism, or seduce others from the approbation thereof, or should leave the Meeting House purposely at the performance of the ordinance, every such person or persons, shall be sentenced to banishment."[43]

In 1651, certain events compelled John Clarke along with Roger Williams to go to England to obtain a charter that would secure the continued existence of the colony. Although Williams later returned to Rhode Island, Clarke remained in England until the Charter was received in 1663 from Charles II. The charter is extremely significant because it represented an experiment in religious freedom. The citizens of Rhode Island desired a place where one could worship God according to the dictates of his own conscience without fear of repercussions from the state or the state churches.

According to the charter, "No one in this colony shall henceforth be molested, punished, disturbed, or brought to trial on account of

219

any difference of opinion in the matter of religion...but each one at the same time shall be able freely and lawfully to hold to his own judgment and his own conscience in what concerns religious questions...so long as he does not violate peace and quietness, and does not abuse this liberty in a licentious and profane manner."[44]

To the throne, it meant that the governmental (tax) support of a state church might become unnecessary if this experiment worked. The experiment, as everyone knows today, was successful, and religious freedom eventually won the day in America.

However, persecution of the colony by their peers continued for several years. It was seen as a society of vagabonds who had deserted the other colonies. In 1695, Cotton Mather said that Rhode Island "was occupied by Antinomians, Anabaptists, Quakers, ranters and every thing but Roman Catholics and Christians; and if any man had lost his religion, he might find it again in this general muster of opinionists...."[45] One official of North Carolina wrote the Chief Justice in 1696, in regard to Providence saying, "Tis necessary that place be taken care of and put under a regular Government, the present pretenders to govern being either Quakers or Anabaptists."[46] A letter addressed to the inhabitants of Providence by an association of Presbyterians in Massachusetts seeking permission to send missionaries to correct their errors was received in October of 1721. In response to this letter, the following paragraph speaks well of the people of Providence:

> We admire at your request, or that you should imagine or surmise that we should consent to either, inasmuch as we know that your ministers, for the most part, were never set up by God, but have consecrated themselves and have changed his ordinances; and for their greediness of filthy lucre, some you have put to death; others you have banished, upon pain of death; others you have barbarously scourged; others you have imprisoned, and seized upon their estates: and at this very time you are rending in pieces, and ruining people, with innumerable

Chapter Fourteen—Migration to Freedom: The Baptists

charges,...and you like wolves, pursue, and whenever you find them within your reach, you seize their estates. And all this is done to make room for your ministers to live in idleness, pride, and fullness of bread. Shall we countenance such ministers? Nay, verily: these are not the marks of Christ's ministry, but are a papal spot, that is abhorred by all pious Protestants....[47]

According to J.T. Christian, the first seventy years of the eighteenth century witnessed a marked growth in the number of Baptist churches in Rhode Island. From 1706 to 1752, at least ten churches were founded, respectively, in Smithfield, Hopkinton, North Kingstown, Scituate, Warwick, Cumberland, East Greenwich, Exeter, Westerly, and Coventry. In 1764, a new church formed chiefly of members from the First Baptist Church of Providence, was established in Cranston. In 1765, churches were started in North Providence and Foster and in 1771, one in Johnston.[48]

Following the Great Awakenings of the early and late eighteenth century, there were some thirty-eight Baptist churches with over 3,502 members in Rhode Island. Chief Justice Durfee at the 250th anniversary of the founding of Providence, spoke of the honor due Providence:

> The great idea here first politically incorporated and showed forth in lively experiment, has made the circuit of the globe, driving bigotry like a mist and superstition like a shadow before it, and sowing broadcast, among men and nations, the fruitful seeds of peace and progress, of freedom and fraternity. The little wisp of glimmering light, which hung, like a halo, over the cradle of infant Providence, has brightened and expanded until it irradiates the world. This is and will be forever the unique glory of our beloved city.[49]

It is apparent that the idea of religious liberty is distinctly a Baptist contribution. Out of the thirteen colonies, only three of the colonies allowed for some religious toleration. Complete religious freedom was found only in Rhode Island. The other nine colonies had formed state-supported religious systems. Religious liberty was clearly viewed as an evil in the early days of America's infancy, and Baptists were often seen as anarchists.

Despite efforts to drive them from the colonies, their numbers only increased. Benedict, in his *General History of the Baptist Denomination in America* (1813), lists fifty-eight Baptist churches organized from 1639 to 1750 in the colonies.[50] Hundreds were jailed or beaten for their beliefs. Much of the history of Baptist persecution during the colonial days comes from the writings of a Baptist preacher named Isaac Backus. Backus was born in Connecticut in 1724. After his widowed mother was jailed for refusing to accept Puritanism, Backus went on a thirty-nine year crusade for religious freedom. He covered sixty thousand miles on horseback stumping from Maine to South Carolina.

Besides his preaching and speeches on the subject of religious freedom, Mr. Backus wrote books and several pamphlets, all with the same theme: *church and state must never be united!* He also spoke before the Continental Congress as well as the Constitutional Convention on the subject.[51]

A Baptist pastor, John Leland of Virginia, was even more responsible for forcing this issue upon the founding Fathers of America. Leland was a very popular pastor in northern Virginia and had become friends with both Thomas Jefferson and James Madison. Leland ran as a delegate to become a member of the Virginia convention called to ratify the United States Constitution. His opponent was James Madison. The two met to discuss the election at a place now known today as the Leland Madison State Park. Leland was sure to win given his popularity as a preacher and Madison knew it. Madison secured the election only after guaranteeing Leland that he would make every effort to introduce an amendment to the Constitution that would secure religious

Chapter Fourteen—Migration to Freedom: The Baptists

freedom for all citizens. Leland withdrew and Madison was elected.[52] By the efforts of Madison and Thomas Jefferson, a Bill of Rights was formally added to the Constitution in 1785. The First Amendment of the Constitution thus guarantees religious freedom in America for all!

By the time of the American Revolution, Baptist influence had grown considerably. Baptists in general caught the spirit of patriotism. They gave their monies to the cause of the Colonies. Their ministers preached the Gospel to the soldiers and led others into battle. They supported the adoption of the Constitution and proposed the First Amendment in support of religious freedom and human liberty.[53] This growth was not due to the church in Newport alone. Many migrating from Europe, especially from the British Isles, brought their Baptist beliefs and evangelistic zeal. Without argument the greatest impact in America during the Colonial days was that of the Welsh. But before we give examples of the Welsh influence, it would be good to understand some historical context.

The oldest account of the introduction of the Gospel to England comes to us from Gildas who affirmed that the Gospel was first introduced into Britain during the reign of the Roman Emperor, Tiberius. Tiberius ruled Rome when Christ was crucified. Gildas' accounting suggests that evangelists sent by the apostles first came by way of France to Britain about AD 63. Rome had invaded Britain about fifty years before the birth of Christ and had established a Roman presence in the Isles.[54] It has already been suggested that the Apostle Simon or even Paul may have come to ancient Britannia according to some traditions.

Although Rome had brought Britain proper into subjection, she never conquered the Welsh people in the west. After a peace with the Welsh was achieved, Roman soldiers lived among the Welsh people for many years, and many of the Welsh soldiers joined the Roman army. It was not uncommon for Welshmen to visit Rome. In AD 180, it is said that two Welshmen (Faganus and Damicanus) who, after visiting Rome, were converted and returned to Wales as ministers of the Gospel. That same year according to Davis, the Welsh king, Lucius, was converted and sought to spread the Gospel among his people.[55]

In the second century, Tertullian wrote, "There are places of the Britains (saith he) which were unaccessible to the Romans, but yet subdued by Christ." Later in the same century, Origen noted that, "The power of God our Saviour is even with them which in Britain, are divided from the world." And Baleus said that, "...the churches (of Britain) also were exactly constituted according to Christ's pattern."[56]

Jeffery of Monmouth, in his book *De Britannorum Gestis*, states that "in the country of the Britains, Christianity flourished, which never decayed, even from the apostles' time, amongst whom, saith he, was the preaching of the Gospel, sincere doctrine, and living faith, and such form of worship, as was delivered to the churches by the apostles themselves; and that they, even to death itself, withstood the Romish Rites and Ceremonies." He continues, "...about the year 448, the English Saxons began to possess Britany; and that about 593, they having made complete conquest of the Britains,...that Gregory, Bishop of Rome, sent Austin the monk to England, to bring the Saxons into conformity to the Church of Rome; for as long as the British churches possessed the country, they kept themselves sound in the faith, and pure in the worship, order, and discipline of Christ, as it was delivered to them from the apostles, or their evangelists."[57]

Austin (AD 597) found that the old Britains (natives) were primarily in Wales, having been driven to the north by the Saxons in about the year AD 448. The Saxons had been invited to take part in conflicts against the Welsh by the Scots and the Picts. However, after driving the Welsh out of their ancient homeland, the Saxons never left. At Bangor (South Wales) Austin found a college containing some 2,100 Christians who had dedicated themselves to

Chapter Fourteen—Migration to Freedom: The Baptists

the work of the ministry. Austin was able to bring many of them to a council where he intended to impress upon them their obligation to embrace the church at Rome as well as the pope. These Christians refused his intimidations, whereupon Austin sought a compromise wherein they would at least conform to three criteria. First, they would celebrate Easter as Rome had determined. Second, they would give Christendom to their children (infant baptism). Third, they should preach to the Saxons (Catholicism).

These humble saints once again refused, believing the faith they had received from the apostles was purer than that of Austin. Austin, in turn, stirred up the Saxons against them to their ruin. Some twelve hundred ministers were slaughtered as well as other delegates representing the Welsh.[58] With this action by the Saxons, the faith that had endured in Britain for nearly four hundred years became nearly extinct throughout the land.

From this time forward, Britain was essentially a divided country. Baptists continued in the north (Wales) and the Catholics in the south. Before Austin's time, infant baptism was not a practice in Britain, but now it became common, except among the Baptists living in Wales. The Welsh historians maintain that these early Christians survived among the recesses of their mountains throughout the Middle Ages. Similar to the Waldenses of the Piedmont, these crusaders of righteousness never received or acknowledged the pope's supremacy.[59] It is from this grand stock of people, the Welsh, that many of the earliest Baptist churches in America were established, some by ministers alone and sometimes by entire congregations accompanying their pastors.

Early in the eighteenth century (1701), William Penn, a Quaker, granted to David Evans and William Davis thirty thousand acres of land to be divided and deeded to settlers from South Wales, some of whom had already settled in Chester County, Pennsylvania. This grant became known as the "Welsh Tract." Some of this tract was located in what is today Maryland, but most of it was located in

225

modern Delaware. The churches of the Welsh Tract have a rich history of church planting and evangelism. The following will hopefully give the reader a sense of the impact that Welsh Tract had on the development of the Baptists in America. The information is primarily from D.B. Ray, *Baptist Succession* (1890).[60]

In 1663, John Miles, along with several members of his church, came to America from Swansea, Wales. The Act of Uniformity (1662) in England had all but forced them and many others from their homeland. With their Baptist principles, Miles also brought their church records. They soon organized a church in Massachusetts that was also called Swansea. This church, located ten miles east of Providence, is the oldest Baptist church in that state and the fourth established in America. Also in 1683, Samuel Jones, with a number of others from Wales, settled in Pennsylvania and organized a church in Pennepek (Davis, *History of Welsh Baptists* p. 39).

Thomas Griffith emigrated to America in 1701, along with the entire membership of the church he pastored in South Wales. Griffith had originally organized the church in Wales that same year with sixteen members before coming to America. They first settled in Pennepek, Pennsylvania. Two years later they moved to the Welsh Tract in Pennsylvania where they formed the Welsh Tract Baptist Church in Delaware. They sent forth many ministers to further the Gospel in America. Among these are Elisha Thomas, Enoch Morgan, Jenkin Jones, Owen Thomas, Abel Morgan, and David Davis. Still other members of this Welsh Tract are responsible for the establishment of many Baptist churches as far away as South Carolina (Philadelphia Baptists Association p. 15).

Nathaniel Jenkins also emigrated to America in 1701. A Baptist minister in Wales, Jenkins became pastor of the Baptist church in Cape May, New Jersey (Davis, p. 114). Hugh Davis along with eight members of the Swansea church in South Wales was sent to Pennsylvania. There in Chester County, Pennsylvania they organized a Baptist church in Great Valley in 1710 (Davis, p. 90). Again from

Chapter Fourteen—Migration to Freedom: The Baptists

Wales came Abel Morgan in 1711. He pastored the Baptist church in Philadelphia (Davis, p. 69). John Burrows, a Baptist minister from West England, ministered in Philadelphia and later (1713) in Middletown, Pennsylvania (Philadelphia Baptist Association p. 12).

In 1737, the Welsh Tract church in Pennsylvania, lettered off (commissioned) thirty members who settled on the Pedee River in South Carolina and formed a church there which they called Welsh Neck.[61]

Griffith Jones, who was the able pastor of Hengoed church in Wales, came to America in 1749 and became a member of the Welsh Tract Church and an associate to Pastor David Davis (Davis, p. 103).

In 1722, Morgan Edwards was born in Wales and was educated at Bristol College (a Baptist institution) in England. Edwards came to America in 1761 and assumed the pastorate of a Baptist church in Philadelphia (Davis, p. 67). Richard Jones from England, settled in Virginia in 1727, where he labored for thirty years in the ministry following after Robert Nordin (Davis, p. 642). Caleb Evans was born in South Wales, educated at Bristol College, and came to America as a Baptist minister in 1778. He settled in South Carolina (Davis, p. 138). As mentioned above, many of the original Baptist churches in South Carolina were founded by ministers that came directly from Wales, while still others were organized out of a Welsh church in Rhode Island.

In addition to the Welsh, ministers came from England such as Robert Nordin, an ordained Baptist minister from London. He came to Virginia in 1714 and soon organized a Baptist church in Burley, which was the first Baptist church in Virginia (Backus, *Church History.* p. 229). Sixteen Baptist churches in North Carolina originated from the missionary outreach of this church.

According to Payne "A branch of the Anabaptists migrated in 1719 from Germany to Pennsylvania, and settled in or near Germantown, Philadelphia; these 'Dunkers' now number 200,000.

In 1874 many Anabaptists of Moravian descent left Russia and settled in South Dakota and Alberta.

"In 1707, the Philadelphia Association was formed. It was an association of five churches organized for fellowship and evangelism, and consisted of churches from Welsh Tract, Pennepek, Middletown, Piscataqua, and Cohansey. In 1742 the Association adopted the Welsh Baptist Confession of 1689 (London Baptist Confession) as their own, demonstrating their link to the ancient Welsh. The confession known as the Philadelphia Confession of Faith was printed for the general public by Benjamin Franklin in 1743. Those Baptist congregations that adhered to this confession came to be known as the 'Regular' Baptists."[62]

The Philadelphia Association had a huge impact on the organization and spread of Baptist principles.[63] However, the danger of such organization was evident, and in 1749 the Philadelphia Association made it very clear that, "Such churches there must be, agreeing in doctrine, practice and independent in their authority and church power, before they can enter into confederation (the Association)...is not to be deemed a superior judicature, or having a superintendency over the churches, but subservient to the churches...."[64] It is obvious that the Association was keenly aware of the importance of maintaining the autonomy of each associated church. The intention of the organization was never hierarchal nor would their member churches allow it!

Although it began small, by 1770 the Association contained thirty-four churches, and by 1791, it contained fifty-three churches. On October 12, 1762, twenty-nine churches gathered together under the appointed leadership of Morgan Edwards and Samuel Jones. It was determined that the Philadelphia Association of churches would commence the building of a college for religious training. It was agreed that Rhode Island would be a suitable location, and thus Brown University was born in 1764. James Manning was the first president of the college, and the first commencement was held in 1769.

The Great Awakening (1734–1745)

Before concluding this portion of our study, an examination of some of the details concerning the first Great Awakening and its impact on Baptist churches in the early eighteenth century in America is needed.

Although Baptists were not directly responsible for or generally involved with the events of the Great Awakening, they did in fact, greatly benefit from it. America was in a very low state spiritually in the early years of the eighteenth century. At the time of the Great Awakening there were but nine Baptist churches in Massachusetts. After the events of the Great Awakening and before the Revolutionary War there were twenty-seven. The Awakening started in 1734 among the third generation of Puritans according to historian J.T. Christian.[65] The descendents of the Puritans had continued to link the church with government, believing that the Bible was not only essential for the well-being of believers but also the benefit of society in general. The Mosaic Law was seen as the means and example of such governance. Many at that time rejected the puritanical rule of such beliefs, being unable themselves to live up to the high standard set by religious leaders. The result was a general decay in the moral fiber of the country.

In 1679, a Reforming Synod was convened to study the reasons for the decay. Thirteen conclusions were reached by the Synod. They determined that there was a decay of godliness on the part of professed Christians; pride and extravagance in dress; neglect of baptism and church fellowship together with a failure to testify against the Quakers and the Baptists; profanity and irreverent behavior in the sanctuary; absence of Sabbath (Sunday) observance; lack of family government and worship; backbitings, censures, reviling, and litigations between church members; intemperance, tavern haunting and putting the bottle to the lips of Indians, besides adultery, lustful dress and behavior, mixed dancing, gaming, idleness, covetousness and love of the world; opposition to reformation and leniency toward sin; a want of public spirit; and finally a general unfruitfulness under means of grace and a refusal to repent.[66]

Congregationalist pastor, Jonathan Edwards wrote in 1730 about his times that, "It seemed to be a time of extraordinary dullness in religion; licentiousness for some years greatly prevailed among the youth of the town."[67] A minister of New Hampshire wrote, "No serious Christian could behold it without a sad heart, and scarce without a weeping eye, to see the solid, substantial piety, for which our ancestors were justly renowned, having long languished under sore decays. Brought low, and seemingly just ready to expire and give up the ghost."[68]

Trumbull, a respected historian of Connecticut described the following sentiments:

> The forms of religion were kept up, but there appeared but little of the power of it. Both the wise and foolish virgins seemed to slumber. Professors (Christians) appeared too generally to become worldly and lukewarm. The young people became loose and vicious, family prayer and religion were greatly neglected...and the Spirit of God appeared to be awfully withdrawn.... Many of the clergy, instead of clearly and powerfully preaching the doctrines of original sin, or regeneration, justification by faith alone,...contented themselves with preaching a cold, unprincipled and lifeless morality;... for when these great doctrines were perspicuously and powerfully preached,...they were offended, and became violent opposers.[69]

Drunkenness had become so prevalent at community events, even at the funerals for the clergy, that the General Court was

Chapter Fourteen—Migration to Freedom: The Baptists

moved to forbid the use of wine and rum at all funerals in 1742. In 1678, Puritan minister, Increase Mather said, "conversions were rare."[70] No doubt the practice of burning witches, commencing in 1692, caused the loss of respect for the clergy and for Christianity in general. In Salem particularly, some one hundred persons were brought to trial. This was finally stopped, but the injury had been done to religion in the colonies.

The Great Awakening began in the midst of this spiritual climate. Specifically, it began in Northampton, Massachusetts with the preaching of the Congregationalist pastor, Jonathan Edwards in 1734. The effect of Edward's sermons was far reaching and began to impact many in the colonies. His most famous sermon was entitled "Sinners in the Hands of an Angry God." The preaching efforts of Edwards were later joined by those of George Whitefield, a Methodist from England who was prone to preach in the open air.

The trend of the preaching of both Edwards and Whitefield was decidedly Calvinistic. Many of the state churches were disturbed by the style and unusual occurrences that were associated with many of these meetings. This often led to protests by the state churches, and an effort to discredit them publicly was not neglected. Edwards was eventually forced to resign his church in Northampton. However, no one could deny the positive effect the Great Awakening had on the spiritual condition of America. The primary beneficiaries of the movement were the Baptists and the Methodists because of Whitefield's involvement. However, much of the gain by the Methodists was lost as the Revolutionary War approached, as we have previously explained.

Baptists were not directly involved with or part of the Great Awakening. The reason for this is threefold. First, the leadership of the Awakening was generally paedobaptist (baby baptizers). Second, the leadership as well as the thrust of the preaching was hyper-Calvinistic. Third, the movement was primarily among those loyal to a church-state system. These were all violations of the Bible-based principles held dear by the Baptists, and for which many in their ancestry had shed blood. However, the leadership of the Great Awakening stressed the importance of the Bible as the supreme authority in life and conduct. As men and women were converted or revived, they attempted to return to their churches but found them dry and cold. They were unwelcome. This resulted in an effort to establish new churches that would accommodate these new so-called *Separatists*. The churches created were termed "New Lights."

These *Separatists* took their newfound faith seriously, especially the admonition to let the Bible be preeminent. As they began to study the Scriptures, they came to realize that paedobaptism was not taught in the Bible. This prompted many of them to become Baptists. Cases of individual conversions to Baptist views were frequent, and the earnestness with which the new opinion was held approved itself not only by debating and proselytizing, but by strenuous and useful evangelizing, especially in the South.[71] Not only were individuals convinced of the correctness of Baptist principles, but many of the New Light churches themselves became convinced, and became Baptist churches by proper means.[72*]

By the end of the Great Awakening in 1745, from a humble thirty-seven churches spread across the Colonies, fifty-eight Baptist churches now existed by 1750. That may not seem like much of an increase, but remember, Baptists at this time were still considered heretical and anarchists. Over the next few years the growth and watershed from the Great Awakening continued, and by 1786, Morgan Edwards, a Baptist pastor, was able to compose a list of 135

[72*] By proper means, we mean to indicate that the members of these New Light churches would have undergone the proper administration of the ordinance of baptism by a proper authority (i.e., a Baptist church) and then the church would have been commissioned by a sending church (i.e., Baptist) that was satisfied that a correct order had been followed in the process.

CHAPTER FOURTEEN—MIGRATION TO FREEDOM: THE BAPTISTS

Baptist churches in America. According to historian John Asplund, by 1790, there were 872 Baptist churches with 64,975 members. By 1812, Benedict reckoned the following: churches, 2,633; ordained ministers, 2,142; members, 204,185; associations, 11. Finally in 1836, Allen gave the following statistics: churches, 7,299; ordained ministers, 4,075; members, 517,524; associations, 372.[73]

The irony of the Great Awakening was that rather than revival and reform benefiting the Protestant state churches, Edwards and Whitefield "were breaking up the fallow ground of their own ecclesiastical systems, and sowing seed from which a sect that was everywhere spoken against (Baptists), would reap a bountiful harvest."[74] Mr. Whitefield once reportedly quipped, "many of his chickens had turned ducks and gone into the water."[75] Whitefield's remark is an obvious reference to the many persons who were admitted to Baptist churches at this time by scriptural baptism, the Baptists having rejected their paedobaptism. Ultimately, thousands were brought to Christ and into New Testament (Baptist) churches. By 1870, there were over five million Baptists in America.[76]

There are many other churches and individuals that could be chronicled here, but the purpose is not to detail every event in the development of Baptist churches in America. The purpose is simply to give a sense of their arrival and growth in early America. From here I urge the reader to continue the study of the development and history of Baptists in America. It is a rich history and one that deserves to be studied by the serious student of ecclesiology.

PART FOUR

The Integrity of the New Testament Church

PERSONAL OBSERVATIONS

The Integrity of the New Testament Church

The study of the New Testament church in some ways is very similar to understanding certain principles of integrity. When we speak of a man's character, we generally focus on the qualities of a person that are most noble in life. We speak of a man's honesty, courage, temperance, and patience. Sometimes we have in mind a man's sense of humor or his kindness to others. Whatever the quality that marks a man's character, we all know that each of us is flawed. No man will be entirely perfect in character. Yet, for a man to be respected, there must be a high degree of consistency in his actions. He must live tomorrow as he lived today! His actions thus reveal his commitment to those qualities we think of as noble. When a man's life reflects such consistency, we speak of that man as a man of integrity, and so it is with the New Testament church.

The doctrinal consistency of the New Testament church down through the centuries reveals its true identity. Although we might find some variance in practice or church polity from one group to another and from one century to another, the fact remains that their doctrinal beliefs are strikingly similar. It is this doctrinal unity in every century that provides the continuity and cohesiveness that allows us to trace the history of New Testament churches.

To this point we have purposely emphasized two perspectives. The first of which is the light that the Scriptures bring to bear on the origin and identity of the New Testament church. In fact we began there because of our complete trust in the Bible and what it has to say concerning the subject. When taken at face value, without the admixture of human tradition and prejudice, it is the final authority. Second, we have examined the heritage or history of New Testament churches. Our purpose was to validate the claims made in the Bible concerning the church that Jesus built. These claims are made by Jesus Himself as well as other writers in the New Testament.

Finally, we want to address the integrity of the New Testament church. I am not the first to write about this subject and most assuredly will not be the last. Many fine writers over the last three hundred years have produced exhaustive works in the area, but they are often unknown in modern times and only come to light when their works are reprinted at considerable costs. Each of these works it seems was instigated during a time of general ignorance on the subject and sometimes even willful neglect by its own people. The same is true of their reproduction in more modern times. We owe much to those upon whom God places a burden to get back to the old paths and to remind others of the ancient landmarks that should not be moved.

We will begin by directing your attention to a brief collection of statements made by individuals worthy of noting not only because of their status among their peers, but also because of the content of their sentiments. They certainly were not all friendly toward the views of the Baptists. However, their views do reflect their honest opinions.

CHAPTER FIFTEEN

The Testimonies of Historians and Persons of Note

Ulrich Zwingli, 1484–1531

Ulrich Zwingli was the Swiss Reformer who, along with Luther and Calvin, spearheaded the Protestant Reformation. Zwingli was involved in several military campaigns in an effort to thwart the power and influence of the pope in Switzerland and was eventually killed in one of these campaigns. In 1525 he made the following statement:

> The institution of Anabaptism is no novelty, but for thirteen hundred years has caused great disturbance in the church, and has acquired such strength that the attempt in this age to contend with it appears futile for a time.[1]

The "church" that Zwingli refers to is the Roman Catholic Church of which he was a part as an ordained priest. With this statement in 1525, Zwingli dates the origin of the Anabaptist to the mid-third century. It was in the year AD 250 that Novatian led a movement out of the Church of Rome (still a New Testament church at this point) over the issue of church discipline.

You may recall that many had recanted their faith during a severe persecution of the early church. A candidate for the vacated pastorate of the Church of Rome was one such individual. After his election to that position, Novatian, who disagreed with his election, led a group of individuals out of that church. Others seeing his action responded in kind in many parts of the empire, thus producing the movement known as the Novatians.

The Novatians practiced Anabaptism and became a very formidable force throughout the empire for several decades to come. These are the people to whom Zwingli refers to as causing great disturbance in the church. Mr. Zwingli also said of the Anabaptists:

> You know without a doubt, and have heard from many, that for a very long time, some very peculiar men, who imagine that they are learned...have preached without the permission and consent of the church, have proclaimed that infant baptism did not proceed from God, but from the devil.[2]

Cardinal Hosius, 1504–1579

In 1554, Cardinal Hosius, who was the Chairman of the Council of Trent and the most powerful person in the Catholic Church outside the pope himself, said that:

> If the truth of religion were to be judged of by the readiness and boldness which a man of any sect shows in suffering, then the opinions and persuasions of no sect can be truer or surer, than those of the Anabaptists; since there have been none for these twelve hundred years past, that have been more generally punished or

CHAPTER FIFTEEN—THE TESTIMONY OF HISTORIANS

that have more cheerfully and steadfastly undergone, and even offered themselves to the most cruel sorts of punishment than these people.[3]

It was at the Council of Trent that the honorable Waldenses were condemned to extinction by the Church of Rome. The statistics reveal that Hosius had in mind the people identified in ancient times as the Donatists. You will remember that Donatist led a group of people out of the church at Carthage, and when he was summoned to appear before the Emperor he refused to do so, saying in effect that the Emperor had no authority over the church, just as the church had no authority over the throne. Those who agreed with Donatist's sentiments aligned themselves with him and withdrew fellowship from all with whom they disagreed. As previously noted, the Donatists practiced Anabaptism, and their influence extended for centuries. Cardinal Hosius then dates Anabaptism as existing at least as far back as the mid-fourth century, just after the union of church and state!

Johann Mosheim, 1693–1755

Because of statements like these from men living in the early centuries of the history of Christianity, the Lutheran historian Mosheim is quoted as acknowledging:

> Before the rise of Luther and Calvin, there lay secreted in almost all the countries of Europe, particularly in Bohemia, Moravia, Switzerland, and Germany, many persons, who adhered tenaciously to the principles of the modern Dutch Baptists…which the Waldenses, Wickliffites, and Hussites, had maintained some in a more disguised, and others in a more open and public manner.[4]

Mosheim, who was a celebrated historian of the eighteenth century and is considered the Father of Modern Church History, was

241

acknowledging that people who held the same doctrinal principles and practices as did the Dutch Baptist of his own day, existed far before the rise of the Protestant Reformation. Mosheim may have had in mind the ancient peoples called the Paulicians, the Albigenses, and the Waldenses. These three groups of peoples represent the ancient ancestry of all those who would follow in their steps down through the Middle Ages. Although called by different names, their identity is secured in history because of their Anabaptist principles. This connection to Anabaptism made the Anabaptists of Holland in the eighteenth century, in Mosheim's mind, the same as their ancient forefathers and spiritual benefactors.

Robert Barclay, Quaker Society 1648–1690

> As we shall afterwards show, the rise of the Anabaptists took place long prior to the foundation of the Church of England, there are also reasons for believing that on the continent of Europe, small hidden Christian societies, who held many of the opinions of the Anabaptists, have existed from the time of the apostles. In the sense of the direct transmission of divine truth and the true nature of spiritual religion, it seems probable that these churches have a lineage of succession more ancient than the Roman Church.[5]

John Clark Ridpath, 1840–1900

Another church historian who was well respected by his peers was the Methodist historian, John Clark Ridpath. Mr. Ridpath, although obviously not comfortable having to admit the fact, honestly writes:

> I should not readily admit that there were Baptist churches as far back as AD 100, although without a doubt there were Baptists then, as all Christians were Baptists.[6]

Alexander Campbell, 1788–1866

Alexander Campbell, the founder of the Christian Church (1824) said in reference to the Baptist sect:

> I would engage to show that baptism as viewed and practiced by the Baptists, had its advocates in every century of the Christian era…and independent of whose existence, clouds of witnesses attest the fact, that from the time of the Reformation, from popery, and from the apostolic age, to the present time, the sentiments of the Baptists, and the practice of baptism have had a continued chain of advocates, and public monuments of their existence in every century can be produced.[7]

Sir Isaac Newton, Scientist, Historian, 1643–1727

> The modern Baptists, formerly called Anabaptists, are the only people who have never symbolized with the Papacy.[8]

William C. King, 1900

Toward the close of the nineteenth century, a textbook entitled *Crossing the Centuries*, edited by William C. King and used at such schools as Harvard and the University of Chicago, deals with the subject of the history of the Baptists as follows:

> Of the Baptists it may be said that they are not Reformers. These people, comprising bodies of Christian believers, under various names in different countries, are entirely independent of and distinct from the Greek and Roman churches, and have an unbroken continuity from apostolic days down through the centuries. Throughout

> this long period, they were bitterly persecuted for heresy, driven from country to country, disfranchised, deprived of their property, imprisoned, tortured, and slain by the thousands; yet they swerved not from their New Testament faith, doctrine and adherence.[9]

Edinburg Cyclopedia

> It must have already occurred to our readers that the Baptists are the same sect of Christians that were formerly described under the appellation of the Anabaptists. Indeed this seems to have been their leading principle from the time of Tertullian to the present time.[10]

Tertullian was a staunch Montanist and was born about fifty years after the death of the Apostle John. In other words, the history of these peoples can be traced to the mid-second century!

J.T. Christian, Dutch Church Historian, Baptist, 1922

> I have no question in my own mind that there has been a historical succession of Baptists from the days of Christ to the present time.[11]

Dr. George C. Lorimer, Church Historian, Baptist, 1838–1904

> That the Baptists are more likely the oldest, is generally conceded and grows more certain with the progress of scholarly investigation.[12]

Dr. J.L. Smith, Church Historian, Baptist, 1881

We have submitted the testimony of more than forty of the world's best historians—not one of them a Baptist—who expressly and clearly point out the movement of these Baptist people through the long centuries back to the apostolic days.[13]

Dr. R.B. Cook, Baptist, 1864

Baptists are able to trace their distinctive principles to the apostolic age…When from the union of the church and state Christianity became generally corrupt, there still remained, in obscure places, churches and sects which maintained the pure doctrines and ordinances of Christ, and hence it is certain that these churches and sects held substantially the same principles which are now held as distinctive views of the Baptists.[14]

Dr. D.C. Haynes, Baptist, 1856

The Baptist church is the primitive church; there has never been a time when it was not in being.[15]

Dr. George W. McDaniel, 1925

Perhaps Dr. George W. McDaniel, past President of the Southern Baptist Convention, best summed up the point:

There is no personality this side of Jesus Christ who is a satisfactory explanation of their origin…. We originated, not at the Reformation, nor the Dark Ages, nor in any century after the apostles…. Our principles are as old as Christianity, and we acknowledge no founder but Christ.[16]

J.T. Moore, 1935, "Why I Am a Baptist"

> No church or denomination that began this side of Christ's personal ministry has any Bible right to make the claim to be a church of Christ. Therefore Christ's promise to the church He built was not made to Catholicism nor to the various sects of Protestantism that originated in and since the days of Luther's Reformation, but it was made to that church that no historian, friend or foe, has ever been able to find its origin this side of Christ's personal ministry, namely, the Baptist church. This is no new theory but a fact that is believed and taught by all loyal and informed Baptists the world over.[17]

The foregoing is not meant to be exhaustive by any stretch of the imagination. It is simply meant to give the reader a sense of the honest opinions of individuals who have expressed themselves on this subject. We have selected these not only because of the content of their sentiment concerning the heritage of Baptist societies but also because of their historical diversity. Many more could easily be provided if required. The perpetuity of Baptist societies down through the centuries—in spite of every effort to exterminate them—is a testimony to God's divine preservation on their behalf, and every credit for their existence to this present day must be attributed to God Himself.

Although statements like the ones we have just quoted are useful and interesting, they still pale in comparison to the authority of God's Word. First and foremost, we have attempted to lay a biblical foundation for the historical claims of this book. We have not approached this subject lightly or casually but with earnestness and sincerity. But still, it is the testimony of the Scriptures that carry the greater weight, and so we will make a final effort to draw the reader's attention to what the Bible has to say concerning our subject as we address the integrity of the New Testament church.

CHAPTER SIXTEEN

The Testimony of the Scriptures

The Common Faith

A matter that is often overlooked or even ignored by many evangelicals is the emphasis that the Bible places on the integrity of the faith. As we see that first church gathered in an upper room the language that is used to describe this fledgling group is revealing. They are described as being in *"one accord."* This little phrase is repeated in Acts 2:1. It is a statement of their oneness together. This statement is more than just a reference to how well they were getting along. It is a declaration revealing their *unity of faith*. They came together believing the same things. They were in agreement among themselves as to the things they had been taught by the Saviour. There was no diversity of beliefs or doctrine among them.

In addition, when some three thousand souls were saved and baptized into this New Testament body on the day of Pentecost, those new converts likewise are said to have continued steadfastly in the apostles' doctrine, continuing daily in *"one accord"* (Acts 2:46).

This principle however, does not originate here in the book of Acts. When we examine the high priestly prayer of Jesus in John 17, we find that unity is dependent on one's acquiescence to the truth of God's Word. In John 17:6, Jesus declared that he had *"manifested"* (made obvious or revealed) the name of the Father to the apostles and that they had *"kept thy word."* In addition, in verses 7 and 8, Christ acknowledges that the apostles had come to know that all things that Jesus had spoken had come from the Father (the Word of God) and the apostles had *"received"* them as such (see also John 14:23–24, 31). As Jesus continued in His prayer in verse 14, He clearly states that He had given them *"thy word"* and because they had received it as the Word of God, the *"world hath hated them."*

The world is no friend to God. However, please note that there is no indication that what the apostles had come to receive was in any way diverse one from another. On the contrary, the passage only makes sense if our understanding is that the apostles believed and thus acted alike! Thus, the world as a whole hated the apostles as a whole.

But that is not all, for Jesus was also addressing the matter of unity in connection with those who would come to know Christ as a result of the apostles' witness. In John 17:11, when Christ first mentions unity, he does so in the context of the Father. As He continues, Jesus makes it clear that His intention is that the apostles (as well as all those who will believe on Jesus through their testimony, see John 17:20) might all be one as the Father and the Son are one (John 17:21–22)! Does this not underscore the expectation of a common faith? I think it does. Thus, for the Christian to be one with Jesus, one with the Father, and one with other believers, there must, of necessity, be a common faith.

Jesus was not just advocating that believers get along despite their doctrinal differences. There is a presumption of commonality

Chapter Sixteen—The Testimony of the Scriptures

in His statements. So, it is the commonality of the faith, not the diversity of faiths, which unites believers together in Christ.

Consider the following verses:

> *Can two walk together except they be agreed?*—Amos 3:3

> *If ye love me, keep my commandments.*—John 14:15

> *He that hath my commandments, and keepeth them, he it is that loveth me: and he that loveth me shall be loved of my Father, and I will love him, and will manifest myself to him.*—John 14:21

It is this **"common faith"** to which the Apostle Paul refers in Titus 1:4. It is the same faith for which Jude exhorts us to "*...earnestly contend for the faith which was **once** delivered unto the saints*" calling it the *"common salvation"* (Jude 3). Now, how can God's people contend for the faith if it is subject to change from one generation to another or from one man to another. Why is it to be considered a common faith anyway? Because the source is a single source; it is from the mind and heart of the Father via the Son to the apostles.

Thus, we have the mind and heart of God revealed to men. We are further admonished in the scriptures that "*the scripture cannot be broken*" (John 10:35), and that "*no prophecy of the scripture is of any private interpretation*" (2 Peter 1:20). Just as God is immutable, so His word remains a constant. A thing cannot be made true nor can a thing become true. It is either true or it is not. For the Christian, something is true because God has declared it so in Scripture.

There is a great verse in the book of Psalms that states this principle very simply:

> *O praise the* Lord, *all ye nations; praise him, all ye people. For his merciful kindness is great toward us: and the*

truth of the LORD *endureth for ever. Praise ye the* LORD.
—PSALM 117:1–2

Moving forward several years in the historical accounts of the book of Acts we find the Apostle Paul and Barnabas *"Confirming the souls of the disciples..."* in Lystra, Iconium, and Antioch, *"... exhorting them to continue in the faith..."* (Acts 14:22). Still later in Acts 15:41, Paul and Silas went through Syria and Cilicia *"confirming the churches."* If there is no common faith in which we are to continue as Christians, then to what was the Apostle Paul *"confirming"* these early believers; diversity is our strength? I don't think so! Indeed, the Bible says, *"so were the churches established in the faith, and increased in number daily"* (Acts 16:5).

It was in Ephesus that the Apostle Paul gave one of his most powerful exhortations concerning error in the churches of Christ. Determined to go to Jerusalem for the Passover and believing that the elders of the church of Ephesus would likely not see his face again, he admonished them as leaders in the following way:

> *Take heed therefore unto yourselves, and to all the flock, over the which the Holy Ghost hath made you overseers, to feed the church of God, which he hath purchased with his own blood. For I know this, that after my departing shall grievous wolves enter in among you, not sparing the flock. Also of your own selves shall men arise, speaking perverse things, to draw away disciples after them. Therefore watch, and remember, that by the space of three years I ceased not to warn every one night and day with tears.*—ACTS 20:28–31

It is a warning for those who would be tempted to allow error to exist among their own company in the name of tolerance. Grace never requires God's people accept doctrinal diversity and human opinion as a legitimate source of divine revelation. In Romans 16:17, Paul concludes the epistles to the New Testament Church of Rome

Chapter Sixteen—The Testimony of the Scriptures

begging the brethren to *"mark them which cause divisions and offences contrary to the **doctrine** which ye have learned; and avoid them."*

The apostle further warns in 1 Timothy 4:1 that in the *"latter times some shall depart from the faith, giving heed to seducing spirits, and doctrines of devils"* and that *"the time will come when they* [God's people] *will not endure sound doctrine; but after their own lusts shall they heap to themselves teachers, having itching ears; And they shall **turn away their ears from the truth**, and shall be turned unto fables* [error]*"* (2 Timothy 4:3–4).

Where does all this tampering with the faith lead? The answer is found in 2 Peter 2:1–3:

> *But there were false prophets also among the people, even as there shall be false teachers among you, who privily shall bring in damnable heresies, even denying the Lord that bought them, and bring upon themselves swift destruction. And many shall follow their pernicious ways; by reason of whom the way of truth shall be evil spoken of. And through covetousness shall they with feigned words make merchandise of you: whose judgment now of a long time lingereth not, and their damnation slumbereth not.*

The end result of minimizing the value and importance of sound doctrine ultimately makes the truth itself the object of scorn and attack while believers become easy prey for every enchanted wind that blows their way.

The Common Error

If the Bible is a book of divine origin, and its entire contents contain the revelation of things God desires men to know about Himself… If God is not the author of confusion (He is the same yesterday, today, and forever) and He never sends mixed messages, then why is it that so many Christians today in the evangelical camp find it so difficult to come to grips with the matter of a common faith? Well, it is my belief that it has to do with an error that most evangelicals have come to accept as the truth. That error is the belief in a mystical universal body often identified by evangelicals as the *"true church."* The implication is that there is only one true mystical church of which all true believers are a part. Individual beliefs are inconsequential, and the local church is merely the natural byproduct of individuals gathering together because they hold the same or nearly the same doctrinal beliefs. Any challenge to those beliefs is seen as unkind and unjustified. A common faith is seen as an absurd concept, except when the subject of salvation is addressed, and then you must be at least close. But other than that, a man may believe pretty much what he feels is doctrinally sound in his own mind (making him the judge of Scripture), regardless of any scriptural contortion he must use to arrive at his conclusion.

This, in turn, has created a kind of merchandising of Christ where churches are marketed to fit human speculation and philosophy. Churches (or fellowships of believers) are purposely designed to meet the declared or perceived needs of the people. True spirituality is replaced by techniques and methods designed to move the masses to a higher level of relationship with God, while at the same time disregarding the necessity of doctrinal soundness.

So, let's deal with this **common error**.

The New Testament church is always viewed in Scripture as local and never mystical.

Let's illustrate the nature of the New Testament church by looking at some passages from the Bible with which the average Christian will be very familiar.

One such passage is found in 1 Corinthians 11. The subject that the Apostle Paul addressed here was that of the proper administration of the Lord's Table, Communion. The local church that he addresses had a reputation that was more carnal than

Chapter Sixteen—The Testimony of the Scriptures

spiritual, not only in this matter but in others also. It is obvious that they were not mature Christians, and their leadership did nothing to correct abuses. The Apostle Paul's task was to set many things in order in this church, and it required at least two letters to them and possibly as many as four, to do so.

The matter begins with an admonition from the apostle to *"keep the ordinances, as I delivered them to you"* (1 Corinthians 11:2). In other words, this was not the first time they had heard the things that were to follow, and Paul begins by emphasizing that there were no options here. They are called ordinances (laws) for a reason, and they are to be followed in a structured manner. The administration of the ordinances is not left to the whims of the membership of the church. This challenge to the church at Corinth was not unique to them, for in chapter 7:17, Paul sets the stage by saying that he had ordained the same things in all the churches. The apostle explains in chapter 4 that Timothy had also been sent to them to *"bring you into remembrance of my ways which be in Christ, as I teach every where in every church"* (1 Corinthians 4:17).

My purpose here is not to debate local church polity but simply to point out some implications in this passage that will illustrate our contention that the true church is local, rather than mystical in nature.

The apostle assumes that in order to celebrate the Lord's Table, it would require that the church members assemble themselves together in a given location. For example, he says, *"For first of all, when **ye come together in the church**, I hear that there be divisions among you..."* (1 Corinthians 11:18; see also v. 19). In verse 20, the same thought is expressed when Paul says, *"When ye **come together therefore into one place**...."* As you follow the discourse you will see this and other similar statements multiple times.

It is obvious that the *place* is a reference to the place of meeting for that particular church. Furthermore, a comparison is made in verse 22, when the apostle asked if they didn't have their own houses in which to eat and drink. Indeed, they had their own individual houses wherein they could eat and drink as they pleased, but the house of God was to be treated differently. Their conduct as they celebrated the Lord's Table was contrary to the very nature of the ordinance. But still, two distinct locations are identified. They had their houses and they had their church—not necessarily a building, but a specific meeting place where the church gathered.

From the foregoing discussion it is quite clear that the New Testament church is not mystical but local. None of the above matters or applies in an invisible church where doctrine and practice is relative and subjective.

Another example of the nature of the New Testament church is found in Romans 12:4–5. Here, the Apostle Paul clearly states that each New Testament body has many members, but not all of the members have the same office (function) in the body (local church). Their individual gifts differ one from another (Romans 12:6). However, although each church is composed of many members who are gifted with various spiritual gifts, the church is still to function as a unit, as individual members are in reality one of each other—a body.

The book of Ephesians reviews the means whereby men are saved (Ephesians 2:1–6); that men are not saved by works but by grace through faith (Ephesians 2:8–9). After being saved, we become a part of a building described as a *"holy temple,"* whose foundation was laid by the apostles and prophets (Old and New Testaments), Jesus, of course, being the *"chief corner stone."* Furthermore, this building is *"fitly framed"* together, suggesting that there is an order by which this building is constructed (see also Ephesians 4:16). It is safe to conclude that it is not left up to the bricks to determine that order! The order is set forth in Scripture, and the believer is to submit to the order it sets forth. Finally, in case you may be thinking that the apostle has in mind the mystical, universal church theory,

Chapter Sixteen—The Testimony of the Scriptures

Paul clearly identifies the church at Ephesus, as an example of the building (*"also"* i.e., among others) of which he is speaking:

> *In whom ye* [plural: members of the church of Ephesus] ***also*** *are builded together* [body] *for an habitation of God through the Spirit.*—EPHESIANS 2:22

The *"holy temple"* (verse 21) to which Paul refers is a reference to the local New Testament church at Ephesus.

The apostle also emphasizes the responsibility that leadership plays in the doctrinal purity of the local church (Ephesians 4:11–16). These men are gifted as evangelists, pastors, and teachers. They have been divinely gifted for the task. These administrative teaching gifts are designed for the purpose of perfecting the saints, the work of the ministry, and the edifying of the body of Christ.

> *And he gave some, apostles; and some, prophets; and some, evangelists; and some, pastors and teachers; For the perfecting of the saints, for the work of the ministry, for the edifying of the body of Christ: Till we all come in the unity of the faith, and of the knowledge of the Son of God, unto a perfect man, unto the measure of the stature of the fulness of Christ: That we henceforth be no more children, tossed to and fro, and carried about with every wind of doctrine, by the sleight of men, and cunning craftiness, whereby they lie in wait to deceive; But speaking the truth in love, may grow up into him in all things, which is the head, even Christ: From whom the whole body fitly joined together and compacted by that which every joint supplieth, according to the effectual working in the measure of every part, maketh increase of the body unto the edifying of itself in love.*
> —EPHESIANS 4:11–16

Even a casual examination of this passage reveals that the local church is the focus. The goal of God-ordained leadership is twofold: first, the unity of the faith, not the diversity of it; and second, Christian maturity. The result of these two principles, is that men will cease being children and will no longer be carried about with *every wind of doctrine*! In conclusion the apostle reminds the reader that the local church derives its life and order from Christ alone. He is the *"head"*! To ignore this as if it is irrelevant and then follow men and their traditions, is to remove oneself from the source of life and light.

So, the integrity of the institution of the local church is likened to the structural integrity of a building (Ephesians 2:20–22). This building, represented by local New Testament churches, is a holy endeavor. Each one is to be built upon a solid foundation (the doctrine of the apostles and the prophets) with Jesus Christ Himself as the cornerstone. It is fitly framed together! When it is built as it should be, it will be the habitation place of God (1 Corinthians 3:16–17). As the body (local church) it is fitly (properly) joined together (tightly) and is compacted (structurally held together) by every joint (connection) that has been supplied (sound doctrine) so that the local church might efficiently operate as it was designed, making increase (Great Commission) of the body (local church). The same concept is taught in Colossians 2:19 in a context of warning concerning false teachers that would spoil God's people through human philosophy and vain deceit (Colossians 2:8).

This description of the church makes absolutely no sense if applied to an invisible, mystical, or universal church. The very nature of an invisible concept of the church defies such an analogy. Paul uses the human body and the engineering of a building to illustrate not an intangible entity but a visible one! This is further illustrated in the concluding chapter, Ephesians 5, as the apostle uses marriage as an analogy of Christ and His church. But still, the nature of the illustration forces an honest man to conclude that the

New Testament church as seen in the Bible must be viewed as being visible and not invisible. There is no invisible, universal church! This is the **common error.** It has plagued Protestant Christianity for some five hundred years to date, and it is responsible for much of the doctrinal confusion that exists today.

The Common Duty

Perhaps the most tragic result of Christian indifference is the failure of God's people to observe the warning given by the Apostle Paul to the church institutionally. We visited this passage earlier, but as we conclude this material, it is fitting to return to the admonition of Paul found in Acts 20. Nearing the end of his own life, or at least his freedom, Paul warned the elders of the church of Ephesus that after his departure (death) *"grievous wolves"* would enter in, and would not spare the flock under their charge. He continued the warning, and in doing so he doubly emphasized that these wolves would arise in their midst, from among themselves. These individuals would speak perverse things and draw away disciples. The apostle's warning was broader in application than that of the church at Ephesus alone, for the historical record of Christianity bears out the reality. Indeed, wolves did come upon the scene, but the warning went largely unheeded and soon much of Christianity was enveloped in error.

The duty of believers in the early centuries was the same as that of believers today. It is a **common duty.** We are to watch! But, have we?

There are so many similar warnings on the pages of the New Testament. Jesus Himself said, *"He that is not with me is against me; and he that gathereth not with me scattereth abroad"* (Matthew 12:30). In the book of Romans, a book that is so rich in doctrine, Paul gave one of his sternest warnings of the New Testament. In this passage (Romans 16:17–18), the apostle commands believers to ***"mark"*** them that cause divisions and offences contrary to the doctrine they had already received.

Now, how could the apostle use such strong language unless in his mind there is only one faith; that believers are to identify those men teaching things contrary or at odds with that faith and avoid them. He also identified the real motive of such people, and it was not pure. With fair speeches composed of good words, they deceive the simple. The *"simple"* are those who have not come to realize that there is but one faith and are open to "new" things. However, it is obvious that the motive behind such activity is self-promotion, and those who do such things *"serve not our Lord Jesus Christ."* Doctrinal diversity does not advance the cause of Christ—never has and never will!

> *Now I beseech you, brethren, mark them which cause divisions and offences contrary to the doctrine which ye have learned; and avoid them. For they that are such serve not our Lord Jesus Christ, but their own belly; and by good words and fair speeches deceive the hearts of the simple.*—ROMANS 16:17–18

Please don't make the mistake of thinking that Paul was merely referring to what we would call "cults." Error is error. No matter how sincerely someone believes something, that does not make it correct. If a man's doctrine is unique to him and those who follow him, whether or not it is cultic is not the issue. How far variant it may be is not the issue. The issue is whether or not its origin is New Testament or more recent than the first century. If any man espouses a doctrine that cannot be traced to the first century and the Bible, it is error, and believers are to mark those who perpetuate such doctrines and avoid them. They are seditious!

That again is why the Apostle Paul could admonish young Timothy to *"charge some that they teach no other doctrine"* (see 1 Timothy 1:1–6). When men teach another doctrine they are described as *"having swerved* [they] *have turned aside unto vain* [empty] *jangling;"* That is not to say that those who teach a doctrine unique to themselves or their movements are not saved. No doubt some or even many are, but they have swerved from New Testament truth, believing what they hold to is genuine when it is not. Yes, we are to mark them who promote error and avoid them, but be very careful. Most Christians who believe something contrary to sound doctrine are just ignorant of the Scriptures. They simply believe what they have been taught. In most cases an honest study of God's Word would correct their error. But remember, we are brethren. Apollos would have continued in his error if was not for Aquila and Priscilla (Acts 18:26). My friends, we are to love the brethren even if we are compelled to separate from those with whom we disagree. May God grant us the grace to maintain a right spirit about these matters!

It would not be unkind or an exaggeration to say that few today seem to concern themselves with the soundness of doctrine. We are in a doctrinal freefall. The issue of wrong doctrine doesn't exist in the minds of many believers unless one is speaking of Mormons or Jehovah's Witnesses or some other questionable group. But how can we condemn the doctrine of others if our position is that doctrine does not matter; that all doctrine does is divide the "body"? C.H. Spurgeon once said, *"if truth is optional then all error is permissible!"* Rather than dismiss the truth as irrelevant, we should be embracing it.

So how is such a state of decay corrected? Well, the answer is simple. Believers in general need to return to the study of the Bible and the Bible alone.

> *Study to shew thyself approved unto God, a workman that needeth not to be ashamed, rightly dividing the word of truth.*—2 TIMOTHY 2:15

I am reminded that just as I have received Christ, so I am to walk. You see, every man who is truly born again is saved because he has put his faith in what the Bible declares concerning Jesus Christ—that He is the Son of God and that He came to this old sin-sick world, born of a virgin, to set the captives free from their sin and its punishment. When men turn from sin and confess with their mouths that Jesus is the Christ (Saviour) and was raised from the dead as evidence of that fact, they are born again into the family of God, and eternity in Heaven is secured! The key is faith. Salvation's journey begins and ends by faith, without which it is impossible to please God. Faith is really a very simple thing. It is placing one's trust in the declarations of God himself in His Holy Word. Now here's the point. Just as a personal relationship with God in Christ begins with faith, so I am to walk by that same principle.

> *That Christ may dwell in your hearts by faith; that ye, being rooted and grounded in love,*—EPHESIANS 3:17

If the Bible does not teach it, I am obligated to reject it and avoid those who teach the error. I am responsible to God alone. He will be my judge; not a preacher, not a friend, not a family member, but God alone. The faith by which you and I will be measured will either find its identity as gold, silver, or precious stones; or sadly, wood, hay, and stubble. We are to be rooted and grounded properly and built up in Christ alone. By doing so, we are established in the faith! But any believer can be spoiled. Any believer who is not grounded in the principles of faith is susceptible. If he fails to direct his heart in obedience toward the declarations of God in His Word, he becomes easy prey for those who, through philosophy and vain deceit, seek to draw him away from the truth.

> *As ye have therefore received Christ Jesus the Lord, so walk ye in him: Rooted and built up in him, and stablished in the faith, as ye have been taught, abounding therein with thanksgiving. Beware lest any man spoil you*

Chapter Sixteen—The Testimony of the Scriptures

through philosophy and vain deceit, after the tradition of men, after the rudiments of the world, and not after Christ.—COLOSSIANS 2:6–8

It is in Christ alone that all the treasures of wisdom and knowledge exist. So many today are led away from the treasures found in Christ by the newest fad or entertainment (rudiments of the world). It is a sad day, for example, when Christians determine where to attend church based on the quality of the band and the style of music or the charisma of the pastor.

In whom are hid all the treasures of wisdom and knowledge. And this I say, lest any man should beguile you with enticing words. For though I be absent in the flesh, yet am I with you in the spirit, joying and beholding your order, and the stedfastness of your faith in Christ.—COLOSSIANS 2:3–5

The distinguishing mark of all religious activity that is human in origin rather than divine, is always the flesh. Water always seeks its own level, and in the same way, carnal men always gravitate to carnal means in religious activity. Men beguile (to deceive by false reasoning) other men with enticing (seductive) words, but it is the steadfastness of true Bible faith that anchors man's religion before God and makes it pure and honorable. Thus we are to:

Take heed unto thyself, and unto the doctrine; continue in them: for in doing this thou shalt both save thyself, and them that hear thee.—1 TIMOTHY 4:16

Just as Paul told Timothy in 1 Timothy 6:20–21 to keep that which was committed unto his trust, so believers in every century are to be faithful to the truth. Believers are to avoid those things that are not of faith. Those who will dabble in diversity will soon find themselves erring from the faith.

If believers in any generation have a common duty to earnestly contend for the faith which was once delivered to the saints (Jude 3), then certainly those who live in these days should be all the more sensitive to this matter, for the Bible clearly states that in the latter days things will wax worse (2 Timothy 3:13). How much more then should believers be willing to accept their responsibility to contend for the faith? Paul told Timothy this very thing and in doing so, emphasized that it was to be clearly understood that some believers will depart from the faith.

> *Now the Spirit speaketh expressly, that in the latter times some shall depart from the faith, giving heed to seducing spirits, and doctrines of devils;*—1 TIMOTHY 4:1

The same thought is conveyed in 2 Timothy 4:1–4:

> *I charge thee therefore before God, and the Lord Jesus Christ, who shall judge the quick and the dead at his appearing and his kingdom; Preach the word; be instant in season, out of season; reprove, rebuke, exhort with all longsuffering and doctrine. For the time will come when they will not endure sound doctrine; but after their own lusts shall they heap to themselves teachers, having itching ears; And they shall turn away their ears from the truth, and shall be turned unto fables.*

What more could be said? C.A. Jenkins (1890) in his wonderful book, *Baptist Doctrines*, makes the following observation, "If Baptists are wrong anywhere, it is in the principles which they have drawn from the Word of God; not in the practical application of those principles. …If their principles are wrong, they should abandon them, by all means. If their principles are right and important, let them have the manliness and fidelity to stand by them, and God and good men will approve their course. In these days of religious latitudinarianism, when, under the cloak of charity, men are crying

Chapter Sixteen—The Testimony of the Scriptures

down creeds and formulas of faith, and calling upon their fellow Christians to give up, or submerge from view, this or that Bible doctrine, that all the Lord's people may appear to be one, is it not worth while that Baptists should stand firm, as the representatives of the grander principle that the Word of God is the supreme rule of life; that to do what God says is of far greater importance than the exercise of a charity that vaunts itself over the Bible, while professing to reverence and love it? To maintain such a position as this at this present time is of the greatest moral value to the world, to say nothing of the sacrifice of principle and conscience involved in yielding their position."[1]

It is tragic to think that we have come to a point in these days where the truth is evil spoken of. That is not to say that Christians do not value the possibility that truth exists. But to say that the general mindset of Christians seems to be that truth is not knowable with certainty. The average Christian believes he should never be so spiritually consumed that others will be made to feel that they are wrong; that would be unchristian!

All of this has brought Christianity in general to a point where a firm belief in the certainty of truth is almost non-existent. For many, truth is ever evolving, ever changing and because it is, they do not see themselves accountable to it. They do not fear being judged by it! And if anyone is forthright in these matters he is dismissed as unloving, or at least unkind. Truth is indeed evil spoken of today, and men seem to do that which is right in their own eyes!

Speaking of God's desire for the church, the Apostle Paul said:

> *That he might sanctify and cleanse it with the washing of water by the word, That he might present it to himself a glorious church, not having spot, or wrinkle, or any such thing; but that it should be holy and without blemish.*—EPHESIANS 5:26–27

The New Testament church has been set aside as a holy instrument of God. Its purity is dependent on its loyalty and commitment to the Word of God, the Holy Bible. When we question the Bible's absolute authority or challenge its integrity, we undermine the very foundation upon which the New Testament church rests. When we treat the Bible casually or as a book of suggestion whose value is determined by the perceived correctness of its interpretation, we have opened the door to a subjective estimation of truth. The proper understanding and study of the church of Jesus Christ reveals that it has always been, and forever will be, a glorious church without spot or wrinkle, or any such thing. Her doctrines have always been and forever will be pure without the taint of human tradition. The wrinkles of human philosophies that often drape themselves as garments fit for the church, have been thoroughly tried and been found doctrinally wanting. Indeed, the marks of carnality that stem from the rudiments of this cursed world have and will continue to be rejected by true New Testament churches, that they might be ***"holy and without blemish"*** before God!

CONCLUSION

We have now covered much relating to the church that our Lord established some two thousand years ago. I trust that it has not only been a blessing to the reader but a challenge as well. I suspect that for many, this may have been the very first time that some of these historic principles have ever been considered. The truth is that very few churches today will even deal with this subject in much detail. Where many Christians are quick to state the historic beginnings of their own particular church, rarely do we examine the historic origin, identity, and heritage of the New Testament church. As a result, some of the issues we have examined may have proved to be a new perspective to some readers. I think it is a shame that we are so quick to point out the human founder of our denomination but know so little concerning the nature and order of the church that Jesus started. It seems to me that without a good and proper understanding of the original, how can we ever be sure that we are a part of Christ's church today?

Recently, after one of our church services, a young man came up to me and asked if I could do him a favor. The young man attended a local non-denominational Christian high school in our area. His class was asked by their teacher to have someone from each of their respective churches write out a brief account of how their churches came into being and to make sure they identified the founder of their denomination or movement. So, the young man asked if I would be willing to write up this paper on his behalf. After explaining to me what the teacher required, I told the young man that I would be happy to do this but that he needed to understand that outside of Christ in the first century, I could not identify a human founder of the "denomination" we identify as Baptists today. I cautioned him this way because I knew that every other student in his class was going to declare a human founder and that each of them would be of fairly recent origin. He responded that that was exactly what he wanted. Then he told me that I must do this in less than two pages. I smiled and thought to myself that I had just taken close to three hundred pages to tell this same story in this book, *A Glorious Church*. I thought, "Someone may be getting cheated here." I sincerely hope you do not feel that way.

I would like to summarize what I have attempted to say. Crucial to our understanding of the New Testament church is the premise that the Bible never describes the New Testament church in *mystical* terms. The church of Jesus Christ is visible, and it is local! It is never described in the sense that all who are saved are a part of a single great and *universal* body called the *church*. This is a fabrication, and I personally believe its source is satanic. Yes, I know that is very strong language, but remember God is not the author of confusion. We have gone to great lengths to make the case that to view the church as universal is to allow for a wide variety and diversity of beliefs. To put it another way, it inherently breeds confusion not order. This position has been the source of great confusion down through the centuries, and it makes man his own "head" rather than Christ. When Christ is supplanted, you no longer have His church. It was Jesus who founded this church, and it is only as we align ourselves with the order and doctrine of that first century church that we align ourselves with Christ ecclesiastically. He is our head, our foundation and our cornerstone.

Surely, there have been times in each of our thoughts when we have quietly asked ourselves, "Where do all of these churches come from? They can't all be right, can they?" The answer is, "No, they can't be." But the general view of Christianity is rooted in a false belief that your doctrine doesn't matter anyway. What is most important is that you are saved and are thus a part of the "one true church in the sky." This unbiblical position keeps us from being able to answer these questions. It is as simple as that.

The Bible maintains that the church that Jesus began in the first century would perpetually exist in its original form and format (Matthew 16:18; Ephesians 3:21). There has never been a time when churches like this one have not existed. In every dark time in history they were there—perhaps hidden for the sake of survival—but just the same, they were there. Later when the hope of a better day sprung forth, so did these witnesses to the true faith. Although some—and perhaps at times even most of those who claimed to be the children of God—rejected the simple truths of Scripture as did Phygelus and Hermogenes of old, these New Testament churches continued to be the *pillar and ground of the truth* (1 Timothy 3:15). We have identified them by a variety of names although they simply preferred to be called Christians. We see them as Montanists in the second century, as Novatians in the third, as the Donatists in the fourth. While these held the light of truth, there were yet others who held the same torch—the Albigenges of Southern France, the Waldenses of Northern Italy, and the Paulicians of ancient Armenia. All of these ancient believers maintained that their existence could be traced to the first century and that they had been true to the faith of the original church. These all stood their ground when a mortal named Constantine secured the Christian crown, uniting church and state in an unholy union. They stood their ground when the church of Rome and their popes claimed supremacy above all others. They stood their ground when hellish doctrines such as baptismal regeneration, purgatory, the mass, and prayers for the dead reared their ugly heads. They stood their ground against the wicked practices of infant baptism, the selling of indulgences, auricular confession, kissing of the pope's feet, and the inquisition. Yes, they stood their ground, but they paid for it in blood.

Over time, their numbers became so great and their doctrines so similar that their enemies called them by a name that identified them as a whole. Being unique to them, it seemed appropriate to their enemies to identify them by a term of derision that spoke of their unique practice, Anabaptism. It was a common practice among them all because they were all pressed by the same Bible conviction—believer's baptism only. The practice of re-administering the ordinance to those who had originally received it in infancy or later, but had come from churches that had long ago aligned themselves with the state, served to be the defining difference between the apostate churches of Rome and the true New Testament churches of Jesus Christ.

As we have said before, these churches rejected the notion and the insinuation that they were re-baptizing anyone. They held that an apostate church has no authority in the first place to administer the ordinances! So, the battle raged on until finally we see the Anabaptists emerge as free men. When they were able, they cast off the name that held them in contempt by the world and identified themselves as the Baptists (baptizers). To this very day, they are seen as a thorn in the flesh in the Christian world. Their insistence on a proper baptism (candidate) by a proper authority and by a proper mode stands as a monument to their unwillingness to compromise the truths of Scripture.

Conclusion

Many of the principles—as well as our freedom in this great land called America—are the direct and indirect result of the struggle that has existed now for some two thousand years. It is a tragedy that so many of our Baptist brethren are woefully ignorant of their own history. Many Baptists have become more Protestant than Baptist. Still, I have not labored in order to lay a foundation upon which men may lift themselves up in pride and arrogance.

If you are a member of a Bible-believing Baptist church where you have been fortunate enough to have been taught these historic principles, thank God for it! These truths should ever humble us and cause us to be filled with gratitude before God. They should strengthen us and cause us to be more committed to our local New Testament churches each day we are privileged to serve within their walls.

It is my prayer that God will be able to use these truths in ways that only God can work. God's people need to be strengthened in this day. There is much error as a result of great ignorance. Many are caught up and captivated by the *style* of religion rather than the *substance*. To those who are searching for something that will make sense out of all the ecclesiastical confusion they see around them, I hope these pages have helped. Sometimes the reason things seem confusing is because pieces of a puzzle are missing. Perhaps this book has been able to return some of those pieces to you.

Let there be glory in the church!

"…Cast ye up, cast ye up, prepare the way, take up the stumblingblock out of the way of my people."
—Isaiah 57:14

Notes

PART TWO
Chapter Six

1. Shackelford, J.A., *Compendium of Baptist History*, Lansing, MI. Calvary Pub. 2006. (Reprint: 1892). p. 23.

Chapter Nine

1. A close reading of the events described in Acts 1 and 2 leads some to conclude that it was the apostles alone upon whom the cloven tongues sat. The fact that the *"cloven tongues like as of fire"* were beheld by some (*"appeared unto them,"* v. 3) may indicate that not all manifested the gift. The fact that *"it sat upon each of them"* does not by itself guarantee a correct interpretation that *"all"* in verse 4 is a reference to *all* present but may refer to *all* the apostles instead. Considering that not all of the 120 would have been

Galilaeans and the fact that those speaking in these languages were all identified as Galilaeans (v. 7), would seem to further support this conclusion. In addition, when Peter addressed the crowd in verses 14–15, he seems to point to a much smaller group (*"these"*) than what would have included all of the 120. Indeed, if the 120 were all responsible for the event, chaos would have resulted and it is doubtful that anyone would have been able to hear anything in his own native tongue. This is further supported by the fact that the passage indicates that once it was noised abroad, people came *together*—that is, to a single location to witness the event. Also, note that the languages represented in the passage is a small number not necessitating the 120.

2. In his commentary on the book of Galatians (Galatians 1:2), Luther writes concerning the church, "Wheresoever the substance of the word and sacraments remaineth, there is the holy church, although Antichrist there reign, who sitteth...in the highest and holiest place of all, namely, in the temple of God. Wherefore, although spiritual tyrants reign, yet there must be a temple of God, and the same must be preserved under them. Therefore...the church is universal throughout the whole world." In essence what Luther was saying is that regardless of the apostasy of the Church of Rome, they still maintained the sacraments and thus maintained their status as the mother church. However, he concluded that any church that maintained the word and the sacraments (i. e., baptism and the Lord's Table) thus retained the grace of God and was thereby legitimized as an agent of the holy church.

3. Indeed Luther, "while being pursued by Pope Leo X, found the only place to hide was among the Picars, a colony of Waldenses who were settled in Bohemia. Luther later reported that after he had more exactly informed himself of their belief, he owned them as brethren and commended them for being faithful Christians. Although he did not agree with them in all things, not being wholly freed from the impurities of the Church of Rome, yet he writes

to them with such affection and esteem, as abundantly shews the respect he had for those who for so long a time had opposed the corruptions of the truth." *Allix's Ecclesiastical History*, p. 321–322.

4. Durant, Will. *The Story of Civilization: Part VI, The Reformation*, New York, NY. Simon and Schuster, 1957. p. 376.

5. Hageman, G.E., *Sketches from the History of the Church*, St. Louis, MO., Concordia Pub. House. date unknown. p. 237–238.

PART THREE
Chapter Ten

1. Shackelford, J.A. *Compendium of Baptist History*. Lansing, MI. Calvary Pub. 2006. (Reprint: 1892). p. 40.

2. McBirnie, William, Steuart. *The Search for the Twelve Apostles*. Wheaton, IL. Tyndale House Pub. 1977.

3. Ibid., (quote: Clement, Bishop of Rome, *Letter to the Church at Corinth*).

4. Armitage, Thomas. *A History of the Baptists*. Watertown, WI. Baptist Heritage Press, 2 Vols. 1988. (quoted from Chandler, *History of Persecutions*). (Reprint: 1886). p. 172.

5. Shelly, Bruce L. *Church History in Plain Language*. Nashville, TN. Thomas Nelson Pub. 1982. p. 71.

6. Orchard, G.H. *A Concise History of Baptists*. Texarkana, TX. Bogard Press. (Reprint: 1855). p. 28.

7. Shelly, Bruce L. p. 134.

8. Orchard, G.H. p. 29.

9. Shelly, Bruce, L. p. 135.

10. Shackleford, J.A. *Compendium of Baptist History*. p. 56.

11. Sargent, Robert J. *Landmarks of Church History*. Book 1. Oak Harbor, WA. Bible Baptist Church Pub. (ref. from Phillip Schaff, *History of the Christian Church*.) (quote by Justin Martyr, AD 100–165). p. 34.

12. Ibid., (ref. Seeberg, *The History of Doctrines*. Vol. 1. quote: Justin Martyr). p. 117.

13. Ibid., p. 82. (quote: Shepherd of Hermas, AD 115–140).

14. Christian, J.T. *A History of the Baptists*. Vol. 1. Texarkana, Ark. Bogard Press, 1922. (quote: Wall, *The History of Infant Baptism* Vol. 1, p. 265). p. 33.

15. Shackelford, J.A. *A Compendium of Baptist History*. p. 168–172.

16. Orchard, G.H. p. 64–67.

17. Armitage. (quote: Niebuhr, *History of Rome*, Lec. lxxix). p. 204–5

18. Ibid., (quote: Cardinal Baronius). p. 205.

19. Ibid., (quote: Polidore Virgil, Lib. iii, ch. i).

20. Ibid., Vol 1. (quote: Guillaume du Choul, *Mons. Drelingcourt, Visage de L' Antiquite*). p. 205–6.

21. Ibid., Vol 1. p. 206.

22. Verduin, Leonard. *The Reformers and Their Stepchildren*. Grand Rapids, MI. Eerdmans Pub. Co. 1964. p. 34.

23. The Montanists maintained that theirs was not a new form of Christianity but a recovery of the old, the primitive church set over against the obvious corruptions of the current Christianity. The old church had demanded purity; the new church had struck a bargin with the world, and had arranged itself comfortably with it, and they (the Montanists) would therefore, break with it. (Moeller, Montanism. Schaff-Herzog Encyclopedia, Vol. 3. 1562).

24. Christian, J.T. Vol. 1. (quote: Schaff, History of the Christian Church., Vol. 2. p. 427). p. 43.

25. Orchard, G.H. pp. 32–34.

26. Christian, J.T. Vol. 1. (quote: Epiphanius, Hoer, XLVIII. 1). p. 44.

27. Ray, D.B. *Baptist Succession*. St. Louis, MO. National Baptist Pub. Co. (ref. Robinson's *Ecclesiastical Researches*. p. 126). (Reprint: 1890). p.189.

28. Sargent, Robert J. *Landmarks of Church History.* Book 1. (quote: Schaff, *History of the Christian Church.* p. 92). p. 62.

29. Christian, J.T., (quote: Robinson. *Ecclesiastical Researches.* Cambridge. 1792. p. 126). p. 44.

30. Armitage, Thomas. p. 200–201.

31. Ibid., (quote: Mosheim). p. 203.

Chapter Eleven

1. Shackelford, J.A., *Compendium of Baptist History.* p. 45.
2. Christian, J.T. *A History of the Baptist.* Vol. 1. p. 49.
3. Newman, Albert Henry. *A Manual of Church History.* Vol 1, Valley Forge. American Baptist Pub. 1903. pp. 380, 381.
4. Christian, J.T. Vol. 1. pp. 48–50.
5. Orchard, G.H. *A Concise History of Baptists.* p. 137.
6. Christian, J.T. Vol. 1. pp. 48–50.
7. Ibid., p. 60.
8. Mr. McBirnie (*The Search*, pp. 126–7) briefly outlines the evidence for this statement citing the writing of Isidore, the Archbishop of Seville (AD 600–636) in which he states that "Philip preached Christ to the Gauls (ancient France), and brought barbarous and neighboring nations seated in darkness…to the light of knowledge and port of faith." (Isidore, *De ortu et obitu Patrum, Cap LXXIII 131*). Bede, born in AD 673, according to Usher (*Antiquities, Cap 2*) assigns Gaul to Phillip in his work *Collections and Flowers.*
9. A full and detailed account of these events is given by many authors but perhaps the most detailed comes from Peter Allix, *The Ecclesiastical History of the Ancient Churches of the Piedmont and of the Albigenses*, Chap. XXI. 1692.
10. Jones, William. *The History of the Christian Church.* Spencer H Cone Pub. New York, NY. 1824. p. 108.
11. Ray, D.B. (quote: Perrin, *History of the Waldenses.* 1847. p. 144). p. 339.

12. Jones, William. p. 135.

13. Christian, J.T. Vol. 1. (quote: Schmidt, History et. Doctrine de la secte des Cathares, Vol. 2. p. 94). p. 64.

14. Ibid., p. 62.

15. From Jones' History we are told that Reinerius Saccho, an inquisitor who lived only eighty years after the time of Waldo, admits that the Waldenses flourished five hundred years before that preacher (Jones' History, p. 232). Allix continues to quote Saccho, "among all the sects that either are, or have been, there is none more dangerous to the Church than that of the Leonists (Waldenses), and that for three reasons: The first is, because it is the sect that is the longest standing of any; for some say it hath been continued down ever since the time of Pope Sylvester (AD 325), and others since that of the apostles. The second is, because it is the most general of all sects; for scarcely is there any country to be found where this sect hath not spread itself." (Allix, *Ecclesiastical History*, p. 192).

16. Ray, D.B. p. 179.

17. Ibid., (quote: Religious Encyclopedia, p. 1148). p. 181.

18. Ibid., p. 185.

19. Ibid., (quote: Jones p. 354) p. 176.

20. Christian, J.T., Vol. 1, (quote: Moreland, *History of Evangelical Churches*, p. 7) p. 73.

21. Allix, Peter. *The Ecclesiastical History of the Ancient Churches of Piedmont and of The Albigenses*. Gallatin, TN. Church History and Research Archives. 1989. (Reprint: 1821, orig. pub. 1690). p. 364.

22. Ibid., p. 209.

23. Ray, D.B. *Baptist Succession*. (quote: Perrin's History). p. 323.

24. Ibid., (quote: Robinson p. 461) p. 325–6.

25. Jones, William. p. 70.

26. Ibid., p. 77.

27. In 1554 the Waldenses drafted a Confession of Faith for the King of France that among other things, addresses their practice

of receiving individuals into their membership. "We believe that in the ordinance of baptism the water is the visible and external sign, which represents to us that which, by virtue of God's invisible operation, is within us, the renovation of our minds, and the mortification of our members through (the faith of) Jesus Christ. And by this ordinance we are received into the holy congregation of God's people, previously professing our faith and the changed of life. (J.T. Christian, *A History*, p. 78. quote: Sleiden, *The General History of the Reformation*, London, 1689. p. 347).

28. Ray, D.B. p. 338.
29. Ibid.
30. Ibid., p. 340.
31. Jones, William. p. 201–202.
32. Ibid., p. 207.
33. Ray, D.B. p. 343–347.
34. Ibid., p. 178.
35. Ibid., p. 349.
36. Jones, William. p. 412–413.
37. Ray, D.B. p. 342.
38. Cramp, J.M. *Baptist History*. Watertown, WI. Baptist Heritage Pub. 1987. (Reprint: 1871). p. 79.
39. Christian, J.T. Vol. 1. p. 87.
40. Ibid., pp. 89, 90.
41. Ibid., (Ref., Cramer and Pyper, *Bibliotheca Reformatoria Neerlandica*, VII. p. 510). p. 92.
42. Ibid., (quote: J.J. Van Oosterzee from Herzog's Real Encyclopedia, IX. p. 346) p. 93.
43. Durant, Will. *The Story of Civilization VI; The Reformation*. New York, NY. Simon and Schuster, 1957. (quote: Kautsky, Karl, 1897). p. 397.
44. Armitage, Thomas. Vol. 1. p. 407.
45. Durant, Will. *The Reformation*. p. 633.
46. Armitage, Thomas. Vol. 1. pp. 411, 414.
47. Durant, Will. p. 634.

48. Armitage. Vol 1. p. 416.
49. Verduin, Leonard. *The Reformers and Their Stepchildren.* pp. 189, 190.

Chapter Twelve

1. Phelan, M. *Handbook of All Denominations.* Nashville, TN., Cokesbury Press, 1929. p. 121.
2. Durant, Will. *The Reformation.* p. 376.
3. Ibid., p. 377.
4. Sargent, Robert J. *Landmarks of Church History.* Book 2. (quote: L. Verduin, *The Anatomy of A Hybrid*, pp. 159, 160). p. 250.
5. Mason, Roy. *The Church That Jesus Built.* Emmaus, PA. Challenge Press, (quote: Johann Mosheim, Lutheran historian, *Institute of Ecclesiastical History*). p. 107.
6. Jarrell, W.A. *Baptist Church Perpetuity.* Baptist Standard Bearer. CD Collection, 2005. (Reprint: 1894) p. 207.
7. Verduin, Leonard. *The Reformers and Their Stepchildren.* (Luther's commentary on Genesis). p. 18.
8. Durant, Will. *The Reformation.* p. 401.
9. Ibid., p. 633.
10. Ibid., p. 545.
11. Ibid.
12. Ibid., p. 547.
13. Ibid., p. 548.
14. Mason, Roy. *The Church That Jesus Built.* (quote: Ulrich Zwingli, 1525). p. 107.
15. Christian, J.T. *A History of the Baptists.* Vol. 1. (quote: Ulrich Zwingli, Reformer, 1525). p. 93.
16. Hageman, G.W. *Sketches From the History of the Church.* St Louis, MO., Concordia Pub. House. date unknown. p. 162.
17. Wikipedia, Michael Servetus. (quote: Toleration and Early Enlightenment Culture. Cambridge University Press, 2006. p. 325).

18. Mr. Calvin clearly understood that the primitive church practiced baptism by immersion. In his comments on Acts 8:38, He says, "They went down into the water. Here we see the rite used among the men of old time in baptism; for they put all the body into the water. Now the use is this, that the minister doth sprinkle the body or the head." He continues, "It is certain that we want (lack) nothing which maketh to the substance of baptism. Wherefore the church did grant liberty to herself since the beginning to change the rites somewhat excepting the substance." (Baptist Doctrines, C. Jenkins. Quote: Calvin's comments on Acts 8:38).

19. Christian, J.T. *A History of the Baptists*. Vol. 1. p. 198.

20. Newman, Albert, Henry. *A Manual of Church History*. Vol 2. Valley Forge. American Baptist Pub. 1903. p. 223.

21. Ibid., p. 236.

22. Ibid.

23. Durant, Will. *The Reformation*. p. 607.

24. Ibid., p. 608.

25. Newman, Albert Henry. p. 242.

26. Ibid., p. 238.

27. Cramp, J.M. pp. 269–270.

Chapter Thirteen

1. Durant, Will. p. 375.

2. Ibid., p. 446.

3. Ray, D.B. *Baptist Succession*. p. 368.

4. The ancient Waldenses consistently identified the Roman Catholic Church with the Great Whore of Revelation 17 throughout the Middle Ages. The Reformers also referred to the Roman Catholic Church as the Great Harlot, "…altogether polluted with all kinds of spiritual fornication." (Durant, p. 611. quote: Knox, History Vol. 2 p. 18).

5. Shelly, Bruce. *The Reformation*. p. 335.

6. Hyde, A.B. *The Story of Methodism.* Springfield, Mass. Willby & Co. 1888. pp 54, 58.

7. Phelan, M. *Handbook of All Denominations.* p. 131.

8. Ibid., p. 132.

9. Durant, Will. *The Reformation.* p. 340.

10. Shackelford, J.A. *A Compendium of the Baptist History.* p. 304.

11. Ibid., p. 305.

12. Cairns, Earle, E. *Christianity Through the Centuries.* Grand Rapids, MI. Zondervan Pub. 1981. p. 324–5.

13. Ibid., p. 139.

14. Hyde, A.B. *The Story of Methodism.* p. 407–411.

15. Ibid., (quote: from Buckley) p. 142.

Chapter Fourteen

1. The Congregationalists were originally organized as Brownists under the teachings of Mr. Robert Browne about 1578. Browne had become convinced that both the Presbyterian and Episcopal forms of church government were unscriptural. He taught that each church should be independent one of another and that each church should practice a pure democracy. Because he believed that each church should be under the headship of Christ alone, their churches withdrew from the Church of England as Separatists. This prompted their persecution by the state. Although holding to many Anabaptist principles, the Congregationalists retained the practice of paedobaptism.

2. Vedder, Henry C. *A Short History of the Baptists.* Paris, Arkansas. The Baptist Standard Bearer Inc. CD Collection, 2005) (Reprint: 1907) p. 138.

3. Mennonites was the name given to certain Anabaptists who organized themselves under the leadership of Menno Simons (1492–1559) from about 1536 onward, primarily in the Netherlands. They are in agreement with Baptists in rejecting infant baptism

but allow baptism by affusion (pouring). They are presbyterial in church order rather than congregational. They are usually identified as Anabaptists historically but this is certainly debatable.

4. Vedder, Henry. p. 140.

5. Cramp, J.M. *Baptist History: From the Foundation of the Christian Church to the Present Time.* (Reprint: 1871) Watertown, Wisconsin. Baptist Heritage Press. 1987. pp. 253–255.

6. Ray, D.B. pp. 130–6.

7. Shackelford, J.A. p. 263.

8. Evans, Benjamin. *The Early English Baptists.* Vol. 1. Standard Bearer. CD Collection, 2005. (Reprint: 1862) Intro. p. 1.

9. Christian, J.T. (quote: Lingard, *The Anglo-Saxon Church.* Vol. 2. 1858). p. 175.

10. Crosby, Thomas. *History of the English Baptists.* Vol 1. Standard Bearer. CD Collection, 2005. (Reprint: 1738). p. 98.

11. Christian, J.T. p. 181.

12. Christian, J.T. p. 182.

13. Christian, J.T. (quote: Knighton, col. 2664). p. 184.

14. Benedict, David. *A General History of the Baptist Denomination in America.* Gallitan, TN. Church History Research and Archives, 1985; (Reprint: 1813). (quote: Bishop Burnet, *History of the Reformation*, Vol. 1). p. 594.

15. Christian, J.T. p. 183.

16. Shackelford, J.A. p. 274.

17. Goadby, J.J. *Bye-paths in Baptist History.* Standard Bearer. CD Collection, 2005. (Reprint: 1871). p. 23.

18. Shackelford, J.A. p. 276.

19. Christian, J.T. (quote: Brewer, *Letters and Papers of Henry VIII*, Vol. 1. p. 285). p. 193.

20. Ibid.

21. Ibid., (quote: Fuller, *Church History of Britain*, Vol. 1. p. 27). p. 195.

22. Ibid., (quote: Ellis, *Original Letters Relative to the English Reformation.* Vol. 1. p 65). p. 197.

23. Ibid., (quote: Bishop Fowler Short, *History of the Church of England,* Vol. 6. p. 543). p. 196.

24. Ivimey, Joseph. *History of the English Baptists.* Vol. 1. Standard Bearer, CD Collection, 2005. (Reprint: 1814). p. 97.

25. Christian, J.T. (ref. state papers, Vol. 1. Library of the Earl of Saulsbury, Samuel Haynes, London. 1740). p. 206.

26. Ibid., (quote: Marsden, p. 144).

27. Ibid., p. 218.

28. Orchard, G.H. p. 375.

29. Shackelford, J.A. p. 277–8.

30. Christian, J.T. Vol. 2, (quote: Millet, *A History of the Baptists in Maine.* p. 21). p. 24.

31. Ibid., Vol. 1. (quote: Cotton Mather, *Magnalia,* Vol. 2. p. 459). p. 359.

32. Ibid., p. 360.

33. Christian, J.T. Vol. 2. p. 32.

34. Crosby, Thomas. *History of the English Baptists.* Vol. 1. (quote: Cotton Mather). Standard Bearer, CD Collection. 2005. (Reprint: 1738). p. 100.

35. Christian, J.T. p. 37.

36. Ibid., p. 38.

37. Ibid., p. 29–30.

38. Armitage, Thomas. Vol. 2. p. 669–672.

39. Ray, D.B. p. 116.

40. Ibid., p. 116.

41. Ibid., Vol. 2. p. 38.

42. Ibid., p. 42.

43. Ibid., p. 43.

44. Armitage, Thomas. *A History of the Baptists.* Wisconsin, Watertown. Baptist Heritage Press, 1988. Vol. 2. (Reprint: 1886). p. 672.

45. Christian, J.T. Vol. 2. (quote: Cotton Mather, *Magnolia*. Vol. VII.) p. 45.
46. Ibid., (ref. Colonial Records of North Carolina, Vol. 1. p. 469).
47. Ibid., (ref: Knight, *History of the General Baptists*). p. 45–46.
48. Ibid., p. 46.
49. Ibid., p. 30.
50. Benedict, David. p. 364–65.
51. Spence, Hartzell. *The Story of American's Religions.* New York, NY. Holt, Rinehart and Winston. 1960. p. 9.
52. Ibid.
53. Christian, J.T. Vol. 2. p. 5.
54. Ray, D.B. (quote: Gildas, *De Victoria Aurelli Ambrossi*). p. 68–69.
55. Ibid., (quote: Fox, *Antiquities of England.* Vol. 1. p. 139). p. 68.
56. Ibid., pp. 68–69.
57. Ibid., (quote: Jeffery Monmouth, *De Britannorum Gestis*p). p. 69.
58. Christian, J.T. (ref: Fuller, *The Church History of Britain*, Vol. 1. p. 101). pp. 178–181.
59. Davis, J. *History of Welsh Baptists.* Standard Bearer, CD Collection, 2005. (Reprint: 1835). p. 14.
60. Ray, D.B. pp 121–129.
61. Shackelford, J.A. p. 223.
62. Durant, Will. *The Reformation.* (quote Payne, *Anabaptist*, p. 16). p. 402.
63. Christian, J.T. Vol. 2. pp. 148–9.
64. Ibid., p. 151.
65. Ibid., p. 167.
66. Ibid., p. 168.

67. Ibid., (quote: Edwards, *Narrative of Surprising Conversions.* Works III). p. 168.

68. Ibid., (quote: Shurtliff, *Defense of Whitefield.*). p. 169.

69. Ibid., (quote: Trumbull, *History of Connecticut,* Vol. 2).

70. Ibid., p. 170.

71. Ibid., p. 180.

72. By proper means, we mean to indicate that the members of these New Light churches would have undergone the proper administration of the ordinance of baptism by a proper authority (i.e., a Baptist church) and then the church would have been commissioned by a sending church (i.e., Baptist) that was satisfied that a correct order had been followed in the process.

73. Ibid., pp 26–27.

74. Ibid., p. 181.

75. Beller, James, R. *America in Crimson Red.* Arnold, MO. Prairie Fire Press. 2004. (quote: William Lumpkin *Baptist Inroads in the South.* p. 20). p. 134.

76. Ray, D.B. p. 121.

PART FOUR
Chapter Fifteen

1. Christian, J.T. *A History of the Baptists.* Bogard Press, Texarkana, TX. 1922. p. 86.

2. Ibid., (ref. Blaupot Ten Cate, Historical Enquiry). p. 93.

3. Sargent, Robert J. *Landmarks of Church History.* Book 1. (ref. Hosius Letters Apud Opera, 112–113). Bible Baptist Church Pub., Oak Harbor, WA. p. 220.

4. Christian, J.T. (quote: Johanan L. Mosheim, Luthern historian, *Institutes of Ecclesiastical History* Vol. 3. p. 200). p. 83–84.

5. Christian, J.T. Vol. 1. (quote: Robert Barclay,*The Inner Life of the Religious Societies of the Commonwealth,* p. 12). p. 174.

6. Jarrell, Dr. W.A. *Baptist Church Perpetuity*, Dallas, TX. Baptist Standard Bearer Inc. CD Collection, 2005). (Reprint: 1894). p. 57.

7. Christian, J.T. (quote: Alexander Campbell, founder, Christian Church, *McCalla-Campbell Debate on Baptism*, 1824. pp. 378, 379). p. 84.

8. Ibid., (quote: Sir Isaac Newton. William Whiston Memoirs p. 201).

9. Mason, Roy. *The Church That Jesus Built.* Emmaaus, PA. Challenge Press. (quote: *Crossing the Centuries*, edited by W.C. King). p. 108.

10. Ibid., (quote: Edinburg Cyclopedia, p. 22). p. 107.

11. Ibid., (quote: Dr. J.T. Christian, *Baptist History*). p. 108.

12. Ibid., (quote: Dr. George Lorimer, *The Baptists in History.* p. 49). p. 104.

13. Ibid., (quote: J.L. Smith, *Baptist Law of Continuity*). p. 105.

14. Ibid., (quote: Dr. R.B. Cook, *Story of the Baptists*).

15. Ibid., (quote: Dr. D.C. Haynes, *The Baptist Denomination*, p. 21).

16. Ibid., (quote: Dr. George W. McDaniel, *Churches of the New Testament*). p. 106.

17. Ibid., (quote: J.T. Moore, *Why I Am A Baptist*). p. 102.

Chapter Sixteen

1. Jenkins, C.A. *Baptist Doctrines*. Watertown, Wisconsin. Maranatha Baptist Bible College. (Roger Williams Heritage Archive CD Collection), Libronix Ed. (Reprint: 1890). pp. 217–218.

Bibliography

Aland, Kurt. *A History of Christianity.* Philadelphia, PA. Fortress Press. 1985.

Allix. Peter. *The Ecclesiastical History of the Ancient Churches of the Piedment*; Reprinted: Dayton, OH.; Church History & Archives, 1989. Originally published, 1821. 2 Vols.

Armitage, Thomas. *A History of the Baptists, Traced by their Vital Principles and Practices, from the Time of our Lord and Saviour Jesus Christ to the Year 1886*; Watertown, WI.; Baptist Heritage Pub, 1988, 2 Vols.

Backus, Isaac. *A History of New England with Particular Reference to the Denomination of Christian Called Baptists*; Newton, Mass.; Backus Historical Society, 1871, 2 Vols.

Backus, Isaac. *Your Baptist Heritage 1620–1804*; Reprinted: Little Rock, AR.; The Challenge Press, 1976. Originally published, 1844.

Beller, James, R. *America in Crimson Red*. Arnold, Missouri. Prairie Free Press. 2004.

Benedict, David. *A General History of the Baptist Denomination in America and other Parts of the World*; Reprinted: Dayton, OH.; Church History Research & Archives, 1922, 2 Vols.

Brown, J. Newton. *Memorials of Baptists Martyrs*, Reprinted: Watertown, WI. Baptist Heritage Press, Originally published, American Baptist Pub. Society; 1854.

Cairns, Earle E. *Christianity Through the Centuries*; Grand Rapids, MI.; Zondervan Pub. 1981.

Carroll, J.M. *The Trail of Blood*; Lexington, Kentucky, Bryon Station Baptist Church, (Ph 606–299–1430); 1999.

Christian, John, T. *A History of the Baptists*; Reprinted: Texarkana, TX.; Bogard Press. Originally published, Sunday School Board of the Southern Baptist Conv., 1922, 2 Vols.

Cloud, David, W. *Way of Life Encyclopedia of the Bible & Christianity*; Oak Harbor, WA.; Way of Life Literature; Bible Baptist Church, Oak Harbor, WA., 1993.

Cramp, J.M. *Baptist History from the Foundation of the Christian Church to the Present Time*; Reprinted: Watertown, WI. Baptist Heritage Pub., 1987. Originally published, 1871.

Crosby, Thomas. *History of the English Baptists*. Vol. 1. (Digital: London, 1738) Paris, Arkansas. The Baptist Standard Bearer, Inc. (Baptist History CD Collection, 2005).

Davis, A.A. *The Baptist Story*; Reprinted: Shelbyville, TN., Bible & Literature Missionary Foundation, 1999.

Davis, J. *History of the Welsh Baptists*. Digital: Pittsburgh, 1835. Paris, Arkansas. Baptist Standard Bearer Inc. (Baptist History CD Collection, 2005).

Durant, Will. *The Story of Civilization; The Reformation*. New York, NY. Simon & Schuster, 1957.

Goadby, J.J. *Bye-paths in Baptist History.* (Digital: London, 1871). Paris, Arkansas. Baptist Standard Bearer Inc. (Baptist History CD Collection, 2005).

Hageman, G.E. *Sketches from the History of the Church*; St. Louis, MO. Concordia Publishing House, date unknown.

Hyde, A.B. *The Story of Methodism.* Springfield, Mass. Willby & Co. 1888.

Ivimey, Joseph. *History of the English Baptists.* Vol. 1. (Digital: London, 1814). Paris, Arkansas. Baptist Standard Bearer Inc. (Baptist History CD Collection, 2005).

Jarrell, Dr. W.A. *Baptist Church Perpetuity*, Dallas, TX. (Digital: 1894). Baptist Standard Bearer Inc. (Bapt. Hist. CD Collection, 2005).

Jenkins, C.A. *Baptist Doctrines.* Watertown, Wisconsin. (Digital: 1890). Maranatha Baptist Bible College. (Roger Williams Heritage Archive CD Collection, Libronix Edition).

Jones, T.G. *The Baptist, Their Origin, Continuity, Principles, Spirit, Polity, Position and Influence.* Paris, Arkansas. Baptist Standard Bearer Inc. (Baptist History CD Collection, 2005).

Jones, William. *The History of the Christian Church.* New York, NY. Spencer H Cone Pub., 1824.

Mason, Roy. *The Church That Jesus Built*; Clarksville, TN; Central Ave. Baptist Church.

McBeth, H. Leon, *The Baptist Heritage.* Nashville, TN. Broadman Press. 1987.

McBirnie, William. *The Search for the Twelve Apostles*; Wheaton, IL.; Tyndale House Publishers, 1973.

McDaniel, George, W. *The People Called Baptists.* Nashville, TN. Sunday School Board, SBC. 1925.

Newman, Albert Henry. *A Manual of Church History.* Valley Forge. Judson Press. 1972. 2 Vols.

Orchard, G.H. *A Concise History of Baptists*; Reprinted: Texarkana, TX.; Bogard Press, 1987. Originally published, 1855.

Phelan, M. *Handbook of All Denominations.* Nashville, TN. Cokesbury Press. 1929.

Porter, John William. *The World's Debt to the Baptists*; Reprinted: Wilmington, OH., Baptist Heritage Press, 1991. Originally published, The Baptist Book Concern, 1914.

Ray, D.B. *Baptist Succession: A Handbook of Baptist History;* Reprinted: Gallatin, TN.; Church History & Archives, 1984. Originally published, 1870.

Sargent, Robert J. *Landmarks of Church History*; Book 1 & 2. Oak Harbor, WA., Bible Baptist Church Pub.

Shackelford, J.A. *Compendium of Baptist History;* Reprinted: Louisville, KY.,Press Baptist Book Concern. Originally published, 1892.

Shelly, Bruce. *Church History in Plain Language.* Nashville, TN. Thomas Nelson Pub. 1995.

Spence, Hartzell. *The Story of America's Religions.* New York, NY. Holt, Rinehart and Winston. 1960.

Stringer, Phil. *The Faithful Baptist Witness.* Haines City, FL. Landmark Baptist Press. 1998.

Torbet, Robert. *A History of the Baptists.* Valley Forge. Judson Press. 1975.

Verduin, Leonard. *The Reformers and Their Stepchildren;* Grand Rapids, MI., William B. Eerdmeans Pub. Co. 1964.

Vedder, Henry, C. *A Short History of the Baptists.* (Digital:1907). Paris, Arkansas. The Baptist Standard Bearer Inc. (Baptist History CD Collection, 2005).

Wayland, Francis. *Notes on the Principles and Practices of Baptist Churches*; Reprinted: Watertown, WI.; Baptist Heritage Press, 1988. Originally published, 1857.

Wickersham, Henry, C. *A History of the Church.* Moundsville, W. VA. Gospel Trumpet Pub. CO. 1900.

Wylie, J.A. *History of the Waldenses.* Middleton, ID. CHJ Pub., date unknown.

Glossary

1. **Byzantine Text:** *Byzantine Text* is a reference to those Greek manuscripts deposited at the city of Constantinople, formerly known as Byzantium, during the early period of the Dark Ages. It was here that many manuscripts were preserved until their removal to the Christian West when the Byzantine East was threatened by the Ottoman Turks in 1453. They form the core of the Majority and Received Text from which the King James Version is translated.

2. **Denomination:** The word *denomination* literally means "to name." In a religious sense, it is an effort to distinguish a religious group by name whose doctrinal uniqueness warrants an identity separate from those that already exist. Mathematically it represents a number that has been divided or multiplied by another.

3. ***Ecclesia:*** The Greek word *ecclesia* originates from two words *kaleo* meaning "to call" and *ek* meaning "out." Thus the word literally means "to call out." It refers to the fact that the church is composed of a people called out from the world to Christ.

4. ***Ecumenism:*** Ecumenism refers to the effort by some to further religious unity among various Christian churches and organizations regardless of their doctrinal differences or polity. It sometimes is used in an even broader sense to include religious groups outside the historic context of Christianity.

5. ***Excommunication:*** Latin for "out of communion," excommunication represents one of the most severe punishments in the Catholic Church. It deprives the guilty Christian from all participation in "the common blessings of ecclesiastical society." Since divine grace is conveyed via the sacraments in the Catholic Church, the excommunicated are thus excluded from or deprived of divine grace, jeopardizing their eternal state.

6. ***Extreme Unction:*** The Catholic doctrine of Extreme Unction refers to the spiritual aid and comfort given to Catholics by a priest when they are seriously ill or their lives are in jeopardy. The Catholic Church claims that the practice provides for perfect spiritual health, including if need be, the remission of sins, as well as the restoration of bodily health.

7. ***The Kingdom of Heaven:*** The kingdom of Heaven speaks of a divine or heavenly order of government, a theocracy. In relation to men, it refers to the divine authority that God exercises among men. Its primary use is found in Matthew because his Gospel is directed to the Jew. Elsewhere in the Gospels, the term *kingdom of God* is dominant. Whereas the former often has a historical connection, both terms deal with the redemptive work of God in real time whereby the authority

Glossary

of God is established in the hearts of men as evidenced in Jesus' discussion with Nicodemus (John 3).

8. ***Local:*** The term *local* is used often in this book. It refers to the existence of New Testament churches that are visible rather than invisible. In other words, they are local in the sense that they have a particular location that is identifiable either in theory or context.

9. ***Manichaeism:*** Manichaeism was one of the major Gnostic religions of the early centuries. Its founder, Mani (AD 210–276), was born in Babylon. Manichaeism thrived between the third and seventh centuries and became a significant religious force. Its theology was dualistic—it believed in two equal and opposite powers, one good and one bad. Augustine (AD 354–430) was converted from Manichaeism and became one of its most severe critics.

10. ***Monotheism:*** Monotheism believes in the existence of one God and that polytheism is merely idolatry.

11. ***Mystical:*** By *mystical* we mean that something is mysterious, unexplained or secretive. The facts are unknown or difficult to ascertain. Because the theory of a universal church involves invisibility we refer to the concept as mystical.

12. ***Non-conformist:*** "Non-conformists" refers to a movement within the Church of England to purify the Church of England of Papal influence and rituals. Non-conformists were loyal to the Church but demanded a purification of it. These dissidents were known as the Puritans, but they never advocated Separatism.

13. ***Para-church:*** By *para-church* we mean religious organizations of human origin that come along side the church either in support of or as a replacement to the church.

14. ***Pentecost:*** Pentecost was celebrated by the Jews as the fiftieth (GK *pentekostos*) day after the presentation of the first harvested sheaf of the barley harvest, i.e., the fiftieth day from the first Sunday after Passover (Leviticus 23:15). It was known among the Jews as the "feast of weeks" (Exodus 34:22; Deuteronomy 16:10) and also as "the day of the first fruits" (Numbers 28:26; Exodus 23:16).

15. ***Polytheism:*** Polytheism is a belief in the existence of many gods usually associated in some way with nature.

16. ***Sacramental Salvation:*** Sacramental salvation is a belief that there is some saving merit in the ordinance of baptism, usually a belief that the act of baptism washes away original sin. First century churches never believed that baptism played any part in the salvation of a new convert. The Bible clearly teaches that salvation is not the result of human merit but is solely by God's grace through faith in Jesus Christ alone.

17. ***Seeker:*** During the seventeenth century a "seeker" was one who believed that the true church would be organized under the authority of an apostle. Since none were to be found, it usually meant that the seeker never united with any society of believers.

18. ***Separatist:*** The term *separatist* refers to certain religious societies that during the latter part of the sixteenth century rejected the authority of the Church of England as well as the union of church-state that often resulted in the persecution of dissenting groups. The Separatists usually consisted of Brownists or Congregational societies as well as Baptist churches.

19. ***Socinian:*** Socinian is a reference to the teachings of Faustus Socinius (1539–1604). Socinius was both anti-trinitarian and

anti-paedobaptist. Socinians rejected Calvinism, believed the Lord's Table was simply a memorial to be partaken by baptized believers only, and that baptism is to be by immersion after an affirmation of belief. Thus he rejected infant baptism. However, Socinius rejected the position that baptism was a perpetual ordinance. He is not considered an Anabaptist although his views were similar in some aspects. His greatest influence was among the Mennonites.

APPENDIX I

Societies of Human Origin

Society	Founder	Year
Reformation		
Luthern Church (Germany)	Martin Luther	1520
Anglican Church (Church of England)	King Henry VIII	1535
Reformed Churches (Switzerland)	John Calvin	1540
Presbyterian Church (Scotland)	John Knox	1560
Congregational Church (America)	Robert Browne	1582
Dutch Reformed Church	Michaelis Jones	1628
Friends Church (Quaker)	George Fox	1650
Church of Brethren (Dunkards)	Alex Mack	1708
Free Will Baptists (Arminian)	Paul Palmer	1727
Seventh Day Baptists	John Beissel	1728
Episcopal Church (Anglican Church in America)	Samuel Seabury	1789

Evangelicalism

Methodism	John Wesley	1744
United Brethren in Christ	P.W. Otterbein & M. Boehm	1800
Evangelical Church	Jacob Albright	1800
Cumberland Presbyterian	Ewing, King & McAdow	1810
Unitarians	W.E. Channing	1825
Churches of God in North America	John Winebrenner	1825
Christian Church (Disciples of Christ)	Alexander Campbell	1837
Church of Christ	Alexander Campbell	1837
Plymouth Brethren	John Darby	1841
Church of God (New Dunkards)	George Patton	1848
Salvation Army	William Booth	1865
Church of God	Daniel Warner	1880
Christian Missionary Alliance (Neighborhood Church)	A.B. Simpson	1881
Brethren Church		1882
Swedish Evangelical (Free Church)		1888
United Evangelical Church		1894
Church of the Nazarene	W.H. Hoople & P. F. Bressee	1908
Bible Churches (IFCA)		1930

Pentecostalism

"Father of the movement"	Charles Parham	1873–1929
Bethel Healing Home, Topeka, KS		1898
Bethel Bible College, Topeka, KS		1900
Houston Bible School, Houston, TX		1905
Azusa Street Mission, Los Angeles, CA	William Seymour	1870–1922
Church of God	Richard Spurling	1886
Church of Christ (Holiness) USA	C.P. Jones	1894
Church of God (Apostolic)	Thomas Cox	1896

Appendix I—Societies of Human Origin

Church of God in Christ	C.H. Mason & C.P. Jones	1897
Pentecostal Holiness Church		1898
Pentecostal Union	Alma White	1901
Apostolic Faith	Florence Crawford	1907
Pentecostal Fire-Baptized Holiness Church		1911
Assemblies of God		1914
Churches of God, Holiness	K.H. Burru	1914
Apostolic Overcoming Holy Church of God	W.T. Phillips	1916
Pentecostal Church of Christ	John Stroup	1917
Church of the Foursquare	Aimee Semple McPherson	1918
Pentecostal Church of God of America, Inc.		1919
Church of our Lord Jesus Christ of the Apostolic Faith, Inc.	R.C. Laws	1919
Congregational Holiness Church		1921
Fire-Baptized Holiness Church		1922
Calvary Pentecostal Church		1931
United Pentecostal Church, Inc.		1945
Elim Missionary Assemblies		1947
Emmanuel Holiness Church		1953
World-Wide Bible Way Church		1957

Charismatic Movement

Full Gospel Business Mens' Association	Demos Shakarian	1956
Trans-denominational Movement		1960s
Fellowship Movement (Calvary Chapel, Costa Mesa, CA)	Chuck Smith	1960s

American Cults

Roman Catholicism	Emperor Constantine/ Pope Sylvester	AD 323

Greek Orthodox Church		869
Mormonism (Church of the Latter Day Saints, LDS)	Joseph Smith	1830
Christadelphians (Brothers of Christ)	John Thomas	1850
Seventh Day Adventist Church	Ellen G. White	1863
Jehovah's Witnesses	Charles Taze Russell	1870
Theosophy Madame	Helena Petrovna Blavatsky	1875
Christian Science	Mary Baker Eddy	1877
Unity	Charles & Myrtle Fillmore	1889
Spiritualism	Katherine & Margaret Fox	1893
Worldwide Church of God	Herbert W. Armstrong	1934

APPENDIX II

Traditions of Human Origin in the Roman Catholic Church

- Presbyters first called priests by Lucian (2nd century).
- Sacerdotal mass instituted by Cyprian (3rd century).
- Infant baptism addressed (AD 251).
- Prayers for the dead (AD 300).
- Making the sign of the cross (AD 300).
- Wax candles (AD 320).
- Veneration of angels and dead saints and the use of images (AD 375).
- Mass as a daily ritual (AD 394).
- Baptism of infants required under penalty, Council of Mela, North Africa (AD 416).
- The term "Mother of God" first applied by the Council of Ephesus (AD 431).
- Priest began to wear special clothing (AD 500).
- Extreme unction (AD 526).
- The doctrine of purgatory introduced by Gregory I (AD 593).

- Latin used in worship (AD 600).
- Prayers to Mary, angels, and dead saints (AD 600).
- First man to be proclaimed "pope" (Boniface III) (AD 610).
  - The title of pope or universal bishop was first given to the bishop of Rome by the wicked Emperor Phocas in 610. This he did to spite Bishop Ciriacus of Constantinople, who had justly excommunicated him for causing the assassination of his predecessor Emperor Mauritius. Gregory I, then bishop of Rome, refused the title, but his successor, Boniface III accepted and assumed the title "pope."
- Kissing the pope's feet (AD 709).
  - Originally, this had been a pagan custom, kissing the feet of the emperors.
- Temporal power of pope conferred by Pepin, King of the Franks (AD 750).
  - After Pope Steven II had called upon Pepin, King of the Franks, to invade northern Italy in order to remove the Lombards, their lands were confiscated by Pepin and given to the church making the church a state within a state.
- Veneration of the cross, images, and relics authorized (AD 786).
- Holy water mixed with a pinch of salt and blessed by a priest (AD 850).
- College of the cardinals instituted (AD 929).
- The baptism of bells, Pope John XIV (AD 965).
- Canonization of dead saints, (Pope John XV) (AD 995).
- Fasting on Fridays and Lent (AD 998).
- The mass becomes obligatory (11th century).
- Celibacy of the priest declared (AD 1079).
- The rosary adopted from pagans by Peter the Hermit (AD 1090).
- The inquisition instituted by the Council of Verona (AD 1184).
- Sale of indulgences (AD 1190).
- Seven sacraments (12th century).

Appendix II—Traditions in the Roman Catholic Church

- Transubstantiation defined by Pope Innocent III (AD 1215).
  - By this doctrine the priest pretends to perform a daily miracle by changing the wafer into the body of Christ. Then he pretends to eat Him alive in the presence of his people during mass.
- Auricular confession of sins to a priest instead of God instituted by Pope Innocent III (AD 1215).
- Adoration of the wafer (Host), decreed by Pope Honorius (AD 1220).
- The Bible forbidden to laymen, Council of Valencia (AD 1229).
- The cup forbidden to laymen at communion, Council of Constance (AD 1414).
- Purgatory proclaimed a dogma by the Council of Florence (AD 1439).
- Tradition declared to be equal in authority with the Bible, Council of Trent (AD 1545).
- Apocryphal books added to the Bible, Council of Trent (AD 1546)
- Immaculate conception of Mary proclaimed by Pope Pius IX (1854).
- Syllabus of errors proclaimed by Pope Pius IX and ratified by the Vatican Council.
  - It condemned freedom of religion, conscience, speech, press, and scientific discoveries which are disapproved by the Roman Catholic Church; it asserted the pope's temporal authority over all civil rulers (1864). Again, Pope Pius X, condemned together with "modernism," all the discoveries of modern science which are not approved by the church (1907).
- Infallibility of the pope in all matters of faith and morals, Vatican Council (1870).
- Assumption of Mary proclaimed by Pope Pius XI (1950).
- Mary proclaimed "Mother of the Church" by Pope Paul VI (1965).

APPENDIX III

Six Reasons to Reject the Universal Church Theory

Many churches believe in a universal church—a belief that the New Testament church is invisible and universal and that everyone who receives Christ automatically becomes a member of this invisible and universal church. It is sometimes referred to as the "body of Christ." The New Testament teaches us that the church which Jesus began has existed down through the centuries as a visible and local church. We believe this for the following six reasons.

1. Our English word *church* comes from a Greek word *ekklesia* which by definition is a visible and local called out assembly of people. In classical Greek it is never used to refer to an invisible, mystical body or group of people. So, when Jesus said in Matthew 16:18, *"I will build my church,"* there is absolutely no indication that the church He spoke of was anything but visible and local, and nowhere in the New Testament do we see a re-definition of the word *ekklesia*. Sometimes the word *ekklesia* is used in an

institutional sense (Ephesians 3:21), but that simply identifies all local churches in a corporate sense, not in a mystical sense.

2. Jesus said, *"the gates of hell shall not prevail against it [His church]."* According to this statement, the institution of the local church would never cease to exist. Indeed, the Apostle Paul says that there would be glory in the church throughout all ages (Ephesians 3:21). So, we understand the Bible to teach the institution of the visible and local church would exist upon this earth to carry out the Great Commission until Jesus comes again. It was the Reformers who had great difficulty with this because they were all Catholic and believed that the church had apostatized and needed reformation. They did not succeed, but neither did they correctly understand Matthew 16:18 or Ephesians 3:21. What the Reformers did do was to take the Catholic doctrine of "universality," and redefine it to describe a "universal body," thus justifying the establishment of Reformation churches and their varied descendants.

3. Baptists understand that the Great Commission was not given to any one man or group of men such as the apostles. If this were the case, then the obligation of the Great Commission would have ceased with the man or men to whom it was given, and when they died the obligation would have ceased. Thus, the conclusion that the Great Commission was given to the institution of local, visible churches that would faithfully teach the doctrine of the apostles is inevitable—that doctrine would therefore be the common link which determined the admission to the institution itself.

4. The letters or "epistles" contained in the New Testament were generally written to encourage or admonish specific local churches or individuals connected with a local church. These letters were then passed on to other local churches for their spiritual benefit. These churches all had a visible location; and thus, the membership could be addressed as a whole.

5. According to Colossians 1:18, 24, as well as many other passages (i.e., Ephesians 4; Ephesians 5:23, 30; Colossians 2:17–19),

Appendix III—Reasons to Reject Universal Church Theory

the body is defined as the local church and the church as the body. Elsewhere in Scripture (1 Corinthians 12:12–27), the local church is described as a physical body that must function in unity (one member not being more important than any other member) to accomplish the will of God and to fulfill the Great Commission. Once again we see that the local church is not invisible or mystical but is composed of a physical body of believers working together. The body in the New Testament is never to be taken as a universal or invisible group of believers.

6. We must be reminded that God is not the author of confusion. To believe that which Jesus instituted in Matthew 16:18 was an invisible, mystical body of which all believers were a part, lends itself to confusion and irresponsibility, and to speak of unity in this type of body is an impossibility. Only when we define the church as local and visible do we set forth all the requirements as defined in Scripture.

APPENDIX IV

The Historic Baptist Distinctives

The Scriptures alone are the sole rule of faith and practice
Rejecting human tradition as being without any divine authority, Baptists believe that the Holy Bible alone is their only source of understanding for all matters of faith and practice; that the sixty-six books of the Bible are considered a perfect treasure of heavenly instruction and are the complete revelation of God to man. (2 Timothy 3:16–17; Isaiah 8:20; Psalm 12:6–7; Psalm 119; 1 Thessalonians 5:21; 2 Peter 1:20–21)

The finished work of Christ
Given their historic opposition to sacramentalism, sacerdotalism, and their insistence on believer's baptism only, we may safely conclude that Baptists have historically maintained that the work of redemption is a finished work of Christ. (John 6:35–40; Acts 2:18–36; Romans 3:24–25, 8:1, 31–39; Galatians 2:16; Ephesians 1:7; 1 Peter 1:3–5, 2:24)

Believer's baptism only

New Testament baptism is meant to be administered to the redeemed alone and only after a good profession of their faith. (Matthew 28:18–20; Acts 2:38–42, 8:26–40; Colossians 2:12; Galatians 3:26–29)

The autonomy (self-determination) of each local church under the headship of Christ

Baptists have historically held that each local church should be completely independent from any outside authority. Their only head is Jesus Christ. (Acts 13:1–4, 14:21–23, 15:19–31; Colossians 1:18; Ephesians 5:23; 1 Peter 5:1–4; Revelation 2–3)

A regenerate church membership

Baptists have historically maintained the position that only the redeemed who have submitted themselves to a scriptural baptism should have any expectation of being received into the membership of the local body of a New Testament church. (Acts 2:41–47; 1 Corinthians 12; Ephesians 2:19–22; 1 Peter 1:18–25)

The priesthood of every believer

Every believer is a priest before God, and thus any mediator (sacerdotalism) other than Christ is unnecessary. (1 Timothy 2:5; Hebrews 7; 1 Peter 2:5–9)

Purity in life and conduct

God's people have a responsibility to lead lives that are in alignment with the stated expectations for all believers in the Scriptures. (Romans 12:1–2, 14:13; 2 Corinthians 6:14–17; Galatians 2:18–21, 5:1, 13, 16–25; 1 John 2:15–17; 2 John 9–11)

Liberty of conscience

Because every man stands before God as an individual, every man should have the freedom to worship God according to his own individual conscience without the fear of reprisal or condemnation by any human authority. (Romans 14:12)

Index

A

"Acephali," 151
Aenon, 30
Affusion, 72, 205, 281
Africa, 110, 131, 133–135, 137, 140–141, 301
Ainsworth, 205–206
Albi, 146
Albigenses, 138, 146–148, 160, 208, 242, 275–276
Alexandria, 110, 117, 121–122, 130, 132
Alexandrian Text, 123, 157
America, 5, 178, 182, 187, 192–193, 195–200, 202, 204, 214–218, 220, 222–223, 225–227, 229, 231, 233, 269, 281, 284, 288, 290, 297–299

Anabaptism, 131–132, 135–136, 138–139, 145, 152, 159–160, 163–164, 166, 179, 239–242, 268
Anabaptist, 113, 131–133, 148, 160–166, 172, 174–175, 178–184, 194, 203–205, 207, 209–213, 215, 219–220, 227–228, 239–240, 242–244, 268, 280–281, 283, 295
Andrew, the Apostle, 29–30, 108, 112
Anglican Church, 88, 178, 192, 194–200, 205, 297
Anglo-Saxon, 281
Antioch, 82, 107, 110, 117, 140, 250
Anti-trinitarian, 184, 294

311

Apostles, 12, 17, 19, 24, 27, 29, 31–34, 40, 45, 47, 52, 55, 58, 60–61, 63, 77, 79–82, 96, 105–108, 111, 139, 143, 148–151, 161, 183, 186, 208–209, 223–225, 242, 245, 248–249, 254–256, 271, 273, 276, 289, 306
Armenia, 109, 112, 141, 143–145, 267
Arminian, doctrine of, 159, 196, 200, 206, 297
Arminius, Jacob, 196
Arnoldists, 159
Asbury, Francis, 196–198
Augsburg Confession, 87
Augustine, 121, 144, 178–179, 293
Austin, 209, 224–225

B

Backus, Isaac, 222, 227, 287
Baptism, xvi, 13–19, 30–31, 41, 45, 55, 68–69, 71–77, 81, 85–86, 91–92, 107, 113, 119–121, 129, 132, 137, 140–141, 145–146, 152, 160, 162, 164, 166, 172–173, 178, 180–181, 183–184, 187, 189, 194–195, 204–207, 211, 213–214, 216–217, 219, 225, 229, 232–233, 240, 243, 268, 272, 274, 277, 279–281, 284–285, 294–295, 301–302, 309–310

    Immersion, 55, 73, 107, 119, 178, 181, 184, 206, 214, 219, 279, 295
    Infant, 86, 119–120, 137, 146, 152, 159, 162, 172, 178, 180, 183–184, 187, 194–195, 205–206, 209, 213–214, 219, 225, 240, 268, 274, 280, 295, 301
    Proper Authority, xvi, 15, 18–19, 69, 73–77, 204, 206, 232, 268, 284
    Proper Candidate, 69, 71, 74
    Proper Mode, 69, 72–73, 269
    Proper Motive, 69, 76
    Regeneration, 72, 119–120, 133, 137, 162, 172, 188–189, 195, 230, 268
    Scriptural Baptism, 68–69, 71–72, 92, 146, 204, 206, 233, 310
Baptist, x, 10–12, 14, 17, 19–20, 29, 58, 108, 118, 124, 143, 145, 159–162, 164–166, 178, 188, 190, 202–208, 210–218, 221–223, 225–229, 231–233, 238, 241–246, 262–263, 266, 268–269, 280, 284, 287–290, 294, 297, 306, 309–310

    America, 214–229, 233
    England, 204–214, 227
    Netherlands, 161–165, 175, 182, 202, 204–205, 280
    Welsh, 214, 223–228, 283, 288
"Baptizo," 73
Bartholomew, the Apostle, 30, 109
Bede, Venerable, 147, 275
Beza, Theodore, 151, 182, 196
Bible, x, xiv–xvii, 4–6, 9–10, 22–23, 25, 27, 37–39, 41, 47–48 51, 54, 56–58, 63–64, 67–69, 72–73,

Index

77–78, 81, 87, 89, 91–92, 96, 98–99, 103, 107, 122–123, 130–132, 134, 137, 150, 152, 158, 162, 170, 173, 186–187, 189, 192, 201, 229, 232, 238, 246–247, 251–252, 257–264, 266–269, 288, 294, 298–299, 303, 306, 309
King James Bible, 47, 58, 150, 291
Bill of Rights, 223
Blacklock, Samuel, 214
Bloody Easter, 155
Blount, Richard, 213–214
Bogomils, 159
Bohler, Peter, 193
Boleyn, Anne, 176–177
Brahmins, 109
Browne, Chad, 216
Browne, Robert, 199, 205, 280, 297
Brownists, 159, 205, 280, 294
Brown University, 228
Byzantium, 129, 150, 291

C

Caesar, 123, 125
Calvin, John, 85–86, 88, 151, 158, 174, 180–181, 183, 170–171, 178–179, 182, 185, 187, 190, 196, 199, 214, 239, 241, 297
Calvinism, 179, 184, 295
Campbell, Alexander, 243, 285, 298
Carthage, N. Africa, 110, 131–132, 134, 140–141, 241
Cathari, 133, 148, 159
Catherine, Queen, 175–177
Catholic Church, v, 85–87, 113, 126, 133, 137, 140, 144, 146, 152, 158, 161, 163, 170–172, 178, 191, 194–196, 199, 204, 209, 214, 239–240, 279, 292, 301, 303
Chalcedon, Battle of, 123
Chaldean, 109
Charles V, Emperor, 87, 164–165
Church of England, 149, 159, 165, 177–178, 188, 192, 194, 197–198, 200, 205, 210–211, 214, 242, 280, 282, 293–294, 297
Church of God, 68, 199, 298–300
Clarke, John, 218–219
Clement, Disciple of Paul, 112
Clement, Pope, VII, 154
Clement, Pope 1534, 177
Cloven Tongues, 46, 80, 271
Coke, Thomas, 197–198
Communion, 121, 131, 215, 252
Congregationalists, 178, 205, 215, 230–231, 280
Congress, Continental, 222
Constantine, Emperor, 123–129, 134–135, 149, 152, 199, 268, 299
Constantine, of Armenia, 144
Constantinople, 129, 144, 150, 291, 302
Consubstantiation, Lutheran doctrine of, 172–173
Corinthian Church, 91–92
Cornelius, 132
Council of Nicea, 117
Council of Trent, 240–241, 303
Cranmer, Thomas, Archbishop, 176–177, 210

313

Cromwell, Oliver, 155–156, 210
Cyprian, Bishop of Carthage, 132, 301

D

Dark Ages, 118, 138, 146, 148, 150, 158–160, 163, 169, 245, 291
Decius, Emperor, 114, 117, 132
Dermout, Dr., 164
Diocletian, 114, 134
Doctrinal Unity, 238
Donatists, 133–135, 141, 143, 208, 241, 267
Duke of Savoy, 150, 156–157
Dunkers, 227

E

Ecclesia, 22, 57–61, 63, 89, 91, 292
Ecumenism, 36–37, 292
Ecumenicalists, 39
Edict of Speier, 161
Edwards, Jonathan, 230–231, 233
Edwards, Morgan, 227–228, 232
Elect (see also Predestination), 179, 214
Elizabeth I, Queen, 212
Emergent Church, 6
England, 88, 153, 155–156, 170, 175–178, 181–183, 193, 195–197, 199, 202, 204–206, 209–215, 218–219, 223–224, 226–227, 231, 283
Ephesus, 33, 53, 82, 93, 107, 111, 250, 255, 257, 301

Episcopalian, Episcopal Church, 197–199, 205, 280, 297
Erasmus, 211
Eusebius, 112, 123, 126
Evangelical(s), 52, 74, 178, 185, 187, 191, 194, 199–200, 202, 247, 252, 276, 298
Evangelicalism, v, 185, 188, 191–192, 196, 298
Evans, Caleb, 227
Excommunication, 86–87, 154, 171–172, 177, 192
Extreme Unction, 137, 292, 301

F

Family of God, 65–66, 68, 201, 260
First Amendment, 223

G

Gaiseric, the Vandal, 136
Galatia, 53, 60–61, 107, 146
Georgia, 109, 141
General Baptists, 206, 283
General Court, 230
Georgia, 193
Germany, 122, 148, 158, 160, 164, 171–175, 199, 209, 227, 241, 297
Gnosticism, 144, 293
Great Awakening, 221, 229, 231–233
Great Commission, v, 19, 22, 31, 34–36, 39, 41–44, 46–47, 61, 73–74, 81, 94–95, 100, 106, 256, 306–307
Grebel, Conrad, 163

Gregorian Calendar, 105
Gregory the Great, 224, 301–302
Guttenberg, 163

H

Harvard, University, 243
Hegessipus, 116
Helwys, Thomas, 205–206
Henricians, 159
Henry II, King of England, 154, 209
Henry VIII, King of England, 88, 170, 175–178, 190–191, 199, 210, 281, 297
Heretics, 39, 87, 119, 127, 146–147, 154–155, 158, 164, 170, 175, 181, 211
Hermas, 120, 140, 274
Herod, 111
Hill Cliffe Church, 210
Holland, 164–165, 196, 199, 204–205, 213, 242
Holy Spirit, 32, 34, 46, 67, 79, 92, 106, 131, 194
Hosius, Cardinal, 240–241, 284
Huguenots, 159
Hussites, 151, 159, 174, 182, 241

I

Ignatius of Antioch, 140
Immersion (see Baptism)
Independents, x, xiii, 40, 106, 118, 205, 228, 243, 280, 310
India, 109, 143
Indians, 192–193, 215, 218, 230

Indulgences, 122, 171, 268, 302
Infant Baptism (see Baptism)
Innocent III, Pope, 121, 146, 303
Institution, 118, 123, 126, 167, 179, 227, 239, 256, 306
Irenaeus, 140
Israel, 16, 32, 72, 98, 186
Italic Version, 150
Italy (Italian), 111, 136, 148–150, 154, 156, 158, 160, 174, 179, 199, 267, 302

J

James I, England, 205, 212
James, the Great, Apostle, 30, 108–111
James, the Less, Apostle, 110
Jefferson, Thomas, 222–223
Jehovah's Witness, 77, 259, 300
Jerusalem, the Church of, 14, 23, 31–33, 43, 45–48, 79, 81–82, 95, 105–106, 111
John, the Apostle, 30, 47, 73, 108–111, 139–140
John the Baptist, v, 10–20, 29–31, 73, 108
Judas Iscariot, 14, 17–19, 30–31, 112
Jude, the Apostle, 109, 111, 143, 249
Justin Martyr, 120, 140, 273–274

K

Key of Truth, 143–144
Kingdom of God, 13, 16, 66–68, 123, 292

Kingdom of Heaven, 12–13, 292
"Kirk," 57, 183
Knox, John, 85, 88, 170, 182–183, 185, 190–191, 199, 279, 297
"Kurios," 57

L

Lateran Council, 133, 146
Leland, John, 222–223
Leo I, Pope, 136
Liberty of Conscience, 167, 310
Lollards, 159, 182, 208–210, 212
Lollard Tower, 209
Lollard, Walter, 209
Lord's Supper (Table), xvi, 74–76, 85, 90, 119, 121, 152, 172–173, 180, 184, 187, 198, 206, 252–254, 272, 295
Lucius III, Pope, 154
Luther, Martin, 85–88, 122, 158, 170–175, 178–179, 183, 185–187, 190, 199, 239, 241, 246, 272, 278, 297
Lutheran, Church, 88, 188, 199
Lyons, France, 140, 159

M

Madison, James, 222–223
Manichaeism, 144, 293
Manning, James, 228
Manz, Felix, 163–164
Marcus Aurelius, Emperor, 114, 140
Martyr, Justin, 120, 140, 273–274
Massachusetts, 215, 218–220, 226, 229, 231

Massachusetts Bay Colony, 215
Mather, Cotton, 215, 220, 282–283
Mather, Increase, 231
Matthew, the Apostle, 110
Matthias, the Apostle, 112
Mela, Council of, 120, 301
Melancthon, 175
Menno Simon, 205, 280
Mennonites, 161, 164, 184, 205–206, 280, 295
Methodism (Methodists), 192, 194–200, 231, 242, 280, 289, 298
Methodist Connection, 194
Methodist Episcopal Church, 198–199
Middle Ages, 113, 122, 128, 148, 159, 163, 179, 182, 191, 204, 225, 242, 279
Miles, John, 226
Milton, John, 156
Monks, 87, 158, 175, 182, 224
Montanists, 130–131, 133, 140–143, 180, 244, 267, 274
Moravia, 174, 241
Moravians, 193–194, 228
Morgan, Abel, 226–227
Mormons, 52, 259, 300
Mosheim, Johann, 174, 241–242, 275, 278, 284
Mysticism, 89, 122–123

N

Nathanael (Bartholomew), 30, 109
Nero, 112–113

Netherlands, 158, 161, 163–165, 175, 182, 202, 204–205, 280
New Lights, 7, 232, 284
Newport, RI, 218–219, 223
Newton, Sir Isaac, 243, 285
Nicaea, Council of, 117
Ninety-five Thesis, 174
Noble Lesson, 150
Non-Conformists, 165, 178, 190, 205, 208, 215, 293
Nordin, Robert, 227
Northumbria, 209
Novatian, 132, 240
Novatians (Novatianists), 132–133, 135, 143, 149, 208, 240, 267

O

Olivetan, Peter, 178
Olney, Thomas, 216–217
Origen, 224

P

Paedobaptism, 120, 183, 185–186, 190, 205–206, 232–233, 280
Paedobaptists, 159, 184, 231, 295
Paganism, 121
Para-church, 93, 293
Parameters, 16, 25, 48, 55, 59, 61–63, 68, 78, 82–84, 96, 100, 179
  Agent of the Great Commission, 94–95, 100
  Body of Christ, 84, 89–92, 95, 100, 255, 305
  Habitation of God, 92–93, 100, 256
  Perpetual Witness, 95, 100, 104
  Pillar and Ground of Truth, 97, 100, 104, 267
  Reflection of God, 98–100
Particular Baptists, 214
Paterines, 159
Paul, the Apostle, 10, 24, 31, 33, 37–38, 40, 43, 47, 53, 60, 62, 74, 76, 90, 92, 97, 105, 107, 112–113, 139, 143, 171, 223, 249–250, 252–258, 261–263, 306
Paulicians, 138, 141, 143–146, 160, 208–209, 242, 267
Penn, William, 217, 225
Pennsylvania, 225–227
Pentecost, 11, 13, 31–34, 42, 44–47, 77, 79–80, 106–107, 199, 247, 294
Persecutions, Roman, 113–119, 123–129, 132–134, 146–148, 151–154, 156–158, 240
Peter, the Apostle, 6, 17–18, 21, 29–30, 45, 52, 77, 80–81, 106, 108–109, 111–113, 127, 272
Petrobrusians, 159
Pharisees, 19, 124
Philadelphia Association, 218, 228
Philip, the Apostle, 30, 108–109, 146–147, 275
Picardism, 161
Picards, 159
Pilgrims, 215
Poland, 145, 148, 158

Polycarp, 112, 139–140
Predestination (see also
    Calvinism), 178–180, 185
Presbyterian Church, 88, 183, 190,
    199, 297
Presbyterianism, 88, 178, 183, 190,
    197, 199, 205, 220, 280, 297
Priesthood of all Believers, 166, 310
Primitive Church, 105, 130–131, 151,
    181, 194, 245, 274, 279
Protestant Reformation, 8, 86, 163,
    169–184, 187, 191, 239, 242
Providence, RI, 215, 217–221, 226
Purgatory, 121, 137, 153, 268, 301, 303
Puritans, 165, 208, 229, 293

Q

Quakers, 220, 229, 242, 297

R

Rankin, Thomas, 196–197
Ray, D. B., 157, 188, 226, 274–277,
    279, 281–284, 290
Re-baptism, 75, 113, 132, 164, 166
Reformed Church, 183, 297
Regular Baptists (succession), 214
Revolutionary War (United States),
    197, 229, 231
Rhode Island, 215, 217–222,
    227–228
Roman Catholicism, 85–86, 113,
    126, 130, 137, 156, 163, 171–172,
    190–191, 199, 208, 220, 239,
    279, 299, 301, 303

Roman Empire, 43, 123, 143
Rome, 85–86, 107–108, 112–117, 119,
    123, 125, 127–129, 132–133, 135–
    138, 140, 148–149, 151–152, 163,
    170, 173, 175, 177, 187–188, 190–
    191, 195, 199, 223–225, 240–241,
    250, 268, 272–274, 302

S

Sacramental Salvation, 107, 294
Salvation, 44–45, 67–68, 83, 107, 120,
    151, 153, 185, 187, 189, 194, 196,
    200, 249, 252, 260, 294
Scotland, 88, 108, 182–183, 195, 199,
    297
Se-baptism, 217
    Roger Williams, 217
Seeker, 216, 294
Separation, Church and State, 123
Separatists, 159, 176, 205, 215, 232,
    280, 294
Servetus, Michael, 181, 278
Simon, the Apostle, 110–111, 207,
    223
Simon, Menno (see Menno
    Simon)
Six Principle Baptists, 216–217
Smyth, John, 205–206, 209
Solomon, King, 55, 97
"Soma," 89–91
Soul Liberty, 167
South Carolina, 222, 226–227
Spain, 110–112, 154, 160, 164–165,
    175–177, 204, 212
Speier, (Speyer) Diet of, 161

Sprinkling, 72–73, 181, 206, 214, 279
Statute of Appeals 1533, 177
Succession of Baptists, 133, 151, 161, 188, 213–214, 226, 242, 244, 274, 276, 279, 290
Swansea, Mass., 226
Swiss Baptists, 161, 164
Switzerland, 163, 174, 179–182, 199, 239, 241, 297
Sylvester, Pope, 149, 152, 199, 276, 299
Synthia (Synthians), 109, 145

T

Tertullian, 131, 140, 224, 244
Tetzel, 122
Textus Receptus, 158
Theodora, Empress, 145
Theodosius, Emperor, 127
Thomas, the Apostle, 109, 143
Tongues, speaking with, 45–47, 80, 106
Tower of Babel, 8
Transubstantiation, Catholic doctrine of, 121, 173, 303
TULIP, 179
Tullian Keep, 108

U

Union of Utrecht 1579, 165
Universal Church, 61, 84–85, 89, 116, 173, 201, 254, 256–257, 293, 305, 307

V

Virginia, 222, 227
Vulgate, Catholic, 158

W

Waldenses (Waldensians), 86, 133, 138, 148–161, 164, 174, 178, 191, 204, 209, 213, 225, 241–242, 267, 272, 275–276, 279, 290
Waldo (Waldus), Peter, 149, 154, 276
Wales, 224–227
Welsh Baptists, 214, 223–228, 283, 288
Welsh, Welshmen, 223–228
Welsh Tract, 225–228
Wesley, Charles, 192–196, 202
Wesley, John, 191–199, 298
Whitefield, George, 231, 233, 284
Williams, Roger, 215–219, 285, 289
William of Orange (William the Silent), 165, 204
Wycliff, John, 209

Z

Zurich, 163–164, 180
Zwingli, Ulrich, 85, 163, 179–180, 185, 239–240, 278

Scripture Index

Genesis
9:1   p. 46
11   p. 8, 46

Exodus
23:16   p. 13, 294
32–33   p. 98
33:3, 5   p. 98
33:20   p. 99
34:22   p. 13, 294

Leviticus
23:15   p. 13, 294

Numbers
28:26   p. 13, 294

Deuteronomy
16:10   p. 13, 294

2 Samuel
12:18–23   p. 121

1 Kings
7   p. 97

Psalms
11:3   p. 7
12:6–7   p. 309
29:2   p. 99
60:4   p. xii
93:5   p. 99
96:9   p. 99

109:8	p. 17	11:11	p. 11
117:1–2	p. 249–250	11:19	p. 191
		12:30	p. 257
		13	p. 134

Proverbs

13:10	p. 169–170	13:23	p. 37
22:20–21	p. 47	16:13–20	p. 108
		16:16	p. 21
		16:18	p. 21, 58, 61, 44, 56, 305–307, 105, 267

Ecclesiastes

3:15	p. 55	17:1–13	p. 112
10:10	p. 76	17:11–12	p. 12
		19:24	p. 67

Isaiah

8:20	p. 309	21:18–21	p. 186
40:3	p. 12	21:31	p. 67
57:14	p. 270	21:43	p. 67
59:14	p. 191	22:21	p. 123
63:15	p. 99	22:37–38	p. 39
		28	p. 31
		28:18–20	p. 22, 39, 43, 61, 71–73, 81, 94, 310

Amos

3:3	p. 39, 91, 249	28:20	p. 25, 73, 95

Malachi

Mark

3:1–3	p. 12	1:1	p. 13
4:5	p. 12	1:1–3	p. 12
		1:5	p. 30
		1:10	p. 73

Matthew

4:18–22	p. 111	1:14–15	p. 67
4:25	p. 31	1:14–18	p. 108
6:23	p. 26	1:21	p. 30
6:33	p. 67	1:29	p. 30, 108
8	p. 15	2:14	p. 110
9:9–11	p. 110	3:13–14	p. 31
10:1–3	p. 110	3:18	p. 109–111
10:3	p. 109	5:37	p. 112

7:9	p. 83	1:34–40	p. 112
9:38	p. 112	1:35–42	p. 108
10:35	p. 112	1:35–51	p. 29
11	p. 186	1:43	p. 29–30, 109
12:34	p. 67	1:44	p. 29–30, 108–109
14:25	p. 67	1:45	p. 29, 109–110
		2	p. 17, 30
		2:19–22	p. 17

Luke

1:11–17	p. 12	3	p. 13, 67, 293
3:4–5	p. 13	3:23	p. 30, 73
5:10	p. 30, 108	3:27	p. 15
5:11	p. 108	3:30	p. 15
6:12–13	p. 31	4	p. 39
6:12–16	p. 105	4:1	p. 19
6:14	p. 110–111	6:5–7	p. 109
6:15	p. 110–111	6:35–40	p. 309
6:16	p. 14, 109	7:16	p. 25
6:39	p. 38	8:32	p. 36–37
8:15	p. 37	10:35	p. 249
9:2	p. 67	11:16	p. 109
10:1	p. 112	11:25	p. 17
11:34–36	p. 26	12:20–33	p. 109
17:20	p. 67	14:5	p. 109
17:21	p. 67	14:6	p. 35
18:17	p. 67	14:15	p. 249
19:10	p. 35	14:21	p. 249
20	p. 14	14:22	p. 109
21:8	p. 37	14:23–24	p. 248
21:31	p. 67	14:31	p. 248
24:49	p. 45	15	p. 188
		15:2	p. 188
		15:6	p. 188

John

1:23	p. 12	15:7	p. 188
1:31	p. 16	15:10	p. 188
1:33	p. 15, 31	17	p. 44, 248
		17:4	p. 44–45

17:6	p. 248	2:2–4	p. 80
17:11	p. 248	2:4	p. 46, 80
17:20–22	p. 248	2:5	p. 32, 80
19:26–27	p. 112	2:14	p. 32, 81
19:35	p. 112	2:18–36	p. 309
20	p. 31, 112	2:37–38	p. 81
20:2, 8	p. 112	2:37–42	p. 68
20:19–22	p. 45–46	2:38–42	p. 310
20:19–23	p. 32, 46	2:41	p. 32, 81, 310
20:19–29	p. 79	2:41–47	p. 310
20:21–22	p. 106	2:42	p. 63, 82, 310
20:24–29	p. 109	2:46	p. 248, 310
21:7	p. 112	3:11	p. 112
21:18–19	p. 108	3:19, 26	p. 14
		4:33	p. 46

Acts

1	p. 31, 80, 112, 271	5:29	p. 39
1–5	p. 108	6:8	p. 46
1:3	p. 80, 271–272	7:58	p. 113
1:4	p. 45, 80, 271–272	8–21	p. 107
1:6	p. 45	8:1	p. 31, 113
1:7	p. 80, 271–272	8:3	p. 113
1:8	p. 41, 45, 47, 80	8:10	p. 46
1:13	p. 45, 79, 110–111	8:14	p. 112
1:14	p. 79, 80, 271–272	8:26–40	p. 310
1:15	p. 45, 79, 80, 271–272	8:38	p. 181, 279, 310
		9:1–31	p. 113
		11:25	p. 113
1:15–26	p. 45	11:26	p. 82, 113
1:20–26	p. 112	12:1–2	p. 111
1:21–22	p. 18, 112	13–28	p. 113
1:25–26	p. 79, 112	13:1–4	p. 310
1:26	p. 45, 79, 105, 112	14:21–23	p. 310
2	p. 45, 77, 79, 80, 106, 271	14: 22	p. 250, 310
		15:19–31	p. 310
2:1	p. 45, 68, 247	15:41	p. 250
		16:5	p. 250

17:30	p. 13	11:18	p. 76, 90, 253
18:26	p. 259	11:19	p. 253
20	p. 257	11:20	p. 76, 90
20:28	p. 250	11:28–30	p. 76
20:29	p. 63, 74, 250	11:33	p. 76
20:30	p. 63, 74, 250	12	p. 90, 106, 310
20:31	p. 74, 250	12:1–12	p. 90
22:16	p. 194	12:12–27	p. 307
		12:18	p. 32
		12:28	p. 31, 95, 105

Romans

1:17	p. 171	13:8–10	p. 106
3:24–25	p. 309	13:9–12	p. 47
6	p. 17	14:33	p. 4, 11
6:4	p. 194	14:40	p. 39, 97
8:1	p. 309	15:5	p. 112
8:31–39	p. 309	16:1–2	p. 60
10:9, 13	p. 44		
12:1–2	p. 310		

2 Corinthians

12:4–5	p. 84, 254	4:2–4	p. 38
12:6	p. 254	6:14–17	p. 310
14:12	p. 310	8:19, 23	p. 118
14:13	p. 310		

Galatians

16:17	p. 250, 257–258	1:2	p. 85, 272
16:18	p. 257–258	1:6–9	p. 37, 53

1 Corinthians

3:9	p. 34, 92	2:1–14	p. 113
3:10–11	p. 24	2:9	p. 108, 112
3:16–17	p. 34, 92, 256	2:16	p. 309
4:17	p. 253	2:18–21	p. 310
5	p. 52	3:26–29	p. 310
5:6–7	p. 92	5:1	p. 310
6:19	p. 92	5:9	p. 92
11	p. 252	5:13, 16–25	p. 310
11:2	p. 253		

Ephesians

1:7	p. 309
1:22–23	p. 23, 84
2:1–6	p. 254
2:8–9	p. 254
2:19	p. 33, 66, 310
2:20	p. 25, 33, 256, 310
2:21	p. 33, 93, 256, 310
2:22	p. 33, 93, 255–256, 310
3:8–13	p. 38
3:15	p. 66
3:17	p. 260
3:21	p. 95, 98–99, 267, 306
4	p. 306
4:1–16	p. 91
4:3–6	p. 55
4:11–16	p. 91, 255
4:16	p. 91, 254–255
4:30	p. 75
5	p. 256
5:22–33	p. 62
5:23	p. 62, 306, 310
5:26	p. 62, 263
5:27	p. 62, 74, 263
5:30	p. 62, 306

Colossians

1:18	p. 23, 84, 306, 310
1:24	p. 306
1:25–27	p. 38
1:28	p. 261
2:17	p. 306
2:18	p. 118, 306
2:19	p. 256, 306
2:20	p. 118

1 Thessalonians

5:21	p. 309

2 Thessalonians

3:6	p. 53

1 Timothy

1:1–6	p. 258
1:3	p. 53
2:5	p. 310
3:15	p. 97, 267
4:1	p. 10, 251, 262
4:16	p. 261
6:5	p. 52
6:20–21	p. 261

2 Timothy

1:7	p. 9
1:9	p. 189
2:15	p. 10, 259
3:13	p. 37, 262
3:16–17	p. 309
4:1–4	p. 74, 262
4:3–4	p. 251

Titus

1:4	p. 201, 249
1:9–11	p. 74
3:3	p. 37

3:5	p. 189	**2 John**	
3:10	p. 39, 52	1	p. 26
3:11	p. 39	1:9–11	p. 310
		1:10	p. 53, 310

Hebrews

		Jude	
2:1	p. 47, 63	1	p. 53
2:1–4	p. 47	1:3	p. 38, 98, 201, 249, 262
7	p. 310		
10:25	p. 22		
12:23	p. 63		

Revelation

1 Peter

		2	p. 83
1:1	p. 108	2–3	p. 53, 310
1:3–5	p. 309	2:5	p. 53
1:18–25	p. 310	2:14–16	p. 53
2:5–9	p. 310	12:13–17	p. 150
2:24	p. 309	12:15	p. 150, 195
5:1–4	p. 310	17	p. 191, 279
5:13	p. 108	17:3–5	p. 7–8
		21:14	p. 112

2 Peter

1:14	p. 108
1:16	p. 6
1:19	p. 47
1:20	p. 5, 47, 201, 249, 309
1:21	p. 47, 309
2:1	p. 52, 74, 251
2:2	p. 52, 74, 251
2:3	p. 74, 251

1 John

2:15–17	p. 310

Also available from
Striving Together Publications

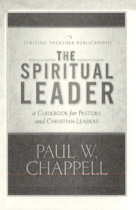

The Spiritual Leader
The Spiritual Leader summarizes a biblical philosophy of spiritual leadership that has been lived out dynamically through the life of the author. Every principle in these chapters flows from the Word of God and from a heart that has effectively served God's people for over twenty-five years. (336 pages, hardback)

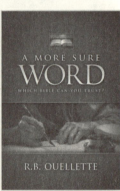

A More Sure Word
This book addresses a very sensitive subject with kindness, candor, authority, and biblical support. Every page points believers to the most biblical, the most logical, and the most historically sensible position regarding the true Word of God for English-speaking people. (216 pages, hardback)

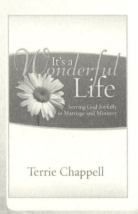

It's a Wonderful Life
From the very first page, your heart will be uplifted by Terrie's candid, humorous, and down-to-earth approach to loving God, supporting your husband, and serving God's people both biblically and joyfully. Discover that it really is a "wonderful life" when your life is dedicated to Jesus Christ! (280 pages, hardback)

strivingtogether.com

Also available from
Striving Together Publications

What Is a Biblical Fundamentalist?
Biblical fundamentalism is being redefined today. Those in secular society, Christendom, and fundamentalism are defining the term with totally different definitions. This book will help any Christian understand from a doctrinal perspective what it means to be a biblical fundamentalist. (80 pages, mini hardback)

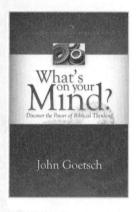

What's on Your Mind?
This book is about letting the mind of the Master become the master of your mind! It is about bringing more than human willpower to bear in controlling and reigning in the power of your thoughts. It is about true, lasting, and biblical life-change. Each page applies God's truth to the battle that every Christian fights every day—the battle of the mind. (184 pages, paperback)

101 Tips for Teaching
Veteran Christian educator, Dr. Mark Rasmussen shares more than thirty-five years of teaching experience in this practical and insightful gift-size, hardback book. This "teacher's toolbox" is also perfect for group study or as a gift to an educator. (224 pages, hardback)

strivingtogether.com

Also available from
Striving Together Publications

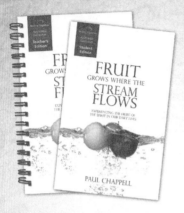

Fruit Grows Where the Stream Flows
Adult Sunday School Curriculum
The only way to truly live the Christian life is to allow the "stream" of the Holy Spirit to flow freely through your life, so He can bear the fruit of spiritual maturity. In this thirteen-lesson study, you will be rejuvenated as you discover what the Holy Spirit wants to produce through you.

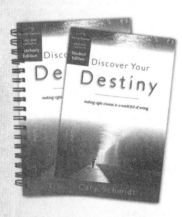

Discover Your Destiny
Teen Sunday School Curriculum
Discover what every young adult needs to know about making right choices in a world full of wrong. This seventeen-lesson series will equip students to discover the perfect will of God for their lives. The teacher's guide contains lesson outlines, teaching ideas, and Scripture helps.

Jonah: A Whale of a Lesson on Obedience
Adult/Teen Sunday School Curriculum
Dr. John Goetsch brings to life a powerful study in this Sunday school curriculum. These thirteen lessons will take your students verse by verse through the book of Jonah. This study is perfect for adult Bible classes as well as young adults and teens.

Visit us online

strivingtogether.com

dailyintheword.org

wcbc.edu

lancasterbaptist.org

paulchappell.com